Exceptionalism and the I
Counter-Terrorism

This book is an analysis and critique of the concepts of 'exception' and 'exceptionalism' in the context of the politics of liberty and security in the so-called 'War on Terror'.

Since the destruction of the World Trade Centre on September 11th 2001, a notable transformation has occurred in political discourse and practice. Politicians and commentators have frequently made the argument that the rules of the game have changed, that this is a new kind of war, and that exceptional times require exceptional measures. Under this discourse of exceptionalism, an array of measures has been put into practice, such as detention without trial, 'extraordinary rendition', derogations from human rights law, sanction or connivance in torture, the curtailment of civil liberties, and aggressive war against international law.

Situating exceptionalism within the post-9/11 controversy about the relationship between liberty and security, this book argues that the problem of exceptionalism emerges from the limits and paradoxes of liberal democracy itself. It is a commentary on and critique of both contemporary practices of exceptionalism and the critical debate that has formed in response. Through a detailed assessment of the key theoretical contributions to the debate, this book develops exceptionalism as a critical tool. It also engages with the problem of exceptionalism as a discursive claim, as a strategy, as a concept, as a theoretical problem and as a practice.

This is the first book to capture the importance of the exceptionalism debate in a single volume, and will be of much interest to students of critical security studies, political philosophy, IR theory and sociology.

Andrew W. Neal is a Lecturer in International Relations at the University of Edinburgh. His PhD won the British International Studies Association best thesis prize in 2006.

Routledge Studies in Liberty and Security
Series editors
Didier Bigo, Elspeth Guild and R. B. J. Walker

Terror, Insecurity and Liberty
Illiberal Practices of Liberal Regimes after 9/11
Didier Bigo and Anastassia Tsoukala (eds)

Exceptionalism and the Politics of Counter-Terrorism
Liberty, Security and the War on Terror
Andrew W. Neal

Exceptionalism and the Politics of Counter-Terrorism

Liberty, security and the War on Terror

Andrew W. Neal

Routledge
Taylor & Francis Group

LONDON AND NEW YORK

First published 2010
by Routledge
2 Park Square, Milton Park, Abingdon, Oxon, OX14 4RN

Simultaneously published in the USA and Canada
by Routledge
711 Third Avenue, New York, NY 10017

Routledge is an imprint of the Taylor & Francis Group, an informa business

First issued in paperback 2011

Typeset in Times New Roman by Taylor & Francis Books

British Library Cataloguing in Publication Data
A catalogue record for this book is available from the British Library

Library of Congress Cataloging in Publication Data
Neal, Andrew W., 1978-
Exceptionalism and the politics of counter-terrorism : liberty, security, and the War on Terror / Andrew W. Neal.
 p. cm.
1. Liberty. 2. National security. 3. Terrorism – Prevention. 4. War on Terrorism, 2001-I. Title.
 JC585.N39 2009
 327.1'17 – dc22
                              2009016196

ISBN10: 0-415-45675-4 (hbk)
ISBN10: 0-415-66453-5 (pbk)
ISBN10: 0-203-86758-0 (ebk)

ISBN13: 978-0-415-45675-3 (hbk)
ISBN13: 978-0-415-66453-0 (pbk)
ISBN13: 978-0-203-86758-7 (ebk)

This book is dedicated to my late grandfathers and namesakes, Andreas Phylactou and William George Neal.

Contents

Acknowledgements   ix

Introduction   1

1   The liberty/security discourse and the problem of the exception   7

2   Freedom and liberty in classic political theory: Hobbes and Kant   35

3   Carl Schmitt and the politics of the exception   57

4   Giorgio Agamben's exception: 'the great historico-transcendental
    destiny of the Occident'   77

5   Securitization theory: practices of sovereign naming   99

6   Foucault in Guantanamo: towards an archaeology of the exception   117

7   The rise and fall of Schmitt at the hands of Foucault and others   135

Notes   151
Bibliography   169
Index   179

Acknowledgements

I could not have written this book without the help and support of some exceptional people. It was made financially possible by a bursary from the Centre for World Dialogue, Nicosia, Cyprus, for my first year at Keele; my appointment to a research assistant position with ELISE (European Liberty and Security), a project financed by the Fifth Framework Research Programme of the Directorate-General for Research of the European Commission; and to a research associate post with CHALLENGE (the Changing Landscape of European Liberty and Security), a project financed by the Sixth Framework Research Programme of the Directorate-General for Research of the European Commission.

An earlier version of Chapter 6 was first published by Sage in the journal *Security Dialogue* (vol. 37, no.1, 2006: 31–46) and in German as 'Foucault in Guantánamo: Eine Archäologie des Ausnahmezustands', in Krasmann and Martschukat (eds), *Rationalitäten der Gewalt* (Transcript: Bielefeld, 2007: 19–46).

Thanks must go to the many members of the ELISE and CHALLENGE projects for providing an encouraging and engaging research environment, to colleagues past and present at Keele University, the University of Birmingham, King's College London and the University of Edinburgh, and to the researchers and staff at the journal *Cultures et Conflits* in Paris, with whom I spent a formative six months in 2004. Thanks also to my publisher at Routledge, Andrew Humphrys, and my very efficient copy-editor, Lisa Williams.

This work is the product of a long intellectual engagement with many inspiring peers and mentors. I would like to thank: the unnamed reading group, mostly held in the George pub behind the LSE, and its core members John Grant, Douglas Bulloch, Lina Dencik and Angharad Closs Stephens, with special thanks to Angharad for countless readings, debates, and conversations, but most of all for sharing the journey; Graham Smith, Jef Huysmans, Thomas Diez, Elspeth Guild, Didier Bigo, Philippe Bonditti, Vivienne Jabri, Seán Molloy, Peter Chambers, Halit Mustafa Tagma, Costas Costantinou, Mick Dillon, Julian Reid, Claudia Aradau, Christian Olson, Emmanuel-Pierre Guittet, Mustapha Pasha, Nick Vaughan-Williams, Luis Lobo-Guerrero,

Debbie Lisle, Peter Burgess, Monica Mookherjee, Kimberly Hutchings and the many members of the c.a.s.e. collective. My greatest gratitude must go to my parents for their unqualified support, to Rob Walker for his exceptional financial, moral, political and intellectual support and guidance, and to my wife Rebecca for her painstaking proofreading, but most of all for her patience, joy and love.

Introduction

How are claims about exceptional events being used to give legitimate authority to exceptional practices? Since the violent destruction of the World Trade Centre on September 11th 2001, a notable transformation has occurred in political discourse and practice. Politicians and commentators have frequently made the argument that the rules of the game have changed, that this is a new kind of war, that exceptional times require exceptional measures. Under this discourse, an array of exceptional measures have been put into practice, such as detention without trial, extraordinary rendition, derogations from human rights law, sanction or connivance in torture, the curtailment of civil liberties and aggressive war against international law. The category of the 'exceptional' has been invoked to legitimize and mobilize an array of violent and illiberal practices. These exceptional policies and practices, legitimated by claims about exceptional events and circumstances, I will call *exceptionalism*.

Many difficult questions are raised by the problem of exceptionalism. What makes an event or situation exceptional? Are there certain recognizable qualities and conditions that mark something out as being so? Does the exception bring about certain necessities and imperatives? Does the exception dictate an exceptional response? What is the relationship between the exceptional event and practices of exceptionalism? How do claims about exceptions work? How are they received? What gives discourses of exceptionalism authority? Who designates the exceptional? How do they overcome political contestation? How is an imperative and mobilizing link made between exceptional events and exceptional practices? What is at stake in the discourse and practice of exceptionalism? What are the politics of the exception?

These post-9/11 transformations in political discourse and practice have not gone unnoticed or uncontested. A broad argument has emerged about the proper relationship between liberty and security. Many urgent and challenging questions have been raised. Should liberal states ever act illiberally? Are there certain situations in which it is necessary to make exceptions to the law and the norm? Or do exceptional security practices destroy the very 'freedoms' they are supposed to protect?[1] I take this 'liberty/security' debate as the starting point for an investigation into the politics of the exception. Does this debate capture what is at stake? I argue that it does not, because many assumptions about liberty and security are problematized by exceptionalism itself.

The need to defend the liberal subject as a historical achievement is taken as a central principle of Western politics, yet the liberal subject, bearing freedom and rights, is thrown into contestation in the liberty/security debate. Is it 'terrorism' that threatens liberty, or the state itself? In this contested field, the discourse of liberty is used both to oppose illiberal security practices and to legitimate them. We must be defended against illiberal and fanatical fundamentalists who are not proper liberal citizens at all, we are told. Terrorist suspects do not deserve liberty and rights, it is claimed. The political implications of liberal principles are being heavily contested. Judgements are put into play about who is liberal and who is illiberal, who is modern and who is pre-modern, and who is normal and who is exceptional. Liberal societies must be defended, we hear, but by and from whom?

The conventional liberal debate contains contradictions that suggest there is something profoundly at stake in the politics of the exception. Exceptionalism problematizes not only the liberal subject, but also liberal society and the principle of liberty itself. How do liberal societies defend themselves, and what is the relationship between their liberal identity and their security practices? How do liberal political authorities make sovereign decisions about who and what is exceptional? How can the sovereign state make exceptions to liberty in the name of liberty, or exceptions to the law in the name of the law? These questions point towards a set of problems that need to be taken very seriously.

One effect of the discourse of exceptionalism and the liberty/security debate has been a resurgence of interest in the sometime Nazi jurist Carl Schmitt. In 1922, Schmitt proclaimed that 'Sovereign is he who decides on the exception'.[2] Schmitt argued that there is always the 'real possibility' of an existentially threatening exceptional event or situation that falls beyond the limits of law, liberty, rights and constitutional government. The exception, according to Schmitt, brings about a more fundamental range of imperatives and necessities that can only be answered by unlimited, unconstrained and unmitigated exceptional sovereign power. For Schmitt, security always trumps liberty and liberal politics; the exception always trumps the norm.

As a spectre haunting contemporary security politics, Schmitt seems to be winning the argument, and has expressed a serious challenge that has not been adequately met by the popular liberal discourse. To ask how and why the claims of Schmitt work is to ask how and why the claims of exceptionalism work. If exceptionalism has taken hold in contemporary political discourse and practice, then how does Schmitt, as one of its sharpest and most uncompromising proponents, make his case? Schmitt's exceptionalism operates as a pointed critique of the political and philosophical limits of liberalism. The reanimation of Schmitt is a symptom of the empirical rise of practices of exceptionalism. This book claims that a critique of Schmitt is also a critique of those practices.

Close engagement with the classic political theory of liberty offers many resources for understanding why Schmitt's claims are so expressive of the apparent contradictions between liberty and security. While the popular liberty/security debate posits the subject and the sovereign as opposites, the more serious political theory, considered here through Hobbes and Kant, holds that liberty is only possible under heavily restrictive political conditions. In this tradition, it is not a case of liberty *or* security, but liberty *under* security. The classic discourse of political theory argues that liberty can only exist in a permanent and necessary relationship with the possibility of its own suspension. Thus the limits of liberty and the possibility of its exceptional suspension appear to play a decisive role in its continuing possibility. Schmitt operates precisely upon this tension, which suggests that he works not as the *opposite* of liberalism but at a *constitutive limit* of liberalism. This apparent place for Schmitt at the heart of the modern Western tradition of political thought is why he must be taken seriously.

It is for these reasons that the challenge of Schmitt has been taken up by critical political thought.[3] The problem of Schmitt and the exception has become a point of departure for critical political approaches that take the contradictions and limits of liberalism seriously. This departure raises two sets of questions. First, what is the value of the discourse of exceptionalism as a *critical* tool? That is, how can the discourse be used to understand and critique contemporary political claims and practices? What does it mean to understand contemporary political practices as exceptional, and what political effect does that designation have? Second, if exceptionalism is a defining challenge of contemporary politics, and Schmitt is representative of that challenge, then how can these critical approaches be used to win the argument with Schmitt? If the empirical experience of exceptionalism and the apparent impotence of liberal opposition mean that Schmitt is in ascendance, can a critical discourse of exceptionalism gain the upper hand? These questions about the possibility of a critical approach to exceptionalism permeate this book.

Schmitt has a particularly strong presence in two influential branches of contemporary political thought, explored in Chapters 4 and 5. The first is the political philosophy of Giorgio Agamben, who attempts to take the problem of the exception seriously by placing it at the centre of the Western political tradition going back to the Greeks.[4] He argues that Western subjectivity has only ever been produced through the sovereign production of a relation between norm and exception. For Agamben, the decisions and judgements of exceptional sovereign power produce a political topology of forms of qualified and disqualified life.

The second influential approach is 'securitization theory'.[5] This dispenses with the idea that security issues or threats are objective, independently occurring things, and instead argues that security issues are constructed through practices of 'securitization'. Issues are turned into security issues through particular political prerogatives and processes. This challenges the idea that the exceptional security threat is an ever-present 'real possibility' that brings forth its own existential imperatives. Instead, an event or situation is made exceptional for political and strategic purposes through discursive processes and practices.

These two approaches go some way towards taking the problem of the politics of the exception seriously. Agamben suggests that the liberal *subject* should not be taken as a stable and fixed point of reference, because the production of liberal subjectivity is deeply implicated in practices of exceptionalism. Securitization theory problematizes the *object* of exceptionalism by theorizing the ways in which events and situations are *named* and *declared* as exceptional. It could be said that Agamben problematizes the *subject* of exceptionalism and securitization theory problematizes the *object* of exceptionalism. They engage with practices of sovereign *subjectification* and sovereign *objectification*. As such, they attempt to take the limits of liberal subjectivity and the constitutive effects of sovereign practices seriously. But there is a danger that although these critical approaches engage with Schmitt, they do not win the argument but ultimately prove him right. Does Schmitt's exceptional sovereign emerge from these encounters seated even more firmly upon his throne?

In search of a more rigorous critique of the politics of the exception I turn to the work of Michel Foucault. In his call to 'cut off the King's head in political theory',[6] Foucault throws down a specific challenge that directly squares up to Schmitt. How can the problem of sovereignty be deposed from its central position in political thought? Can Foucault offer a critical response to the politics of the exception that does not allow Schmitt to win the argument? Can exceptionalism be critiqued in a way that does not reify exceptional sovereign power, as Agamben and securitization theory ultimately do?

The methodology of Foucault's early work corresponds particularly well with the problematic categories of the discourse of exceptionalism. His method of 'archaeology', articulated in *The Archaeology of Knowledge*, first published in 1969, engages with the modern categories of knowing and being that are, I argue, discernibly in play in the politics of the exception. 'Archaeology' is a concept that emphasizes the analysis of practices, knowledges, structures, principles and discourses as dispersed historical sites. This allows a close engagement with the multiple modes and sites of the discourse and practice of exceptionalism, such as: the ways in which exceptional events are made into objects of political thought and discourse; the ways in which different subject positions are constituted through exceptionalism such as the sanctified liberal subject and the knowing, naming, judging and deciding sovereign; and the ways in which key terms such as 'exception' and 'security' have been constituted as concepts that imply their own political imperatives and necessities.

'Archaeology' as a mode of analysis is closely engaged with Kant's notion of critique.[7] It is a way of rigorously understanding the conditions under which authoritative knowledge-claims are possible. This is particularly appropriate for this project because the problem of the exception is a Kantian problematique in two specific ways. First, in the pervasive insistence on the salvation of freedom, or liberal subjectivity, whether from the dangers of uncivilized enemies or from illiberal tyranny; and, second, in the sovereign imposition of categories of knowledge upon the world. In Kantian fashion, the liberal subject maintains a sovereign presence at the heart of Western modes of being and thought; its faculties of knowledge and understanding shape and order the chaotic and contingent world into knowable categories according to its own image.[8] In political terms, this is manifested in such dualisms as liberal and illiberal, modern and pre-modern, civilized and barbarous, friend and enemy, and norm and exception. Exceptionalism is a problem of the limits of liberal life; a problem of the sovereign imposition of categories of interpretation onto contingent events and situations; and a problem of a King's head that is Kantian in its modes of being, thinking, judging and acting. It is therefore particularly enticing that Foucault's method of 'archaeological' critique attempts to explicitly depart from Kant by deposing the sovereign subject from the centre of Western critical thought. It is for this reason that I take my questions about the politics of the exception to the early Foucault.

Exceptionalism and the Politics of Counter-Terrorism pursues three broad questions: what is at stake in the politics of the exception? What kind of critique is called for? Can Foucault be used to defeat Schmitt?

Chapter 1 begins by identifying exceptionalism as a contemporary political problem that is present in empirical events, situations and practices, and in the discourses being used to interpret, represent, legitimate and criticize those empirical sites. It establishes points of contention in the popular debate about liberty and security and the notion of 'balance', noting symptomatic contradictions and blind spots. The chapter uses three case studies to develop an understanding of the general problem. These are: the civil liberties discourse in the United States; the legal argument over exceptionalism in the European Union; and the issues raised during the drafting process of new civil contingencies legislation in the UK. The end of the chapter reflects on the issues and difficulties raised and establishes a theoretical framework for the book.

Chapter 2 analyses two canonical theorists of the politics of liberty: Hobbes and Kant. These thinkers engage seriously with the political and philosophical implications of the problem of human freedom at both the individual and social levels. The chapter investigates the problem of the exception as a symptom of liberal politics rather than an aberration of liberal politics. Departing from the problematic understanding of exceptionalism as a dualistic problem of liberty and security, it reads the relation between liberty and security as a mutually constitutive dialectic rather than an either/or dualism. The aim is to understand how Schmitt effectively captures and deploys the difficulties that occur at the limits of liberal politics, and to ask what it might mean to consider Schmitt as the constitutive limit, rather than the opposite, of liberalism.

Chapter 3 is a detailed critique of Schmitt that engages in a careful textual analysis of his key exceptionalist texts: *Political Theology* and *The Concept of the Political*. The chapter works towards a more rigorous understanding of the problem of the exception in its different forms, testing the immanent validity of Schmitt's arguments. The most important aim is to understand what is at stake in Schmitt's work and thus what is at stake in the politics of the exception.

Chapter 4 deals with the work of Giorgio Agamben. It tries to establish how Agamben grapples with Schmitt and the problem of the exception, why his work is important and what it means for this study. Through Agamben, the chapter explores the work of key theorists in further detail, including Schmitt, Foucault and Walter Benjamin. The aim is to establish how far Agamben's work can be used to critique Schmitt and the problem of the exception, what its limitations are and why the problem needs to be addressed differently.

Chapter 5 assesses the implications of securitization theory for the problem of the exception. What resources does securitization theory provide for tackling the problem? The chapter analyses the theory's constructivist approach to security and its relationship to Schmitt, questioning their closeness and whether the methodological and political choices of securitization theory allow it to break free from Schmitt's central claims and their political implications. The final part of this chapter begins to introduce an alternative 'archaeological' approach derived from the work of Foucault.

Chapter 6 explores Foucault's archaeological method in detail, establishing how it might be used to tackle the politics of the exception. It then applies these methods to the issue of extra-legal imprisonment and torture with specific reference to the experiences of the 'Tipton Three' in Guantanamo Bay.

Chapter 7, the concluding chapter, is a definitive statement on Schmittian and Foucauldian approaches to the problem of the exception and exceptionalism. It discusses a range of contemporary scholars, dividing them into these two camps. It explains the reasons for the rise of Schmitt amongst critical scholars of security, critiques that debate for its failings, and establishes in detail a Foucauldian methodology and response to the politics of the exception and the problem of exceptionalism.

1 The liberty/security discourse and the problem of the exception

Since September 11th 2001, the 'exception' has become central to political discourse and practice. Many policymakers and commentators have sought to define 9/11 as an exceptional event that brought about an exceptional set of circumstances, which in turn both require and justify exceptional responses. As such, governments and their agents have unleashed huge levels of violence both domestically, against citizens and aliens it deems threatening, and externally, with seemingly global reach. It is possible to describe an extensive array of exceptional measures that have been legitimated and put in practice under claims about exceptional circumstances. This trend has been a particular feature of the political landscape in the UK, the US and the EU, made all the more notable as these are places that claim a liberal heritage. Much of this has consisted of a series of illiberal antiterrorism laws enacted, often quickly and with little opposition, under the aegis of urgency, necessity, emergency and exception, but many contemporary transformations have occurred outside and away from the field of law, instigated by executive fiat, changes in operational policy, and a generalized sentiment of exceptional legitimacy and mobilization not simply in government, but at multiple levels of governance, governmentality and public practice. Under the same series of claims about the rules of the game having changed, the US and UK have waged aggressive international war contrary to international law.[1]

Most disturbingly, this pattern of *exceptionalism* extends far beyond these visible areas into what has been called a 'global archipelago of the exception'.[2] It has become clear that Guantanamo Bay is only the best-known instance of a network of extra-legal practices of kidnapping, detention, abuse and torture that reaches into both Western and Eastern Europe, North and sub-Saharan Africa, the Middle East, Central Asia, and innumerable military and intelligence bases, prisons and camps in other untold locations.[3] The stories of former prisoners are both horrendous and similar.[4] The revelations continue apace.

There has been a concerted effort to document these exceptional policies and practices at the legal, institutional and sociological levels,[5] accompanied by widespread anxiety about an apparently growing gap between the realms of norm/law and potentially arbitrary and often unseen assertions of illiberal and violent practices of exceptionalism. These empirical trends are readily visible in public discourse and political practice. They have spawned many different responses and interpretations, the most dramatic, profound and interesting of which is an appeal to the concepts of exception and exceptionalism. There is much significance in the fact that these concepts have returned to scholarly discourse, having last been significantly in play in interwar Europe.

There is an implicit exceptionalism in the many contemporary claims and commentaries that refer in one way or another to a well-established account of the relation between liberty and security. This chapter will show that the limitations and contradictions in this discourse are both palpable and well exercised critically. In portraying the relationship between liberty and security as one of trade-off or striking the right balance, there is a profound failure to grasp the contradictory, aporetic or perhaps dialectical nature of that relationship, as understood by more serious theoretical approaches. The most interesting theories and critiques of exceptionalism illustrate that beyond these problems of liberty and security there is more at stake. This first chapter, therefore, has three main aims, to be pursued together: first, to describe the empirical existence of exceptionalism as a discourse and practice; second, to describe the empirical existence of the prevailing liberty/security discourse and subject it to critique; and, third, to show that in these first two areas of concern there is something more profound at stake. This will lead, in later chapters, to a sustained critical engagement with the merits and failures of key theoretical departures on exceptionalism. Ultimately, the aim in the final chapter (Chapter 7) is to sketch a radically different theoretical response to the problem.

9/11 and the liberty/security discourse

Since September 11th 2001 an intense debate has sprung up about liberty and security. Within that debate there appear to be two poles. At one pole there is political authority, often in the form of states and their agents, but also increasingly manifested in forms of governance and governmentality that exceed the traditional boundaries of the state. The leaders, agents, ideologues and commentators of these political authorities claim that we need to sacrifice some liberty for security because of the renewed threat of terrorism. Hence governments have responded to large-scale acts of murderous political violence by implementing what they call necessary renegotiations of the liberty of their citizens, or more likely a specific minority, in order to meet the demands of security. At the other pole there is a broad coalition that claims to speak for civil society by standing up for liberty and rights against the encroachment of the state and other political authorities. From civil liberties campaigners to international lawyers, it is anti-terrorism itself that is seen as the threat to liberty. Many suspect that the threat of a ubiquitous 'terrorist' enemy is being used to legitimate contentious, illiberal and violent policies and practices across the globe. Post-September 11th anti-terrorism measures and legislation have raised anxieties that the 'proper balance' between liberty and security has been lost. Many fear that in the process of 'defending our freedoms' political authority is damaging the very freedoms it claims to protect, and that the constitutional, legal and historical limits normally placed on political authority have been violated. These are the basic terms of debate for the prevailing liberty/security discourse. The key question has become: what is the proper balance between liberty and security?

This relationship between liberty and security has been posed both as one of balance, where liberty and security are considered inversely proportional, and therefore requiring the sacrifice of one for the defence of the other; and as mutually reinforcing, where improving the proliferation and protection of rights and freedoms is thought to improve security, because it addresses the grievances and resentment of those who may otherwise turn to violence. There is no distinction to be made between these two positions when the language of freedom and rights can be used both to legitimate and to oppose violent and illiberal security practices. 'Liberty' and 'freedom' are not stable referents, but highly mobile, contested and co-optable political discourses. To frame the problems of post-9/11 world politics in terms of liberty and security is to remain firmly rooted in a highly problematic liberal dualism that is incapable of responding to the problem of sovereign exceptionalism without becoming mired in contradictions; contradictions that the dominant liberal discourse has the simultaneous, characteristic effect of obfuscating and silencing, but also, and more interestingly, contradictions symptomatic of the profound paradoxes that reside at the heart of modern discourses of politics.

Simply put, claims about the need to protect freedom from the overzealous pursuit of security are massively vulnerable to the Hobbesian counter-claim already contained within that discourse: without security there can be no freedom.[6] This is demonstrated empirically when calls for the observance of constitutional and legal checks and balances are decisively silenced or pushed aside by claims that those checks and balances must be suspended in the name of a temporary or even indefinite state of exception. This presents us with a contradiction: the hegemonic discourse of liberty is the rationale for both practices undertaken in the name of freedom and practices undertaken in the name of security. The epigraph over the gates of Camp Delta in Guantanamo Bay reads: 'Honor Bound to Defend Freedom'. The problem is that the liberty/security binary is empirically, historically and theoretically hierarchical – claims about freedom always risk being trumped by claims about the necessity of security, which often appear as claims about security *in the name of* freedom.

This problem is not restricted to hypocritical and contradictory illiberal security practices conducted in the name of freedom. The examples presented here demonstrate that there is no adequate response to the primacy of security over liberty if one remains within this liberty/security discourse. The civil libertarian side of the debate is not able to overcome this contradiction. As Chapter 2 will elaborate, the concept, discourse and tradition of liberty already entail limits. One can only be free under certain conditions. One can only be free under conditions of security. Some positions within the civil liberties discourse are silent about this problem, while others insist that exceptions be made to liberty only under conditions of *real* danger and *genuine* emergency, thus accepting a hypothetical rationale for exceptional measures, but not the rationale offered today. Similarly, the pursuit of security in the name of liberty cannot but be paradoxical. Liberty is secured under the possibility of its own suspension. To oppose liberty and security, especially in a 'balance', is part of the problem. In both theory and practice, the two principles belong to a single discourse. At the limit, under exceptional conditions, and at the extreme point, the dualism of liberty/security collapses into a monism in which security trumps liberty.

These contradictions are well rehearsed critically.[7] Aside from marginal accounts of liberty such as anarchism, the classic political theory of liberty is always an account of liberty under certain conditions and within certain limits. Within the canon, liberty has been imagined under God, under sovereignty, under security, under the law and within its own logical limits. The principle of liberty is grounded within tight limits and upon the exceptional possibility of its own suspension.

Within contemporary liberal discourse, there is a silence and failure to come to terms with the problem of the inherent limits of liberty. At the heart of the dualistic liberty/security discourse there is an obfuscated, radical silence about what is at stake in practices of sovereign exceptionalism. The central claim of this chapter is that liberty and security are inherently part of the same discourse – a single liberty/security discourse. Within this discourse many positions are possible, but the discourse is defined by inherent contradictions. The position of liberty does not form an adequate position of opposition or critique; it is already co-opted and complicit in the illiberal practices of its own defence and suspension.

There is a more profound difficultly here too. The opposition of liberty to security does not capture what is at stake in declarations of exceptions and practices of exceptionalism. This problem exceeds the liberty/security discourse. Questions must be asked about the sources of exceptional authority and legitimacy; about the capacity to name and declare exceptions; and about the historical, social and political conditions under which exceptionalism is possible. Later chapters will engage with key theoretical departures on these questions. Here, the problem will be framed through an analysis of three textual sites or case studies that are characteristic expressions of the 'liberty/security' discourse and its contradictions, which at the same time provide further empirical detail about the problem of exceptionalism. The regularity of their contradictions, and the symptomatic failure to come to terms with them, points towards the deeper profundity of the problem of the exception and exceptionalism.

The first of these textual sites is a selection of literature from the post-9/11 civil liberties debate in the United States. The second is a high-level legal report into liberty and security in the European Union. The third is an analysis of the drafting process of the Civil Contingencies Act in the UK, which in its course stumbled across certain fundamental political questions.

Civil liberties in the United States

In the US civil liberties discourse, the general critical sentiment is that although 9/11 has been officially characterized as an 'attack on freedom', the governmental response appears to hold 'freedom' itself in scant regard. The three books analysed here are typical of this literature of dissent: Nancy Chang's *Silencing Political Dissent: How Post-September 11 Anti-Terrorism Measures Threaten Our Civil Liberties*;[8] Stephen J. Schulhofer's *The Enemy Within: Intelligence Gathering, Law Enforcement, and Civil Liberties in the Wake of September 11*;[9] and an edited collection entitled *It's a Free Country: Personal Freedom in America after September 11*.[10]

Although these books reveal the far-reaching social and legal consequences of the USA PATRIOT Act (the Uniting and Strengthening America by Providing Appropriate Tools Required to Intercept and Obstruct Terrorism Act) and other illiberal government policies, they betray a characteristically narrow conception of what might be at stake in contemporary world politics. They operate entirely within the parochial discursive frame provided by the United States Constitution. Although this discursive frame has its origins in classical liberalism, any intellectual awareness of problems of limit or contradiction seems to have been lost.

Nancy Chang, a senior lawyer at the Centre for Constitutional Rights in New York, seeks to impress upon her readers the inappropriateness, unconstitutionality and indeed immorality of the USA PATRIOT Act and associated executive measures undertaken without recourse to the usual constitutional and institutional limits since 9/11. She offers a concise account of historical abuses of civil liberties enacted by US governments in times of fear and crisis, such as the internment of Japanese-Americans after Pearl Harbour and the FBI's attempt to disrupt and discredit the civil rights movement, in order to illustrate that these past violations are being repeated and indeed exceeded.[11]

As Chang explains, the USA PATRIOT Act establishes an ambiguous and potentially arbitrary definition of terrorism, sweeps protest and civil disobedience into the nebulous category of 'domestic terrorism', institutes guilt by association, facilitates secret property searches and wiretaps, and makes an explicit distinction in the constitutional liberties and rights of full US Citizens, other US residents and foreigners. The Act's shockingly swift and barely challenged passage through Congress has been well documented,[12] but, as Chang notes, much of what has been done since September 11th has not even been carried out through legislation.[13]

The fate of what Chang calls 'America's disappeared' points towards just such arbitrary or prejudicial violent practices; as many as 2,000 Muslim men resident in the US were arbitrarily detained in a 'dragnet' in the months after September 2001, predominantly without criminal charge at the time or subsequently.[14] Efforts by families and civil liberties groups to obtain information about these men was persistently obstructed by the Justice Department, signalling the (re-)emergence of a culture of secrecy contrary to US traditions and laws on freedom of information. Detainees were held incommunicado, moved without notice and denied access to counsel. *Habeas corpus* was effectively suspended. Although many were charged with minor immigration violations, none was charged with any offence relating to terrorism.

Despite her empirical rigour and an explicit call for protest and resistance against these developments, Chang betrays a characteristic blind spot about what might be at stake in practices of exceptionalism. Her civil libertarian approach takes her straight back to the US Constitution, which she consistently lauds as a sacrosanct work of genius representing the pinnacle of human justice and liberty. The result is that she seems unable to engage in critical questioning of what 'freedom' or 'liberty' might actually mean in the US, let alone in countries that do not have the good fortune to have a United States Constitution of their own. Her liberal-nationalist flag-waving, albeit dissenting, has the effect of simultaneously concealing and exacerbating the contradictions that reside at the heart of the liberty/security discourse. Is 'liberty' the collection of political rights enshrined in the Bill of Rights, or is 'liberty' the right of the US government to put security before the rights of minority groups and foreign populations? The Hobbesian impasse endures as a particularly sharp articulation of the problem; liberty and security cannot easily be separated from each other. Civil liberties campaigners claim to defend liberty against the government, whilst the government claims to defend the security necessary for that liberty to exist.

Stephen J. Schulhofer adopts a different approach in *The Enemy Within*, by taking on the more difficult task of evaluating anti-terrorism policy not just in terms of its liberality or constitutionality, but on its own terms. Rather than exalting America's mythical founding ideals or invoking lessons from history, Schulhofer goes beyond case law with a deft command of policy, procedure and practice. That is, he actually asks the question: will post-September 11th legislation and executive measures actually succeed in preventing acts of political violence? The answer is mostly 'no'.

Schulhofer's interpretation is that legal and public policy developments since 9/11 can be described in terms of updates to out-of-date elements of law enforcement (regarding telecommunications, for example), illiberal right-wing opportunism and genuine but ill-considered anti-terrorism measures. He charts what he calls 'bad compromises',[15] where civil liberties have been damaged in return for no significant anti-terrorism gain; 'September 11 opportunism',[16] where new investigative and law enforcement powers with no relation to terrorism have been 'slipped into' the new legislation to take advantage of the sense of emergency that has gripped the nation and Congress; and 'unchecked executive power',[17] where the checks and balances of the American Constitution have been circumvented. The danger is that the US government's determination to make terrorism investigations and pro- secutions into 'exceptional' cases is counter-productive as it may undermine the due process needed for the criminal convictions that could otherwise be secured if acts of violence were genuinely being planned.[18]

By analysing policy developments in relation to the practices they replaced, rather than in relation to constitutional ideals, Schulhofer avoids the soapbox tone that plagues some radical writers. Yet although not overtly fighting a particular corner in the way that much of the popular political literature does, Schulhofer offers little reflection on the discursive use of the terrorism label or indeed the concept of liberty. By engaging with the liberty/security debate simply at face value, Schulhofer's text symptomatically serves to reify the concepts of 'security' and 'liberty' as unproblematic and desirable, and fails to come to terms with the contradictory nature of the relationship between those principles. There is more at stake in the problem of exceptionalism than a mere technical evaluation can reveal.

It's a Free Country, an edited collection of over fifty contributions, presents many famous names and heavy hitters, including Michael Moore, Judith Butler, five members of Congress, several executive figures from the American Civil Liberties Union (ACLU), journalists, professors, law enforcement and intelligence agents and the odd musician. The book aims to show that civil lib- erties 'transcend traditional left/right divisions' and illustrate that liberty and security need not be an either/or trade-off. What it actually reveals is that the 'broad spectrum' of political opinion on civil liberties is in fact extraordinarily narrow.

The overwhelming consensus of the contributors is that America's ideals are a beacon for liberty and justice in the world, and need only be followed faithfully. This approach typically fails to grasp any sense of contradiction in the concepts of liberty and security. The contributions are characteristically libertarian but often distastefully nationalistic; the book presents a very American, libertarian left/right alliance that rarely offers any suggestion that there may be anything at fault or contradictory in its ideals. Again the political imagination does not venture far beyond the US Constitution.

Only one of the book's pieces hints at the more profound implications of practices of exceptionalism, and only descriptively rather than critically. Andrew Kirkland, Assistant Police Chief in Portland, Oregon, became a minor celebrity – perhaps folk devil is a more appropriate label – when he was quoted in the *New York Times* as having said 'No' to then Attorney General John Ashcroft's edict that all men of Middle Eastern origin should be taken into custody and interviewed.[19] Kirkland describes how, in the after- math of this contentious 'No', hundreds of phone calls and emails flooded his office. Many were press enquiries into his grounds for dissent, to which Kirkland responded by referring to received legal advice about Oregon state law. He would not interview people without grounds for suspicion, nor was he willing to jeopardize the good work of anti-racial-profiling community policing programmes. Outside of journalistic enquiry, the majority of correspondence was passionately negative, calling him a 'traitor' and telling him to 'do his job'.[20] Kirkland explains that one question stood out for him in particular: he was asked why, if state law prevented him from conducting the interviews, he could not just ignore the law this one (exceptional) time, in light of the scale of the national crisis?[21]

Kirkland's experiences suggest a constitutive 'democratic' element at work in practices of sovereign exceptionalism. His experiences suggest that 'democratic' forces – not particularly votes, but the will or assent of a group of people, the 'weight of a nation' as Kirkland's title puts it – can trump normal political structures and the rule of law. This raises questions about how political decisions and judgements work, and about the sources of authority and legitimacy upon which they draw. It also evokes the potential paradox in liberal democracy at the intersection of individual rights and democratic rule suggested by Chantal Mouffe.[22] If 'the people' (the question of who the people are and who rightfully speaks for them is another question) want certain individuals or minority groups to suffer illiberal and illegal practices, then that is potentially what will happen, and apparently what has happened in the US. Indeed, in the UK ministers publicly made the argument that the democratic demand for security justifies exceptions being made to the rights of particular individuals.[23]

There is a distinction to be made between changes to the law that are temporary suspensions, legally inconsistent or unconstitutional, and the call to disregard the law completely in the name of an emergency. Beyond a state of exception declared in relation to law, beyond the *legal exception*, there is possibly a more profound *exceptionalism* operating in general political discourse, in governmental practices and in social relations. This raises questions about how political authority functions and what its sources are in the broadest possible sense. The popular civil libertarian discourse in the United States is blind to these more profound problems.

'Fundamental rights' and the balance of freedom and security in the European Union

In March 2003 a report was published entitled *The Situation of Fundamental Rights in the European Union and its Member States in 2002*, with an extended supplement on the 'The Balance between Freedom and Security in the Response by the European Union and its Member States to the Terrorist Threats'. This was produced for the European Commission by a group of lawyers called the European Union Network of Independent Experts on Fundamental Rights. It is an exemplary and sophisticated expression of the liberty and human rights discourse. It is also a telling symptom of the contradictions and radical silences that surround the problem of exceptionalism. Although to some degree the document shows an awareness of these problems, its response is no more than a restatement of legal principles. A critical analysis of this document reveals what is at stake in the characteristic contradictions and occlusions of the discourse of liberties and rights.

The report argues that the central problem with EU anti-terrorism measures is the lack of an adequate, established and commonly agreed definition of terrorism. A precise and stable definition, they argue, is essential if 'terrorist' actions are to be distinguished from regular criminal activity, as governments are inclined to insist they are.[24] Without this distinction, the application of exceptional rules and procedures in the detection, detention, prosecution and punishment of 'terrorists' cannot be justified. Without a precise definition, the experts argue, 'the measures adopted in fighting terrorism will lack clear legal basis'.[25] Tellingly, the document effectively maintains that such a definition must be possible, even if it is not currently available.[26] From the perspective of law, proper definitions are necessary if rights and freedoms are to be 'fundamental' and not simply precariously subject to political whims.

This insistence on stable definitions reveals a more fundamental problem. The group of lawyers cannot – *qua* lawyers – entertain the idea that the designation of 'terrorism' might not have an independent, essential, legal meaning. Presupposing such a definition has the effect of occluding the political questions raised by practices of exceptionalism: how and by whom is terrorism authoritatively defined? Under what conditions? What violent practices does such a definition make legitimate?

The liberal-legal discourse presupposes a kind of transparent deliberative rationality in practices of defining and naming. However, exceptionalism, and in particular sovereign decisions about what is and is not 'terrorist' and what is and is not exceptional, suggests that sovereign practices of naming, representing and defining the 'truth' of a situation or thing are precisely what are brought into question by contemporary political transformations. These practices of naming lead directly to the sanction, authorization, legitimation and enactment of violence.

The lawyers' report also seeks to reject the idea that freedom and security are inversely proportional, i.e. that increasing the one means reducing the other.[27] However, although this is a reasonable proposition, the discourse of liberty and rights remains ambiguous. The principles deployed in the attempted legitimation of the recent war in Iraq suggest that a discourse of liberty, rights, moral conviction and righteousness might actually be more effective for legitimating illiberal, violent or bellicose aims than an old-fashioned discourse of military-strategic necessity. The group of lawyers, even in their modified adoption of the liberty/security pairing, do not seriously engage with the contradictions implied in the potential complicity of the principle of liberty with illiberal practices.

Practices of exceptionalism highlight the political foundations of law, because they expose the sovereign political decisions, and not simply technical legal procedures, involved in the declaration of exceptions. Yet what seems to be at stake for the group of lawyers is not so much the violence of practices authorized by claims about exceptions, but the autonomy of the rule of law itself. Whereas the 'proper' use of state violence was perhaps once convincingly legitimated by the invocation of law, political practitioners are finding it either increasingly necessary, useful or effective to legitimate violent practices through the invocation of 'exceptions' to the law.

Today there is a burgeoning debate about phenomena that exceed the existing capacities of the state and the law, such as transnational crime, people-trafficking, 'international terrorism', movement of people and so on.[28] A corresponding host of new institutional arrangements have been established to address these phenomena, such as the ambitious and sensitive Justice and Home Affairs (JHA) policy agenda set out by the EU in the 'Tampere scoreboard' of 1999. However, this expanded frame of policy and analysis does not alter the difficulties that a legal approach has in critically engaging with, in Giorgio Agamben's terms, a widening 'zone of indistinction' between the realm of norm and law and the arbitrary assertion of force and violence – a growing rift between the law and the force of law, the law and actual practices on the ground.[29] The legal approach to post-September 11th anti-terrorism measures cannot – *qua* legal analysis – address the way that the idea of 'exceptionalism' calls into question the limits of freedom and the boundaries of law/violence.

As a final symptom, the group of lawyers appear to be overwhelmingly against sovereign exceptionalism and the arbitrary use of power by states and their agents, yet they step back from this position in their final conclusions. They do not condemn the violence and violation of privacy, freedom and rights caused by profiling, detention without trial, surveillance, restrictions in the right of defence, etc., as one would expect. Rather, they declare that these violations should be carried out only when they are 'absolutely necessary',[30] kept to a 'strict minimum',[31] be of a 'temporary character'[32] and 'targeted sufficiently precisely'[33] to 'avoid a risk of arbitrariness'.[34] Consequently, the lawyers end up in support of the very same exceptional practices that they consider a problem, and also undermine the idea that rights are 'fundamental'. Furthermore, they are unable to address the compelling political question of who decides what constitutes 'necessity' and the 'minimum', and indeed how and by whom exceptions to 'fundamental' rights are made.

What is apparent from this analysis is the profound difficulty in attempting to reassert principles of law, liberty and rights against practices or discourses of exceptionalism. It is not hard to argue that these ethical principles *ought* to be fundamental, but this thrust is constantly thwarted by the potential capriciousness of politics and the 'threat' presented by violent contingencies. The fact that the Network of Independent Experts steps back from its analyses to give quarter to exceptionalism is symptomatic of this problem. Politics and contingency appear to be in excess of law and ethics; attempts to reduce the former to the latter, and the exception to the norm, are ultimately flawed or contradictory. There is a need for a theorization of exceptionalism that does not simply reproduce its symptoms.

The UK Civil Contingencies Act

The Civil Contingencies Act, which received Royal Assent on 18 November 2004, raises further questions about the excess of politics, sovereignty and authority over law and its limits. The Act was the result of an extensive review of emergency powers and legislation that began prior to, but was given new impetus by, the events of September 11th 2001. It was considered that the emergency planning and logistical capacity of the UK would have been unable to cope with such an event. The Act replaces the previous legislation on emergency powers and civil protection (defined as defensive measures against attack by a foreign power other than actual combat) contained in the Emergency Powers Act 1920 and the Civil Defence Act 1948. These were for the most part directed towards trade union strikes and the perceived Soviet threat, respectively, and as such were considered outdated. The Act expands the definition of an emergency to include, for example, environmental disasters, disruption of telecommunications and financial markets, and threats to public health. It also creates a new logistical and planning framework that incorporates local and regional authorities, the emergency services, and utility and transport companies.

This section focuses less on the Act and more on the drafting and consultation process of the initial Bill, first published in June 2003. The process exposed fundamental questions about political authority, declaratory power, sovereignty and limits (those found both in the law and in less tangible sites). As such, the development of the Bill captured many of the key challenges posed by the problem of sovereign exceptionalism.

The stakes involved in the drafting of the Bill were high, as signalled by the great furore provoked upon its initial publication. A *Guardian* newspaper leader from 20 June 2003 opened by noting the 'accusation that the Blair Government is planning to enact the most sweepingly authoritarian piece of official legislation in modern peacetime' and concluded by describing the Bill as 'potentially the greatest threat to civil liberty that any parliament is ever likely to consider'.[35] The major concern shared by the *Guardian*, the civil liberties group Liberty and the Parliamentary Committee entrusted with scrutiny of the Bill was that the new definition of emergency was far too wide. The report of the Joint Committee on the Draft Civil Contingencies Bill read: 'Witnesses and responses to the Cabinet Office consultation have commented that the definition is so wide as to encompass events which are already routinely dealt with by emergency services'.[36] The Committee directed its strongest unease at the part of the Bill that defined an emergency as 'an event or situation which presents a serious threat to … political, administrative or economic stability'.[37] It noted that the 'political stability' provision could give a future government carte blanche to 'protect its own existence when there may be no other threat to human welfare'.[38] The report argued:

> Emergency powers could therefore be triggered by events which threaten the essentials of life for the government, as well as events which threaten

the essentials of life for the community. These two points of focus are not necessarily compatible. In protecting the government, emergency powers could potentially be used against the civil population.[39]

The Joint Committee also recommended that the definitions of 'serious', 'threat' and 'stability' should be much more clearly focused, emphasizing that 'the core of an emergency is the threat to human welfare'.[40] To this end it urged that the government's proposed 'triple lock' safeguard conditions of 'seriousness', 'necessity' and 'proportionality' should be 'significantly strengthened'.[41] In fact, the government responded positively to these recommendations, narrowing the definition of 'emergency' and removing the reference to 'stability', thus largely mollifying its critics.[42]

Nevertheless, the government did not address a concern expressed by Liberty about the 'subjective' nature of defining 'security threats'.[43] Liberty pointed out that assessments of security threats are frequently based on intelligence which remains secret, the 'questionable reliability' of which was 'highlighted by the recent controversy surrounding the Iraq dossier'.[44] No doubt, the apparent 'error' of the intelligence used to construct the rationale for invading Iraq has (further) undermined the legitimacy of truth-claims made by the governments of the UK and elsewhere.[45] That debacle has reinforced the need for scepticism and scrutiny of the truth claims deployed in the legitimation of exceptional practices.

Moreover, in its criticism Liberty touched upon more profound questions about the relationship between political power and 'truth'. The declaration of security threats and exceptional situations hinges on much more than the inherent truth or falsehood of such claims. The distinction between 'objective' and 'subjective' judgements is helpful only up to a point. In terms of the effectiveness of these judgements in authorizing, legitimating and mobilizing illiberal political practices, it is more important to consider how such claims come to function as 'true'. Under what conditions do claims about security threats have authority? Who has the authority to make authoritative claims about security threats? How are political practices structured around institutional and social prerogatives of declaring, defining and naming? How do such decisions function as 'sovereign', i.e. as the highest and final source of authority?

The controversy over the Civil Contingencies Bill also raised questions about the limits that operate upon political practices and sovereign decisions. Constitutional government, in its many forms, is an institutionalized system of checks and balances that serves to limit political power, ideally preventing it from becoming tyrannical or arbitrary. The UK is guided by the constitutional principle that Parliament is sovereign. This means that only Parliament can pass primary legislation that has full sovereign status, while the executive can only create secondary legislation, or delegated legislation.[46] The distinction is that the law courts can declare the secondary legislation of the executive illegal and issue injunctions against it, but, in deference to the sovereignty of

Parliament, the courts can only declare primary legislation *incompatible* with other laws or international commitments such as treaties and conventions. An injunction can be directly enforced, while a declaration of incompatibility cannot.[47]

The initial Civil Contingencies Bill proposed that executive regulations made under a declared state of emergency be treated as primary, rather than secondary, legislation. The intention of the government was to remove the possible hindrance of human rights challenges to, and injunctions against, its emergency powers. As the Liberty response to the draft Civil Contingency Bill explains, '[t]he purported justification is that, unless treated as primary legislation, injunctions against regulations allegedly breaching the [European] Convention [on Human Rights] would interfere unduly with the Government's emergency powers'.[48]

Both the Joint Parliamentary Committee and Liberty had major concerns about this proposal, because the implications would have been far-reaching indeed.[49] If emergency regulations were to have the status of primary legislation, it would effectively mean that 'a Secretary of State's utterances could legally become statutes',[50] which Liberty described as 'truly remarkable'.[51] Not only would any 'balance' between liberty and security be undermined by removing the judicial compulsion on the executive to follow the law on human rights, but the system of constitutional limits intended to hold executive power in check would be removed. In order to stress the profundity of this possibility, it should be noted that in twentieth-century legal thought the idea of executive word automatically becoming law was a key innovation of Nazi juridical theory, which also grew out of a declared state of emergency.[52]

Although the government conceded these concerns and withdrew the clause, its response reveals some of the stakes involved regarding the prerogatives of sovereign power. The government stated (thus confirming the original fears of Liberty and the Joint Committee):

> this provision would not have enabled the maker of emergency regulations lawfully to make regulations that contravened the Convention rights. Nor was this the Government's intention when it suggested the inclusion of this clause in the Bill. ... [The clause] served only to limit the remedies available on a successful challenge to human rights grounds. In particular, the regulations could not be struck down by a court on human rights grounds. Instead, the court could have issued a declaration that the regulations were incompatible with the Convention rights. The Government considers that emergency powers should always be operated within the confines of the Human Rights Act.[53]

The key point is not the commitment of this government or a future government to the Human Rights Act, but that a government could decide for itself if its actions were compatible with human rights or not. If the courts could not issue an injunction, but instead only make a declaration of incompatibility, then the government could not be compelled to act or desist. The question is one of where sovereignty ultimately resides. The draft Civil Contingencies Bill sought to remove a limitation on the sovereign capacity of the executive to judge, decide and act in an emergency situation (which the executive itself would declare). In this scenario, a government would not be constrained by the rule of the law, but by its own judgement of itself, demonstrating a circular logic and process.

Accordingly, the Bill was changed so that emergency regulations made by the executive must be approved by Parliament within seven days, and only then will they have the status of primary legislation. If approval is not forth-coming, the regulations will lapse.[54] However, even this schema does not entirely remove the legal difficulties posed by emergency powers. The section of the Bill/Act regarding parliamentary approval contains the proviso that '[n]othing in this section … shall affect anything done by virtue of regulations before they lapse, cease to have effect or are amended under this section'.[55] This means that even if parliamentary approval is not given and the emergency regulation lapses, the status of anything done under emergency regulations prior to their lapse will not be affected. Even if emergency regulations fail to win approval, they cannot be subject to retrospective legal challenge. They will not have been illegal during the time they were in force. Thus they dwell in a legal grey area. Even if greater legal recourse were possible post facto, this would not necessarily undo the practical consequences of acts committed under the assumed legitimacy of a declared emergency.

The Civil Contingencies Bill/Act demonstrates how sovereign exceptionalism, manifested here as emergency powers, exposes the limits of positive law (that is, law understood as deriving from human reason, but rationally coherent and immanently valid, as opposed to law by executive fiat, or natural law deriving from precepts about nature). It appears that it is both practically and logically impossible to fully contain sovereign power within the limits of law, despite efforts to do so.

The Act prompts further questions about limits on sovereign power other than those found in the law. If sovereign exceptionalism cannot be entirely contained in formal legal terms, does the high status and long tradition of the rule of law in the UK make it unthinkable that emergency powers could be used to undermine the constitutional foundations of the country, for example?

In its critique, the Joint Committee suggested that 'past legislation which makes up the statutory patchwork of the British constitution' (including, for example, the 1297 Magna Carta, the 1688 Bill of Rights and the 1998 Human Rights Act) should be 'protected' as 'not being liable to modification or dis-application under [the clauses of the Civil Contingencies Bill]'.[56] The govern-ment replied: 'the Government does not consider that it is possible to prepare and maintain a list of enactments which should be "protected" from amend-ment … Parliament is sovereign and is free to amend and modify any pre-vious enactment it considers fit'.[57] This is why it was so necessary to remove the provision in the draft Bill that would have allowed emergency regulations to be treated as primary legislation. If this had been so, the executive could effectively assume the sovereign legislative authority of Parliament. The executive could then theoretically use emergency powers to alter the constitutional fabric of the UK by repealing statutes of constitutional importance. Indeed, the government is right to point out that Parliament itself could fundamentally alter the constitutional fabric of the UK regardless of any state of emergency. Nevertheless, this remains more or less unthinkable.[58]

The questions of limits to sovereign power, some formal, some less tangible, suggest that there is a strong cultural and discursive aspect to constitutional law and the status of law generally. There are sources of political authority and limit beyond the law and beyond governmental institutions. What is the role of this more nebulous limiting power with regard to the declaration of states of emergency? Can this limiting power act as a rejoinder or bulwark against the juridical logic of exceptionalism? Or, going back to the 'democratic demand' for exceptionalism in the Oregon case above, does this nebulous force function more like a constituent power?

What are the shortcomings of the liberty/security debate and what is at stake in exceptionalism?

Claims about liberty and claims about security, as understood in the context presented here, are inseparable. I have argued that they form a single 'liberty/security' discourse. The popular debate on liberty and security is beset by contradictions. Does 'liberty' act as a cover for actions that threaten the possibility of a community of liberty? If we need security to defend liberty, what happens when security undermines the very liberty it was meant to defend? If the principle of liberty is sacrificed, what is to distinguish between security practices and plain old violence? If liberals sacrifice the principle of liberty, what is to distinguish their violence from the violence of their illiberal enemies?

Practices of exceptionalism have problematized the relationship between liberty and security. Despite the dominant dualistic understanding, their relationship is not one of balance. It is a relationship wracked by problems of limit. Traditionally, the relation of the individual to the state has been resolved through some kind of constitutional settlement that defines the 'proper' limits of individual subjectivity and the 'proper' limits of sovereign political authority. This settlement is challenged by practices of exceptionalism. And although this settlement is questioned in the liberty/security debate, there is little comprehension of what is really at stake. The debate is little more than a symptom of the problem. Practices of exceptionalism have taken the liberty/security relation to the limit. At the limit, the liberty/security relation appears as something other than dualistic; perhaps monistic, perhaps dialectical.

I shall now summarize and clarify the key themes raised so far, and begin to sketch how some critical purchase might be regained:

1   Many disturbing contemporary political developments and tendencies can be placed under the umbrella term of 'exceptionalism'. Although this concept is for the most part limited to a particular thread of critical responses that draw upon the ideas of Carl Schmitt and Walter Benjamin, the term captures both the spirit of much contemporary political discourse and the empirical experiences of many of those on the receiving end of the often violent practices legitimated by that discourse. More importantly, the concept of 'the exception' captures the radical way in which popular and dominant theorizations of liberty, security and politics more generally have been exceeded or undermined. I will develop a more sustained investigation of the ideas of 'the exception' and 'exceptionalism' in later chapters.

2   When discussing accounts of liberty, political theory has tended to distinguish between 'negative freedom' and 'positive freedom', where the former is a concern with freedom from forms of repression and oppression, and the latter is a concern with the freedom to have the opportunities that depend on basic material provisions like education and healthcare.[59] Although it would be fair to argue that in the contemporary post-9/11 debate the liberties concerned are mainly 'negative' civil liberties and human rights, the negative/positive distinction is not particularly important or interesting in this context. What *is* interesting and revealing is that whichever way liberty is understood, and whatever its content, it is always understood as something to be achieved in relation to the state, whether by imposing limits on state action or by making material demands upon the state; often it is both. For the liberal discourse of liberty, the state giveth and the state taketh away. The relational nature of the concept of liberty means that it should not be considered as a thing or condition that can be held or lost, but as a political rationale, an authoritative principle and a historically situated discursive practice. Indeed, the question of political authority, in its many forms, seems to be a much greater problem than the relation between liberty and security.

3   Existing, dominant theorizations of liberty and security betray a characteristic but highly problematic dualism. The attempt to ascertain the 'proper' relationship between liberty and security posits two poles: the 'sovereign' individual – 'sovereign' because of his/her 'fundamental' rights and liberties; and 'sovereign' political authority – 'sovereign' because it has the 'final say', backed with violence, which it needs in order to guarantee the conditions under which liberal political community and individual freedom are possible. Exceptionalism exposes the contradictions of this dualism in two ways. One is the Hobbesian critique that security always trumps liberty, because without security there can be no liberty. The other is that violent practices are often effectively legitimated through the language and rationale of liberty itself ('Honor bound to defend freedom', 'defending freedom-loving people', 'fighting those who hate freedom', etc., but also more sophisticated invocations of tolerance and intolerance, multiculturalism and fundamentalism, and so on).

4   While it is not surprising that the discursive legitimation of security practices
    is often profoundly nationalistic ('National security', 'Homeland security',
    'Defending our borders and ideals', etc.), claims about civil liberties also
    display a profound nationalism. This is especially true in the US, where
    claims about civil liberties almost without exception invoke the US Con-
    stitution or the 'genius' of the Founding Fathers. This, of course, feeds
    straight into claims about enemies who don't share/don't understand/hate
    the American ideals that, although certainly contestable, are unswervingly
    considered as the pinnacle of freedom and political achievement. Europe
    has a more diverse stock of ideas about what liberty and rights might
    mean, to some extent expressed in ideas about multiculturalism and in a
    developing body of human rights law at the national, European and
    international levels. This has not stopped European discourses of threat
    and fear from invoking similar ideas of an unenlightened or pre-modern
    enemy. Discourses of liberty all too often reinforce discourses of security.
5   The liberty/security discourse presupposes boundaries but does not take
    the problem of boundaries seriously. In Rob Walker's terms, the modern
    presupposition of sharp lines is in trouble.[60] Traditionally, accounts of
    security have tended to make a distinction between 'internal/domestic'
    (crime, order, political stability) and 'external/foreign' (national security,
    espionage, overseas interests) domains. There is now a wide consensus
    that this internal/external distinction has been rendered meaningless (if
    indeed it ever held much meaning) by September 11th and the 'threat' of
    a 'new type' of 'terrorism'.[61] Post-9/11 anti-terrorism measures have
    conflated internal and external security to a greater degree than ever. The
    'terrorist training camp' in Afghanistan or Iraq is supplied with 'recruits'
    from the British mosque, we are told, and the immigrant who infiltrates
    our sacred borders brings hatred of our ideals and recipes for ricin. Poli-
    ticians and state agencies have enthusiastically applied to their own citi-
    zens and residents surveillance practices long used by foreign intelligence
    agencies, attempting to make what was once a schoolboy fantasy world
    of distant intrigue and 'reasons of state' into a 'necessary' feature of
    everyday life. The conflation of the 'foreign enemy' and the 'enemy
    within' is a recurring feature of the history of states of emergency.
6   It is widely held that the characteristic spatial and temporal claims of
    modern accounts of politics sound ever more implausible in light of the
    increasing porosity, fluidity and ambiguity of territorial, cultural and
    legal borders.[62] Challenges to traditional spatial, predominantly statist,
    assumptions are being posed in terms of increasing movement of poten-
    tially dangerous people, finances, technology and ideologies. A similarly
    modern account of temporality is invoked in discourses of threat, as in
    claims about 'post-modern societies' and 'pre-modern societies', religious
    fundamentalism, the tide of globalization, development or a pathological
    lack thereof. These ideas about spatial and temporal transformations are
    being colonized by the liberty/security discourse: in claims about either

new threats to liberty which require new security practices or the need to actively spread liberty throughout the world in order to reduce security threats. These trends are being explicitly played out in both the US and the EU. Accordingly, there has been a concerted extension of military sight and reach, growth of transnational and supranational institutional arrangements, proliferation of surveillance and weapons technologies, increased cross-border intelligence and police cooperation, and novel new forms of global governance and development.

Yet it seems that institutional and discursive responses to these spatial and temporal readjustments have been jolted into a tailspin. Philippe Bonditti has documented and analysed conflicting trends within the US bureaucracy manifested in inter-agency competition and contestation over resources and discursive authority in the 'war on terror'.[63] Whilst the CIA has sought to 'de-territorialize' threat and move away from the traditional enemy state by invoking enemy individuals, groups, networks (e.g. Al Qaeda) and cyber-terrorism, the State Department and Pentagon have sought to secure their role in the 'war on terror' by 're-territorializing' threat in the form of rogue states that sponsor terrorism and have the capability to build 'weapons of mass destruction' (e.g. the 'Axis of Evil'). This discursive contestation at the institutional level serves to further undermine the possibility of stable distinctions between 'here' and 'there', 'friends' and 'enemies', 'norm' and 'exception'.

7   It is symptomatic, therefore, that the overwhelming popular and intellectual response to the mounting difficulty of drawing sharp lines of distinction, truth and judgement has been to bring a renewed vigour to just that task. Hence the European Union Network of Independent Experts on Fundamental Rights stresses the need for a proper definition of terrorism so that proper decisions can be made about when to deploy 'exceptional' anti-terrorism measures. It seems that the entirety of the civil liberties discourse in the US seeks to confront challenges to liberty by reasserting the inalienable truth of the rights enshrined in the US Constitution. The tendency of these responses is to attempt to rein exceptional practices back in to the established framework of normality and legality. These responses underestimate the challenge of exceptionalism.

The theoretical implications of the liberty/security discourse and the exception

The dominance of the contradictory 'liberty/security' binary within the current debate undermines the possibility of an effective critical or political response to contemporary practices of violence and exceptionalism. Despite the existence of impassioned criticisms of illiberal and violent political practices, we should be uncertain of our ability to contest or resist those practices. If the language we speak and the principles we invoke in our political contests are the same as those claimed by our adversary, then not only are we unable to offer an alternative vision, but we must consider the possibility that the terms of our discourse make us complicit in the legitimation of violence. While we may embrace the language of liberty and rights as resistant and critical, our leaders claim that the violent security policies they pursue are driven by those very principles. For example, not only did Tony Blair attempt to legitimate his military adventurism through claims about the removal of human rights-abusing regimes and the 'liberty' we have brought to the world, but this military adventurism seemed to be driven by genuinely heartfelt conviction in the very principles that others claim he violated. We must consider whether the reification of liberty and rights might be grist to the discursive mill of the very same violent practices that we oppose.

The implications for critical discourse posed by practices of exceptionalism are not grasped by the renewed rigour brought to the question of the 'proper' balance between liberty and security. Intellectual contestation over the 'proper' meaning of 'liberty', 'security' and indeed 'terrorism' presupposes the possibility that there is a 'proper' meaning to be found. The capacity to authoritatively define such concepts and principles is precisely what is at stake in practices of sovereign exceptionalism. Who decides on the proper meaning of liberty? Who decides what or whom is to be a necessary exception to liberty? When do the norms of liberty apply and when must they be exceptionally suspended? These are not simply technical questions. They bring into question the discursive structures (in the broadest social, historical, cultural and political sense) which serve as the conditions of possibility for such judgements and decisions.

This problem has been most sharply captured by Carl Schmitt in his declaration that '[s]overeign is he who decides on the exception'.[64] Schmitt polemically declares that the exception says everything and the norm says nothing. If this is the case, is it useless to reassert the norm if politics is happening as an exception elsewhere? If the exception lives off the norm, as Schmitt claims, what does it mean to continue to reaffirm the norm, as in the case of the seemingly parasitical relationship of security to liberty? Schmitt poses a profound challenge to proponents of liberty, when, seemingly paradoxically, it is liberty that is being used to justify exceptions to liberty.

Schmitt prompts such questions as: who decides on the exception? Are they themselves exceptional? Do they exist beyond the realm of law and norm? What is the status of political decision in the arena of the exceptional, when it cannot be reduced to or contained within the arena of the norm, of liberty, of positive law? Upon which sources of authority does the exceptional sovereign decision draw? What are the conditions of possibility for the sovereign decision on the exception?

The dominant intellectual approach to the problem of defining liberty, security and terrorism does not seem to have answers to these questions that are not overwhelmed by contradictions. The 'defence of liberty' seems ultimately to affirm the same sovereign exceptionalism that threatens to undermine liberty. If Schmitt is wrong, it does not appear possible to prove him so from within the contradictions of the dominant liberal discourse.

To borrow a concept from the philosopher of science Gaston Bachelard, the dominant 'liberty/security' dualism is an 'epistemological obstacle'.[65]

Commentaries on the sovereignty of the individual, manifested in 'inalienable' or 'fundamental' rights and liberties, allow us little, if any, critical purchase on the problem of sovereign exceptionalism and even hinder us in that critical task. On top of the empirical problem of 'exceptional' practices, our dominant ways of thinking about politics compound our political predicament by hindering our ability to comprehend and perhaps resist these developments. Bachelard writes: 'It is in the act of cognition that we shall show causes of stagnation and even of regression; there ... we shall discern causes of inertia that we shall call epistemological obstacles'.[66] It is tempting to suggest that dominant ways of thinking about liberty and security have stagnated and become just such 'epistemological obstacles'. The 'liberty/security' discourse is an inherited, historical mode of cognition that has inertia: it continues on a path resistant to change and has become an obstacle to new ways of thinking. Yet this particular 'epistemological' characterization of the problem does not go far enough.

We should be wary of jumping too quickly to the conclusion that there is something profoundly new about our current set of political circumstances (that characterization holds its own dangers). The 'exception' is subject to a multiplicity of practical and discursive contestations. Are we or are we not living under a set of 'exceptional' circumstances that require 'exceptional' measures? Are those who have had their liberties and rights taken away 'necessary' 'exceptions' to the norm, or do their experiences imply something more profound about the status of the norm itself? Is the 'state of exception' temporary or permanent? Has the exception become the norm? If in our critical enquiries we unreservedly characterize the present as 'exceptional', is there anything to distinguish our position from that of the illiberal governmental rhetoric that claims the present 'need' for just such 'exceptional' practices? We should be careful of simply arguing over what is exceptional (new threats, or new responses to new threats?) without considering the political implications of attempting to name the present as exceptional.

The 'exception' is much more interesting than a simple characterization of the present. Certainly, the contemporary situation is a pressing, indeed urgent, political problem, but it is only one moment within the historical constellation of politics and political thought. The concept of the 'exception', as shorthand for both the empirical and discursive developments of the present (a present largely characterized by its own 'exceptional' moment in the 'historical rupture' of 9/11),[67] is interesting because it captures some of the most profound and enduring political and philosophical problems of modern thought – problems that hold deep epistemological implications, but also ontological, metaphysical and even theological significance.

The stakes and new terms of engagement: violence, subjectivity, discourse, sovereignty

In light of the singular discursive terrain of the liberty/security discourse that I have described, and the widespread failure to come to terms with its contradictions and occlusions, it is clear that a more sustained critical approach is needed. The failure to come to terms with the limits of the prevailing narratives of the liberty/security discourse is symptomatic of the problem of exceptionalism itself. Exceptionalism – as a discursive claim, as a strategy, as a concept, as a principle and as a practice – is a problem that feeds on the limits of the liberal tradition. It forces us to take seriously the relation between liberty and security as more than a simple problem of balance. The conceptual figures of liberty and security are expressions of political subjectivity and sovereignty. There is a need to take this relationship more seriously, and, more specifically, to take its dialectical and historically contingent nature more seriously. There is nothing 'fundamental' about the liberal subject except when treated as such by dualistic liberal principles. That principle should not be blithely reasserted but interrogated as a historical and political effect. The ways in which the relation between subjectivity and sovereignty has been understood, and the ways in which violence plays a part in that relation and understanding, should themselves be an object of study.

If the discourse of liberty and security is itself deeply implicated in the transformations which that relation is undergoing, then a critical investigation into 'exceptional' transformations in that relation needs to do more than reassert basic or 'fundamental' principles like rights or liberty. It needs to engage with discourse itself as a field of study, where discourse is taken in the broadest possible sense: as a historically contingent series of relations between objects, subject positions, statements, concepts and strategies.[68] It is from Michel Foucault that I draw this methodological guidance. If Carl Schmitt expresses the challenge of exceptionalism in the sharpest terms, and contemporary debates on liberty and security have fallen prey to him, then I propose to test Foucault as a potential saviour. The stakes and terms of engagement for an encounter between these two theorists are laid out below. The subsequent chapters will engage more thoroughly with the concepts of liberty, security and exceptionalism, and will interrogate the arguments of Carl Schmitt and those theorists who would deploy him, establishing their weaknesses before exploring the work of Foucault to sketch a different response. Going beyond the terms of the liberty/security discourse, I propose different terms of debate, grouped below under the headings of violence, subjectivity, discourse and sovereignty. These, I hope, will capture the stakes involved in the problem of the exception and exceptionalism.

Violence

While I still reserve judgement on whether or not we should characterize the present as 'exceptional', it is certainly some kind of topological shift, or rather an attempt to reinscribe the topology of boundaries and limits – be they legal, political, social, discursive, spatial or temporal – that has stirred the current pressing need to ask these questions. The problematization of violence in its many forms is central to all of this. This study has so far taken journalistic, sociological, legal, political and allegorical accounts of contemporary violent practices as its starting point, and has gone on to critique the weaknesses, silences, contradictions and even complicity of these common responses with regard to these practices. But whether violence is an ever-present feature of human life is not the question that needs asking. Violence itself is not novel. It is transformations in the ways in which violence is manifested in political, international, discursive, ontological and metaphysical relations that are interesting.

New manifestations of violence reveal shifts in the relationship between forms of subjectivity, discourse and sovereignty. The limits of political subjectivity have been transformed by the curtailment of civil liberties in new ways, with violence unleashed against subjects in ways that would have previously been less acceptable. The authoritative principles deployed in the legitimation of violent political practices have shifted. Violence is manifested in transformed modes of sovereignty that, for example, pay less respect to established spatial and conceptual limits, the most obvious of which are state borders and law, respectively. An enquiry into the violence of the present is an enquiry into the violence manifested interstitially in transformed relations between subjectivity, discourse and sovereignty.

Subjectivity

The liberal subject is immediately at stake in contemporary practices of violence, illiberality and exceptionalism. Beatrice Hanssen quite rightly characterizes the speaking subject as central to liberal political theory, in terms of both the immanent political power and the immanent rational validity of speech.[69] The problem of the exception implicates subjectivity in problems of political speech and action, because our dominant modes of enquiry and critical speech seem unable to satisfactorily respond to violent contemporary practices, and are perhaps even incriminated in them. More importantly, violent practices are altering the material conditions under which subjectivity has been considered possible, by violating or at least altering the constitutional, legal and political settlements that have long been regarded as its historical cornerstones.

Causes for concern regarding liberal subjectivity under conditions of exceptionalism can be described as follows: (1) the 'free' subject is threatened with arbitrary, or at least extra-legal, incarceration, degrading treatment, and perhaps even torture or death; (2) the political voice of the 'speaking' subject has become at best ineffectual, at worst compromised and complicit in the very exceptional practices which threaten to undermine political subjectivity; (3) the rational validity of knowledge, discourse or language presumed by liberal thought to be immanent within political speech has been brought into question by potentially arbitrary declarations of exceptionality.

Anxieties about the current material circumstances of political subjectivity cannot but invoke the longstanding centrality of subjectivity to modern political thought; liberal political thought especially. The individual subject is enshrined in such key historico-political sites of the liberal tradition such as the US Constitution, the French Revolution, and twentieth-century human rights conventions. Yet the popular liberal discourse, which has grown out of this tradition, conceives of subjectivity in foundational and dualistic terms, criticized here as part of the problem. What is needed is to question the relation between forms of subjectivity and sovereign political power. How does the one constitute the other? In the prevailing contemporary discourse of liberty and security, these questions are lacking. The contemporary debate does not do justice to its politico-theoretical ancestry, which took questions such as these seriously (the subject of Chapter 2).

The problems raised by the exception and exceptionalism show that modern subjectivity is not a stable and foundational figure but a historically and politically contingent one. Subjectivity should be understood, more generally, as part of a manifold relational problem in modern political thought. That relational problem is threefold: first, as a relation with discourse, as the condition for the subject to think, know, name and judge; second, with sovereignty, as both guarantor of subjectivity and threat to subjectivity; and, third, with violence, manifested as the empirical and perhaps discursive enforcement of modern conditions of subjectivity, judgement and sovereign decision.

How has the relation between subject and sovereign been constituted, and how is that relation being transformed by practices of exceptionalism? What part do specific forms of subjectivity play in the constitution of practices of sovereign exceptionalism? In what ways is the subject – liberal, modern, national or some other prefix – implicated in the problem of the exception? For Carl Schmitt, the problem of the exception exposes the limits of liberal subjectivity and freedom. In Schmitt's vision of exceptionalism, the conflated sovereign 'subjectivity' of the nation-state must necessarily take precedence over the liberal subject. Is this a principle that is in operation in contemporary practices of exceptionalism? If so, how can it be addressed? I have shown that the contemporary liberty/security discourse betrays a kind of statism, nationalism, or both, often in spite of itself.

The central argument of this book is that the work of Michel Foucault has a special significance for the problem of the 'exception'. In terms of subjectivity, Foucault's work on practices of 'subjectivization' seeks to subvert the 'sovereignty' of the subject, emphasizing instead the historically and socially contingent practices through which subjectivity is constituted.[70] Foucault ties these practices of 'subjectivization' to the operation of language, knowledge, institutions, discourse and power. Following this Foucauldian vein, it is a key point of departure for this project that, contrary to the reifying tendencies of much contemporary liberal discourse, subjectivity can only be seriously considered as relational, historical or discursive, and not as essential, necessary, 'inalienable' or 'fundamental'. Under what historical conditions of possibility, and through the invocation of which discursive principles, has violence against the subject been legitimated? What forms of subjectivity have served to constitute the principles and practices of violent sovereign exceptionalism?

And, in turn, how do practices of exceptionalism serve to constitute forms of subjectivity?

Discourse

One point of contention for this study is the problem of law, specifically the lack of a stable and accepted legal definition of terrorism from which political authorities can legally proceed with 'exceptional' anti-terrorism measures. Yet the legitimation of practices of exceptionalism cannot easily be summed up in terms of law; this is what distinguishes the problem of exceptionalism from the 'norm' of criminal justice. Indeed, the whole concept of the exception rests on an excess of politics, fact, necessity or contingency over law. It has become clear that the modes of judgement and decision that operate in the legitimation of exceptionalism draw upon far less tangible sources than law.

Exceptionalism is a problem that exceeds law in both conceptual terms and empirical terms. Practices that claim exceptionality explicitly attempt to draw upon sources of authority other than law. And insofar as legitimations of exceptionalism have been successful, in empirical terms, such sources of authority have been forthcoming. Security rationales seem to hold a special status that allows them to trump all other concerns through a classic existential imperative captured by Hobbes and latterly by Schmitt (one must be secure to survive, but particularly to survive in ways that are 'free', or perhaps 'modern').

The problem of exceptions and exceptionalism exceeds legal codes by definition. The legitimacy of exceptionalism stems from claims about exceptional events that require extra-legal responses. The attempt to legally codify a domain of exceptional prerogatives and practices regarding 'terrorism' and 'security threats' is fraught with difficulties. It becomes apparent that the designation of exceptions is itself extra-legal; it does not directly draw upon the law as its source of legitimacy, but upon more emotive claims about threat, civilization, security and so on. Emergency laws specifically attempt to designate a jurisdiction domain beyond normal legal limits, and in their legitimation draw upon extra-legal discourses. They operate beyond the normal scope of law. The 'exceptional' sovereign designation of particular subjects, groups, places and even ideas as 'enemy' – inscribing a whole topology of friends and enemies, freedoms and dangers, norms and exceptions – is used to enable and legitimate forms of violence with little respect to established laws. This is precisely how Carl Schmitt's arguments about the exception work; he seeks to establish the principle that beyond the law there are more profound sources of political authority. What are they? How are they put into practice? And what is the relationship between legal authority and extra-legal forms of authority?

The problem of exceptionalism cannot be addressed through dualistic approaches that try to establish clear boundaries between liberty and security, norm and exception, legal and extra-legal. The task is not to establish clear distinctions, but to question how such distinctions are made. From where do those distinctions acquire their authority, if not from legal codes? The problem is not one simply of establishing the truth of the situation through the proper procedures, but of questioning the operation of truth and authoritative claims within wider discourses. What is interesting about our current predicament is that it renders highly visible just what is at stake in problems of knowing. It reveals the implausibility of the classical imperative of speaking truth to power. It is precisely through sovereign distinctions, sovereign judgements and sovereign authorizations of 'truth' that practices of exceptionalism function. The question is: *how* do these sovereign authorizations work?

Foucault's provocative problematization of truth and power is especially relevant here. For Foucault, power derives its authority from authoritative accounts of what must be true.[71] Sovereign power requires sovereign knowledge. As he argues in *The Order of Things*, it was Nietzsche who shattered the conception of language as a transparent medium between man and the world. For Nietzsche, it is no longer a question of what is and is not, but a question of who owns the possibility of designating, in language, what is and is not. As Foucault writes:

> it was not a matter of knowing what good and evil were in themselves, but of who was being designated, or rather *who was speaking* when one said *Agathos* to designate oneself and *Delios* to designate others. For it is there, in the *holder* of discourse and, more profoundly still, in the *possessor* of the word, that language is gathered together in its entirety.[72]

The problem of knowing and speaking expands through the problem of language and representation into the problem of discourse. The relationship of ideas to the world cannot, if indeed it ever could, be considered transparent and unproblematic. 'Discourse' becomes Foucauldian shorthand for the lack of any real distinction between the empirical and the theoretical or abstract.

The identification of specific discourses – the terminology I have used throughout this chapter in the identification of a largely singular 'liberty/security' discourse – is the identification of particular, historically contingent expressions of the mediated relationship between man and the world; a relation that is the historical, not transcendental, condition of possibility, not simply for knowing, but, more importantly, for particular modes of being (e.g. being 'free', 'civilized' and 'modern') and particular modes of acting, sometimes in very violent ways (e.g. against declared exceptions to those modes of being). The enveloping centrality of discourse in the problem of man's being is therefore far more than some kind of linguistic puzzle. The problem of discourse is central to the questions of violence, politics and, in this case, exceptionalism.

Sovereignty

The Nietzschean question 'Who is speaking?' illuminates a final set of questions regarding sovereignty. Much political and international thought remains anachronistically fixated with the problems of state sovereignty symbolized by Germany in 1933: fascism, authoritarianism, unchecked modernization (particularly weapons production and proliferation), imperialism and the almost mythical figure of the sovereign, the *Führer*, the king, the superman, the statesman or the great Leviathan. Call it Napoleon, Hitler, Robert Mugabe, Saddam Hussein or George W. Bush. To an extent, this project is no exception. Certainly, concerns about state sovereignty and the things done in its name are more pertinent than ever. The recent resurgence of interest in Carl Schmitt, the theorist of state sovereignty posed in the starkest terms, is surely a symptom of this concern. If Schmitt represents the challenge posed by exceptionalism, then the question is: how is it possible to win the argument with him? What kind of riposte to exceptionalism is possible? The dominant liberal discourse, with its contradictions, occlusions and lack of historicity, has failed in this respect. Schmitt shrewdly articulates problems that dwell precisely at the legal, political, philosophical and discursive limits of the liberal tradition. If, as Schmitt states, '[s]overeign is he who decides on the exception',[73] then we need to engage more seriously with sovereignty as a principle, practice and problem.

As an important qualification, it must be noted that sovereignty and state sovereignty are not synonyms, although they are often treated as such. State sovereignty, as an object of analysis, has come under much critical reappraisal in recent years, pulled this way and that in debates about either the decline or perseverance of the state, or the need to think about state sovereignty in new ways because of new global conditions. In response to these seemingly endless contestations, Rob Walker argues for the need to consider sovereignty as 'a complex process that works as a reality precisely as a claim about what *must be*'.[74] Sovereignty is not a positive 'reality', but a powerful set of normative claims about what is 'necessary' and how the world and human life 'must' be shaped and ordered. It is precisely this powerful normativity that is manifest, for example, in claims about the 'necessity' of the exceptional pursuit of 'enemies' by the state in order to 'secure' the 'free' or 'civilized' 'world'.

Modern state sovereignty is only one particular historically situated articulation of a sovereign 'regime' of truth and power. Claims about the decline of the state or new forms of sovereignty should be taken as a demonstration that modern state sovereignty has only ever been a particular idealization of the form that the resolution of the problem of sovereignty should take. It is for this reason that interrogating modern state sovereignty as a normative ideal is so productive, because it makes more visible the regulative, authoritative principles – the 'truths', if you like – that are powerfully implicated in contemporary and indeed historical political practices. Interrogating sovereignty in a way that does not repeat the contradictions and occlusions of the liberty/ security discourse means problematizing language, representation, discourse and the relation between man and the world.

As a historically specific articulation of a relationship between language, the world, subjectivity and authority, modern state sovereignty can be characterized as a spatio-temporal cartography that idealizes sharp lines drawn between 'here' and 'there', 'then' and 'now'.[75] That the possibility of drawing and sustaining these spatio-temporal distinctions is 'in trouble'[76] only serves to further emphasize that sovereignty is a mysterious practice that has not only geopolitical implications, but also ontological, epistemological, metaphysical and even theological significance. Sovereignty (to include modern state sovereignty) is a problem of transcendence, in that it both poses and resolves questions about the place of human life in the universe. Sovereignty, in its innumerable expressions, is an answer to questions about the highest sources of authority. One could never hope to comprehensively capture all the complexities of its many historically contingent expressions, least of all because our own ways of knowing cannot easily be separated from prevailing epistemic conditions. However, through interrogating different historical and empirical sites where the depths of these profound problems are discernible, it is perhaps possible to make these compelling mysteries glow more brightly through the imposing shadows of epistemic certainty or 'totalitarian theory', as Foucault called it.[77]

The questions that must be brought to the workings of this powerful abstract and empirical practice concern how such sovereign claims work. If we are alarmed about the present, then we must concern ourselves with the discursive, ideological or hegemonic operation of those 'sovereign' claims, judgements and decisions that enable and legitimate the violent practices with which we wish to take issue. Sovereignty somehow works within the discursive arena; that is, within an almost seamless interplay of subjective positions of authority and powerful authoritative claims about the world, which in turn appear to be inseparable from the violent human practices that order, define, divide and judge the world. This is why the question of 'Who is speaking?' is so important, whether the 'who' is construed as a singular entity or as a complex collective subjectivity such as nation, culture, community, civilization or humanity. Pursuing questions regarding the 'proper definition' (read 'truth') of who is 'evil', 'enemy', 'exceptional', 'terrorist' and so on can only obfuscate the mysterious workings of sovereignty and sovereign 'truths'. In Foucauldian terms, sovereignty is a complex phenomenon that operates within both truth and power – a phenomenon that simultaneously enables truth and is enabled by truth.

To ask 'Who is speaking?' is therefore much more than to pin down singular sources of political authority. However powerful the actions or dictates of particular 'world leaders' might be, the physical enactment of the force of their words is only possible through already-existing, historically contingent social, political and institutional arrangements. 'Sovereign' figures are only able to authoritatively claim ownership of the language of rights, freedoms, civilizations or security because of the existence of prior discursive structures, in the broadest possible sense, that make this kind of authority possible. Hence sovereign claims are never simply taken 'at their word', like some kind of divine commandment. Rather, sovereign claims work because they operate within already established, authoritative schemas of 'truth'. As Foucault famously argues: '"Truth" is linked in a circular relation with systems of power which produce and sustain it, and to effects of power which it induces and which extend it. A "régime" of truth'.[78] Foucault prompts a certain kind of questioning that will prove extremely productive for thinking about problems of sovereign exceptionalism. How does sovereign authority work? From whence does it derive its authoritativeness? What makes a judgement, a decision, or a designation 'sovereign'? Under what conditions are sovereign decisions possible? How does a discursive landscape authorize sovereign regimes of truth and power? By pursuing the problem of 'discourse' in the broad Foucauldian sense, this book will shed light on the truth claims, philosophical and historical narratives, subject positions, strategies and concepts that work to authorize practices and principles of sovereign exceptionalism.

2 Freedom and liberty in classic political theory
Hobbes and Kant

The stakes involved in the problematic liberty/security discourse can be made clearer by looking more seriously at the political theory of the concept of liberty. The canonical theorists of liberty had a much better idea of the limits and contradictions implied by the concept. The contemporary debate would do well to pay more heed to its ancestry. By understanding how the contradictions in the concept of liberty were resolved by these canonical theorists, it will be possible to gain a much better grasp of the implications and consequences of a *politics* of liberty. The aim of such an enquiry is to understand exceptionalism not simply as an anomaly in a politics of liberty, but as a *symptom* of a politics of liberty. How does the political principle of liberty work to produce illiberal political effects? How was the concept of liberty incorporated into now-canonical accounts of politics? How did the canonical theorists of liberty tackle the apparent contradictions in the concept? What relation of liberty and political authority was imagined and produced?

The main argument of this chapter is that, unlike the derivative and unreflective claims of contemporary protagonists in the liberty/security discourse, the canonical theorists of liberty and the Western political tradition were well aware of the limits and contradictions of freedom. To this end, part of what is offered here is an analytical account of the idea of freedom as it appears in key sites in the history of Western political thought. This will be an exposition of what it must mean to be 'truly' free according to Thomas Hobbes and Immanuel Kant. The purpose is both to explain why this account is so powerful and to establish a clearer understanding of its immanent contradictions and political implications.

Reading these political theorists gives us a good idea of what is at stake in a politics of liberty. What is fascinating is how each deals with the contradictions in the concept. The previous chapter argued that the contemporary liberty/security discourse displays a symptomatic dualism whereby two contradictory positions are held at the same time: liberty must be defended both *by* security practices and *from* security practices, without destroying liberty in the process. Hobbes and Kant deal with these contradictions in a rigorous and uncompromising way. Beginning from precepts about what *must be* – theologically, metaphysically, existentially and rationally – they derive political accounts of what, consequentially, freedom *must be*. They structure their theorizations of human freedom through accounts of metaphysical and political necessity. It is this theme of *necessity* that demonstrates how powerful accounts of the relation of liberty to sovereign political authority have worked both theoretically and historically.

Understanding the workings of canonical accounts of freedom *under* conditions of necessity is a way of understanding why calls for the observance of constitutional and legal limits seem weak in the face of claims that those limits must be suspended, perhaps temporarily, perhaps more permanently, in the name of a state of emergency or state of exception. According to the logic of freedom under conditions of necessity, sovereign authority has the capacity to declare exceptions to liberty and law not because it is corrupt, tyrannical or arbitrary, but because liberal freedom *necessarily* entails the 'security' that sovereign authority imposes. Thus necessity both trumps liberty and is its prior condition.

The argument that liberty must come after security is commonplace, more so under declared conditions of exceptionalism. The aim of this chapter is not to legitimize that argument philosophically. Nor is it a case of describing the authoritarian position in opposition to the liberal one. Rather, the aim is to show how, in the philosophical tradition, the conditions under which liberty is considered possible are extremely rigid. A restrictive account of liberty is not an obstacle to liberty, but a 'product' of liberty. The aim is not so much to establish a determinate relation between the philosophical tradition of liberty and its contemporary fate, but to demonstrate why arguments about necessary compromises and suspensions of liberty work so powerfully. The initial conclusion would be that the principle of sovereign exceptionalism is immanent to the logic of the concept of liberty in the case of both canonical accounts discussed here. This does not mean that sovereign exceptionalism is a timeless principle, but rather that exceptionalism is implicit in a well-established discourse that is philosophically, politically and historically powerful.

Therefore, while the contemporary discourse on liberty, security and the exception is largely silent about its internal contradictions, these contradictions are symptomatic of a deeper theoretical problem. There is more at stake in these silences than the familiar political positions of contemporary protagonists reveal. Exceptionalism is not only a pressing political concern, but raises more profound politico-philosophical questions. It is not derivative of the problem of freedom, but primary to it, and indeed primary to politics itself. Hobbes and Kant engage precisely with what is at stake in these current political concerns. The immanent logic of the concept of liberty does not, indeed cannot, resolve the problem of exceptionalism.

By understanding how a discourse of sovereign exceptionalism is philosophically implied by the discourse of liberty, this chapter will establish the grounds from which an understanding of Carl Schmitt – the theorist of exceptionalism posed in the starkest terms – is possible. More specifically, what is needed is an understanding of the politico-philosophical conditions under which the claims of Schmitt work. The aim is not simply to tar Schmitt as an abhorrent figure at the wrong end of a spectrum of possible political positions (which is too easy, has been done many times before, and avoids questioning what is really at stake),[1] but to understand the politico-philosophical conditions under which Schmitt seems to win the exceptionalism argument. To simply oppose 'liberty' to Schmitt and exceptionalism is not enough; once the philosophical contradictions and implications of the concept of liberty are appreciated, it becomes clear that a more radical argument is needed to defeat him. Once the basic philosophical problems of liberty, sovereignty and modernity have been established, and armed with the resources that the classic discourse of liberty offers for refusing the banal contradictions of the contemporary liberty/security debate, the task in later chapters will be to deal with the widespread failure to gain some critical purchase on these contemporary political developments, and ultimately try to win the argument with Schmitt.

Hobbes and Kant

Hobbes and Kant proceed from claims about the nature of man and the universe to abstractions about what it must mean to be free. They construct an understanding of what freedom must be if it is to be proper freedom at all, and construct a kind of necessary progression from a basic and dangerous freedom as a natural human condition to a heavily qualified form of liberty that is entailed by the necessities of social and political human life. Thus the possibility of 'true' freedom depends on certain necessary conditions being met: for Hobbes it is sovereignty and security; for Kant it is sovereignty and individually internalized reason. Each account of freedom is posed in terms of the logical and necessary impossibility of freedom being otherwise. This is why Hobbes claimed that his was a doctrine that 'admitteth no other Demonstration'.[2]

The 'freedom' that resides at the heart of each account is extraordinarily restrictive, and hence implies something of a paradox. What is freedom if it can simply be taken away? What does freedom mean if it is only true freedom *under* strict conditions? What kind of freedom does a political subject have if they must either be free in the only way there is to be free, or else be subjected to the immense but necessary costs of sovereign punishment or death? In more philosophical terms, what kind of freedom does a human being have if the only way to be free is to be tightly subject to the dictates of necessity? What is the relation of human freedom to metaphysical determinations and political necessities? The authority of these accounts stems precisely from their apparent resolution of the dualism of freedom and determinism into a dialectic or perhaps even a monism where freedom *is* determinism. What follows is an elaboration of how this apparent contradiction between freedom and determinism has been so powerfully framed and resolved.

Hobbes and Kant both proffer the same solution: political subjects are only *truly* free when they obey. There is always a progression from a dangerous natural freedom to a politically qualified, highly restrictive form of liberty. For Hobbes, life without subjection to sovereignty would be a hellish anarchy: 'nasty, brutish and short'.[3] Freedom without authority would be no freedom at all. Humans are only truly free under the security of universal obedience to a sovereign power, and this is shown by the dictates of reason. For Kant, true enlightened freedom means obedience to the dictates of reason, internalizing the laws of moral freedom and being one's own lawgiver. The institutions of law and sovereignty become the external expression of this internal moral law of freedom. Irrational man is no more free or autonomous than a child. Thus the dualism of 'freedom and determinism' becomes the monism of 'freedom *is* determinism'. How does each thinker reach this resolution?

Hobbes

Hobbes creates the first modern account of what it must mean to be free. His political philosophy begins by systematically destroying both classical and Christian metaphysics. This enables him to draw radical new conclusions about human life, which are at the same time radical new conclusions about political life. Through this account of metaphysics and human life, Hobbes establishes principles of necessity that authorize and delimit a realm of qualified liberty. As such, he posits an account of how one can be free under specifically modern determinations – a specifically modern account of what it must mean to be free.

In the first ten chapters of *Leviathan* Hobbes systematically assembles the principles of a new metaphysics which is effectively informed by Galileo. Instead of the Platonic realms of crude appearances and divine forms, and instead of an Augustinian City of God and fallen earthly city in its shadow, Hobbes's universe consists only of bodies and motions. Hobbes replaces divinely ordered qualities with scientific quantities. Things are to be known not by their relation to God, but by measurement. A singular, geometric universe replaces the classical and Christian metaphysics of heaven and earth. Hobbes's universe is established across lines drawn in space and time, not between heaven and earth.

What then of God? In the early Christian period, Augustine had raised God to a position of awesome and unfathomable mystery – an opaque source of sovereignty.[4] For Augustine, humans could only know God and the world through the traces of His commands in scripture and in the existing order of things. Hobbes faced a similar problem of knowledge in Calvinism. Samuel I. Mintz informs us that 'the Calvinists held that all events proceeded directly from God's arbitrary decrees'.[5] This position would deny any reliable knowledge of the universe, because any discernible patterns or order would be subject to change at God's whim. This would render the causal principles of Galilean science impossible, and humans would effectively be God's pawns. Hobbes's position was rather different. God, he thought, was the *first cause*, the initiator of an endless chain of causality.[6] Indeed, God was the creator of causality itself. God created the laws of causality, motion, perception, reason and science – he was, in later terminology, a 'clockmaker'. All knowledge about nature could then follow from these first principles, 'the Art whereby God hath made and governes the World'.[7]

Hobbes's Galilean metaphysics brings about some radical political implications. The Platonic moral imperative of 'knowing your place' loses its authority. The differences between individuals are no longer by design or according to a natural order. Instead, human ontology, their mode of being, is simply as a collection of atoms and motions. All humans are subject to the same physical and causal laws as the rest of the matter in the universe. Therefore, according to nature and *in* nature, all humans are equal. There is no natural or essential difference between a lord and a peasant, for example.

Hobbes's Galilean metaphysics means that humans are by nature free; free to do whatever they have an inclination to do. Whereas for Augustine, a person following their free inclinations would be in danger of sinfully stepping out of their place in the pre-ordained order, no such constraints are given by Hobbes's cosmology. For Hobbes, the only given constraint is that of physics. Physics, however, is a massively restrictive constraint. Humans, as part of the universe, must be subject to the laws of causality. Therefore every act of will, desire and inclination must have a cause, which has in turn proceeded from another cause. Human inclinations simply follow the necessities of causality. Explaining this chain of causality, Hobbes writes: 'to him that could see the connexion of those causes, the *necessity* of all mens voluntary actions, would appear manifest'.[8] Radically, Hobbes concludes that man is 'free' merely if he is not artificially constrained from following the necessities of causality: '*A FREE-MAN, is he, that in those things, which by his strength and wit he is able to do, is not hindered to do what he has a will to do*'[9] (Hobbes's italics). This position leads to a very limited idea of freedom that makes it impossible for man to be the *first* cause of any action or event – it makes it impossible for man to will anything 'freely' and independently of prior causes.

More important than the philosophical problem of free will are the *political* implications of an individual freedom that is limited by the mechanics of the universe. What is politically important is the idea of being 'hindered' in one's freedom. Hobbes writes that men have created 'Artificiall Chains, called *Civill Lawes*'.[10] Although in nature, man may only be as free as the laws of physics and causality allow, in civil life he is artificially constrained further, and by his own hand.

Why have we bound ourselves in artificial chains? 'For the atteyning of peace', Hobbes tells us.[11] In nature, because there are no rules other than those given by physics, humans have a right to anything they want. If they have the inclination, strength and wit to attain something, there is nothing to prevent them from taking it. This is no different to how an animal would pursue its impulses and desires, except that humans also have the faculty of reason that they can put to the service of their desires.[12] Because of their faculty of reason, therefore, humans do not simply reach for their desired end when it is before them, but can plan for the future attainment of ends too: 'For the Thoughts, are to the Desires, as Scouts, and Spies, to range abroad, and find the way to the things Desired'.[13] They can use all their 'wit' as well as simply their 'strength' in pursuit of their ends. Hobbes has already established that all individuals are equal and similarly free, and from this follows an equally unhindered propensity for them to pursue the objects of their will. Yet human equality goes further than this still. Hobbes states that although there are some natural differences in human strength, 'the weakest has strength enough to kill the strongest'.[14] Furthermore, in terms of 'the faculties of the mind',[15] each will 'hardly believe there be many so wise as themselves'.[16] Hence it is not simply that humans are free and equal under the laws of physics, but that they have the equal capacity to kill each other, that they equally believe themselves to be able to outwit the other, *and* that they have an equal right to everything they desire. This combination of factors leads Hobbes to conclude that in this 'state of nature' humans would very quickly come into conflict, and violent conflict at that:

> From this equality of ability, ariseth equality of hope in the attaining of our Ends. And therefore if any two men desire the same thing, which neverthelesse they cannot both enjoy, they become enemies; and in the way to their End ... endeavour to destroy, or subdue one an another.[17]

Man, unhindered in nature, is a very dangerous animal. Thus Hobbes concludes that man in a 'state of nature' is akin to man in a 'state of war'. Man would live in 'continual feare, and danger of violent death'; and, famously, his life would be 'solitary, poore, nasty, brutish and short'.[18]

The solution that Hobbes offers is the contract or 'covenant'. Fear of violent death prompts men to realize that their common enemy is not other men, but death itself. This fear of violent death cuts through selfish impulses, and it is in this moment of clarity and rationality that the decision is made to institute a contract. In this contract, people agree to lay down their right to all things, including the taking of the lives of others. Instead, a limitation is accepted on natural liberty. People agree to have only as much liberty as they would allow others to have. Since none would allow others the liberty of killing them, it follows that all would agree to lay down their right to take each other's lives in pursuit of their ends.

Vitally, Hobbes adds that 'Covenants, without the Sword, are but Words, and of no strength to secure a man at all'.[19] His understanding is that such an agreement could not be made to hold of its own accord. Men could not trust each other to stay true to their word, especially since each man's desire to pursue his own ends, even at the expense of others, would simply reassert itself. Hobbes's solution to this problem is to erect a 'Common Power' to 'make their Agreement constant and lasting'.[20] This common power will protect men from each other and from invasion from abroad, and so provide them with *security*. And the only way to do this, Hobbes writes, is for men 'to conferre all their power and strength upon one Man'.[21] This 'artificial man' is the sovereign. The sovereign acts to keep men in a state of peace and security. He can do this because, with the transferred power and strength of all men at his disposal, he who is sovereign has the capacity to compel men to keep to their contract on pain of death.

Hobbes makes a profound distinction between natural and 'artificial' life. In *Leviathan*, he tells us (in the very first line in fact) that although nature is the art of God, man has copied this art and so can make artificial things: 'NATURE (the Art whereby God hath made and governes the World) is by the Art of man, as in many other things, so in this also imitated, that it can make an Artificial Animal'.[22] By this Hobbes means that modern political life and the modern political subject – in his terms 'Common-wealth' – are artificial. It is in this artificial condition that man now lives; he is not natural man, he is artificial man – modern man. This is the profoundly modern move of Hobbes. Hobbes's modernity does not simply stem from his Galilean metaphysics. Nor does it stem from nature and an objective and true natural law theory of politics and right. Rather, as Leo Strauss explains, Hobbes's politics stems not from claims originating in nature, but from claims originating in the subjective will of man.[23] Humans have not followed the natural art of God ('whereby God hath made and governs the World'),[24] but have instead imitated that art for their own purposes. Humans have made and govern their own artificial world. Hobbes's political thought is premised on a fundamental separation between modern life, which is modern because of its artificial creation by humans, and natural life, in which humans are subject to no artificial constraints. (This means that Hobbes is not a natural law theorist but a positive law theorist.)

Hobbes's distinction between the modern state ('commonwealth') and the state of nature is based on lines drawn in both time and space. On this side of the line is modernity, on the other side its negation: a terrifying anarchy. The 'state of nature' is a terrifying account of how we must have been 'before' modernity, before the institution of a contract and sovereign. The temporal line is a rhetorical or mythical rupture in time between now and then, between modernity and pre-modernity. The temporal, developmental move from non-modern human to modern human must occur before the spatial move of keeping the non-modern behind the border. The spatial line is a physical border. It is the line beyond which the foreign aggressor cannot pass; the line behind which the modern subject is secure. These two categories of time and space are entwined. The foreign aggressor, the savage and the barbarian exist both beyond the spatial line that separates here from there, and behind the temporal line that separates civilized modern man from uncivilized pre-modern 'natural' man. The line is drawn in space-time – it is spatio-temporal.[25]

The fundamental tenet of this account is that natural freedom is terrifying. Natural freedom is war, savagery and brutality. Instead, Hobbes offers civil liberty. Civil liberty is liberty under artificial limits. It is secure and peaceful. As Hobbes famously argues, in a state of war without civil liberty there can be no industry, no agriculture, no navigation, no building, no knowledge of the earth, no arts, no letters and no society.[26] Yet in a state of civil liberty man can do whatever he has the will to do, as long as it does not threaten the *security* of the commonwealth. The authority of Hobbes's conception of political life comes from the terror of its absolute negation. The negation of political modernity, the state of nature, is posited as a terrifying vision.

Hobbes leaves us with an account of politics and freedom that operates under an elegant early modern aesthetic. The principle of security establishes the minimum necessary conditions under which one can be 'free'. The principle of security also establishes a specific understanding of what that 'freedom' must be. It is not, indeed *cannot*, be natural freedom, but rather civil liberty. It is the task of the sovereign to guarantee the conditions under which civil liberty is possible. Sovereignty, and the security it provides, is the minimum condition under which modern life is at all possible. Yet only the sovereign can decide what constitutes a threat to that security. This is because the danger that sovereignty protects man from is himself. Danger is the outcome of man's natural condition of freedom. Modern sovereignty ensures that the modern subject does not revert to his dangerous natural freedom. Modern sovereignty must ensure a condition of civil liberty over natural freedom. Hobbes sets up a powerful political imperative whereby if sovereign authority were to disappear, life would revert to a state of natural chaos and terror. Thus the modern sovereign must draw lines in time and space (for in a Galilean universe what other medium is there?). These lines divide safety from danger, peace from war, modern from savage, here from there, us from them, friend from enemy and norm from exception.

Of course, Hobbes's account of the transition from the state of nature to the commonwealth is not without its contradictions: if humans were so rapacious in nature, how could they find a moment of rational sobriety in which to agree to institute a contract and sovereign? And if they could find such rational sobriety within themselves, then the state of nature can't have been that bad after all. The state of nature is simply a powerful rhetorical device. It is not an account of history. It is a way to justify, legitimate and give authority to a normative idea of political order.

There are two ways of understanding Hobbes that hold profound relevance for the problem of liberty and security. Initially his universe appears profoundly dualistic, dividing the world between a modern realm of qualified 'civil liberty' and a pre-modern world of dangerous 'natural freedom'. This reading mirrors the either/or function of the liberty/security discourse, in that liberty is seen as a progressive achievement which is compared to the uncivilized condition of barbarians; pre-moderns who are threats to the security and the continuing possibility of modern life (read fundamentalists, haters of freedom, terrorists, etc.). As such, civil liberty functions as a political principle that reifies a kind of ontological superiority in modern subjects, and mobilizes practices to defend and secure that liberty from its enemies. This leads to the familiar problem of security practices destroying the very liberty they are supposed to protect. This is the conventional story of liberty and security, which is present with great clarity in Hobbes.

Read more critically, however, and Hobbes's political system is more dialectical, providing resources for refusing the dualistic paradox of liberty/security. The relationship of Hobbes's commonwealth to its rhetorical outside and past is of key political importance. Modern civil liberty does not simply exist in natural opposition to savage pre-modern freedom. Departing from the very obvious point that Hobbes's 'state of nature' is not a historically identifiable condition, it is clear that this terrifying anarchy is a rhetorical projection of the negation of modern subjectivity. Although in Hobbes's *narrative* a condition of modern civil liberty comes *after* a condition of terrifying natural freedom, in terms of the *immanent structure* of his political theory it is clearer that the *modern subject* comes *first* and the terrifying but imaginary possibility of its negation comes *second*. At the root of Hobbes's political theory is not savage anarchy, but modernity and the fear of its negation. The pre-modern terror of the state of nature is a projection of a specifically modern fear that is a *product* of modern subjectivity, not a real condition to be excluded. In other words, Hobbes's terrifying vision of the 'state of nature' is a rhetorical device that works to entrench the principle of modern subjectivity under conditions of modern state sovereignty. In this discourse, modern liberty is actually a dialectical principle that implies and provides its own mirror-image from the beginning. This principle works by projecting an imagined negation of modern subjectivity onto 'non-moderns'. A political insistence on modern subjectivity projects and produces an imagined realm of negative difference and terror. These 'outsides' are a projection of the inside. They are a projection and designation of the not-properly modern by the modern on the basis of the fear of its own negation.

Two conclusions can be drawn from Hobbes therefore. The first is that the dualistic contemporary liberty/security discourse operates around a reified principle of modern liberty that leads to paradoxes about destroying liberty to defend liberty. This was demonstrated in Chapter 1; Hobbes provides us with an elegant account how these balances, trade-offs and paradoxes play out. Through Hobbes, one can glean a sharp articulation of the political necessities that lead to restrictions on freedom. This leads to the second conclusion, which is that all roads marked freedom lead to necessity, sovereignty and security. It is not that freedom is impossible, but that logically the security of freedom depends on the possibility of its suspension. Freedom implies the possibility of its own negation from the moment it is enshrined as a political principle. Once modern civil liberty – liberty 'properly so-called' – is enshrined as a political principle, the fear of its negation *projects* and *produces* that negation. And therefore without an insistence on modern subjectivity there would be no imagined negation. In a politics of liberty, all political implications *follow* from the principle of liberty, despite the fact that, discursively, liberty is portrayed as a *progression* from barbarism.

Consequently, three points regarding the principle of liberty can be taken from Hobbes:

1   When liberty is dualistically opposed to security it results in political and philosophical contradictions.
2   The discourse of the modern subject of liberty dialectically produces a vision of its own negation. In light of the danger posed by this dialectical opposite, which for this discourse is man in his natural, pre-modern condition, modern civil liberty is only considered possible under heavily restrictive conditions of modern sovereignty. The condition of possibility for the modern subject of liberty is the possibility of its own exceptional suspension.
3   In its necessary capacity to define and defend the limits of the properly qualified liberty of the modern subject, the problem of modern sovereignty is far in excess of the principle of liberty. If modern sovereignty is to decide upon the limits of modern subjectivity, who or what is to decide upon the limits of modern sovereignty? What is there to prevent the execution of modern sovereignty becoming arbitrary? The guarantee of modern subjectivity provided by modern sovereignty seems something of a Faustian bargain.

Schmitt and the problem of the exception grow out of this problematique. A concern with the possibility and limits of political modernity implies an account of the conditions of danger under which the productive dialectic of modern politics must be exceptionally resolved in favour of exceptional sovereign power. This politico-theoretical tradition says much about the conditions that must obtain for Schmitt to always win.

Kant

For Hobbes, true freedom meant heteronomy: being subject to some kind of external law, rule or authority, be it the laws of the universe or the 'artificial chains' of civil society. *Leviathan* works around a progression from 'natural' freedom, which is dangerous, to a qualified form of freedom that only works under restrictive political conditions. This kind of qualified freedom or 'civil liberty' works through a subject/sovereignty dialectic which at the point of contradiction resolves into a monism where freedom *is* obedience, necessity or determinism.

Ostensibly, Kant marks a radical break with this tradition. Instead of describing the properly qualified subject of liberty as dependent on an external source of authority, which is *heteronomy*, Kant reasoned that true freedom is *autonomy*. Instead of the subject being dependent on an external source of authority and law, Kant's idea of freedom as autonomy meant *being one's own lawgiver*. Instead of being governed by others, man could govern himself. As J. B. Schneewind explains, it was Jean-Jacques Rousseau who impressed the idea of man as his own lawgiver upon Kant.[27] It was Rousseau who wrote: 'the impulse of appetite alone is slavery, and obedience to the law one has prescribed for oneself is freedom'.[28] Kant set about theorizing how such autonomous lawmaking was possible, by deriving moral laws from rational precepts.

Yet, despite Kant's stress on autonomy, his version of freedom works around the same point of resolution as Hobbes's; ultimately, true freedom *is* necessity. And similarly, by establishing an ideal principle of what true freedom means, Kant sets up a productive dialectical relation between this principle and its negation. What begins as a philosophical principle of freedom properly so-called very quickly translates into a series of political relations which can be read both positively and negatively. The aim of this section is therefore to demonstrate, once again, how the principle of freedom or liberty is not naturally opposed to political necessity or the dictates of sovereignty but, rather, implicated in the problematique of sovereign power from the beginning. The aim is to show that the problem of exceptionalism is not something that appears in dualistic opposition (both theoretically and politically) to the principles of liberty, but something that relates to the limits, contradictions and aporia of the liberal political discourse itself. The problem of the exception, as expressed through the problem of Schmitt, is not a political aberration that can be dispatched with a reaffirmation of political principles, but a problem that is intrinsic to the modern Western political tradition in general. As such, Schmitt should be understood as a product of this tradition, rather than simply appearing in iniquitous opposition to it. Following the format of the previous section on Hobbes, I will work through the basic moves of the conventional story in order to arrive at a point where the political stakes become clear.

If, for Kant, properly qualified liberty was to be based on the internalization of rationally derived moral laws, from what principles could one derive such laws? They could not be based on desires, because that would mean slavery to one's impulses. For the same reason, they could not be based on instrumental reasoning to reach such ends as happiness. The outcomes of one's actions could not reliably be predicted anyway. Neither could principles of lawmaking be derived from kindness or altruism, as they were for Rousseau, because Kant believed that benevolence bred dependence, paternalism, servility and hence heteronomy. For Kant, true freedom could only be derived from one's own use of the principles of reason.[29]

If, for Kant, freedom could not mean slavery to desires or outcomes, true freedom would not be possible under a system of purely instrumental or hypothetical reasoning. (Hypothetical reasoning takes the form of 'if you want *x*, do *y*' – it is a means–ends maxim.) However, Kant was aware that human desires could not be theorized away altogether. Instead he devised a mechanism that could be used to test one's instrumental maxims in order to establish whether they were also moral. The aim was to establish whether the instrumental maxims used to pursue one's selfish desires could be made to conform to a universal moral law. If the subject pursued only those desires that conformed to the universal moral law, then the subject could be considered to be acting according to his own internal use of reason.

The test that Kant derived was the 'categorical imperative'. In contrast to hypothetical imperatives, it is not a means–ends formulation. Its most basic form is: 'Act only according to that maxim through which you can at the same time will that it should become a universal law'.[30] The key test is whether the maxim (the expression of proposed conduct) can be universalized. Would it be possible and logical for the maxim in question to be pursued universally, without resulting in contradiction? For example, it would not make sense to follow the maxim of breaking one's promises, because if promises were broken universally, the concept of promise-making would collapse. The original maxim of breaking one's promises would no longer make sense, because there would be no promises to break. Maxims are not moral if they cannot be universalized rationally.

The categorical imperative can also be thought of as that which a 'perfectly rational' being would will. For Kant, maxims that conform to the categorical imperative have the same *a priori* truth status as Newton's laws, because, independent of any empirical application, they must be analytically logical. Of course, humans are not perfectly rational, so in order to be moral they must test their empirical, hypothetical maxims against the perfect rationality of the categorical imperative. By following the categorical imperative, the individual agent can be sure that he is not merely pursuing his own selfish ends or desires. Rather, he is acting according to maxims that could be followed rationally by all; maxims that could become universal laws. The agent is not simply a 'slave' to his desires or impulses, but is instead obeying reasoned moral laws that he has understood and internalized autonomously. Therefore the agent is free in the proper, autonomous sense. According to Kant, being moral, by limiting one's actions according to one's own use of reason, is being free.

A problem ensues from these precepts, however. Henry Allison describes it thus: '[if] only genuinely autonomous actions are free ... it follows that we are not responsible for our immoral acts'.[31] Kant theorizes that we are only free when acting autonomously, which means obeying the rationally derived moral law of the categorical imperative. This means that if we act immorally, and hence irrationally, we are not being free. Because it is not our autonomous, properly free choice to commit wicked acts, we cannot be held morally responsible for them. The reason for this problem is that Kant's philosophical idea of freedom is tautological: it is a circular truth. Schneewind describes Kant's reasoning as follows: 'if we are free we are under the moral law, and if we are under the moral law we are free'.[32] Being moral is by definition being free, and vice versa. It follows inversely that if one is not being moral, one is not being free, and hence cannot be held responsible.

This is exactly why Hobbes, who could not admit to his material universe the idea of a causally independent free will, did not believe in moral responsibility.[33] Instead, moral responsibility was simply something that society had to presuppose for the necessities of order and security.[34] Although the conceptions of free will in Hobbes and Kant stem from a different set of philosophical precepts, the effect of the problem of free will is the same. The problem of moral culpability, specifically a lack of moral culpability for acts which do not qualify as being freely willed, propels the problem of freedom into the social and political realm. How can moral principles be sustained if those subjects who cannot be considered truly free cannot be held responsible for their inability to obey moral laws?

In response to this problem, Kant later argued for what he called the 'fact of reason',[35] which operates as follows. We know from experience that unconditional moral obligations exist. We know of the existence of the categorical imperative and the means to use reason to establish what is moral. Although often we don't obey moral laws because we are not perfectly rational beings, we know we *can* obey them, because if it were impossible to obey unconditional moral obligations they would be irrational. Although for Kant, immorality, irrationality and lack of freedom all amount to the same thing, the 'fact of reason' means that immoral people, although not properly autonomous, can still be held morally responsible for their actions. This is because the immoral person knows from experience that it is *possible* to be moral, rational and free. Because we are aware that we must *be able* to follow rational morality, even when we do not, we know we *can* be free and therefore morally responsible. We can be held morally responsible regardless of whether we are being properly free and moral or not, because we are aware that we *can* be free and moral. The person's lack of these qualities is his own responsibility, and therefore they can be held responsible and morally culpable.

This is where Kant transfers his notion of freedom from the realm of private moral autonomy to the public realm of politics. The justification for attributing moral culpability to those who are not properly qualified as autonomous and free is a justification for punishment and coercion. As I will explain, this justification extends further, to the punishment and coercion of the not-properly free in order to protect the freedom of the properly free. This is Kant's concept of *Recht*, or right. Wolfgang Kersting explains that the concept of right is based on the same universalization argument as the categorical imperative.[36] Kant defines right as follows: 'Right is therefore the sum of the conditions under which the choice of one can be united with the choice of another in accordance with a universal law of freedom'.[37]

Rationally speaking, universal freedom is possible only if each individual's use of freedom does not interfere with that of others. Like morality, right is a purely formal principle. It simply ensures that freedom is compatible with itself. In this sense right is a purely negative law; it cannot provide any guide to what the content of freedom should be. Kersting explains:

> Indifferent to all the elements of content in human actions, [right] is concentrated solely on the question of the formal compatibility of the external freedom of one person with that of others, and thereby limits individual action within the boundaries of possible universalization.[38]

Kant believed that the concept of right could provide principles for a just form of government. This is the *Rechtsstaat*, or the republican constitution. Under a republican constitution, a legislative will must act as if its laws could be universally accepted by a society of perfectly moral, free and autonomous beings. This leads to a model of limited government, because all the state can rightly do is set limits on non-universalizable uses of freedom. The *Rechtsstaat* guarantees each person their own sphere of autonomy. Because impinging on the freedom of others is not a universalizable maxim, right establishes the outer limits of a personal sphere of freedom for each citizen. Under the concept of right, freedom must be universal. For these reasons, the republican constitution authorizes the use of coercion. As Kant writes:

> if a certain use to which freedom is put is itself a hindrance to freedom in accordance with universal laws (i.e. if it is contrary to right), any coercion which is used against it will be a *hindrance* to a *hindrance of freedom*, and will thus be consonant with freedom in accordance with universal laws – that is, it will be right.[39]

A *Rechtsstaat* is only sustainable if individuals have a mutual right to have their 'spheres of freedom' defended by coercion.[40] In a *Rechtsstaat*, a sovereign will must support this right. Only a society of morally perfect beings would not require some form of coercion in order to maintain the principles of right.

Once the reasoned laws of morality and right are established, the imperatives held within those laws demonstrate that despite Kant's attempt to ground freedom in autonomy in contrast to dependent heteronomy, the same reduction of freedom to necessity takes place that is found in Hobbes. Because the categorical imperative and the concept of right have the quality of formal laws that are incontrovertibly rational, governing oneself using one's own rationality can only mean obeying morality and right. Although for Kant freedom means obeying the law that one has prescribed for oneself, the formal quality of a law is that it is universalizable. Hence using one's *own* understanding is something of a misnomer. There is only one kind of understanding, and that is universally valid rationality. For this reason we move swiftly from freedom as obeying one's self-prescribed law, to freedom as obeying the universal law of rationality. As it was in Hobbes, the only way to be properly free is to obey a singular and necessary mode of being. Once again, the problem of freedom and necessity is resolved by the solution that freedom *is* necessity.

Moreover, this philosophical resolution of freedom and necessity translates directly into a political resolution of liberty and security. It is apparent that if one does not choose to obey the universal laws or the *Rechtsstaat*, then it is politically justifiable to be compelled to obey. Political law and the principle of right are the external public expression of the internal moral freedom achieved in the transition from heteronomy to autonomy. In Hobbes, a principle of properly qualified freedom is predicated on a *temporal* move from natural freedom to civil liberty, followed by a *spatial* move that encloses a realm of freedom-properly so-called behind secured borders. In Kant, the spatio-temporal move is given direct expression by the problematique of enlightenment. This is worth expanding upon. Kant's famous piece 'An Answer to the Question: "What is Enlightenment?"' opens as follows:

> *Enlightenment is man's emergence from his self-incurred immaturity.* *Immaturity* is the inability to use one's own understanding without the guidance of another. This immaturity is *self-incurred* if its cause is not lack of understanding, but lack of resolution and courage to use it without the guidance of another. The motto of Enlightenment is therefore: *Sapre aude!* Have courage to use your *own* understanding.[41] (Kant's italics)

Enlightenment corresponds to the principle of autonomy; it means using one's own faculty of understanding to govern oneself. Under a perfectly realized republican constitution, the enlightened, the moral, the free and the autonomous need never come into contact with sovereign coercion, because the rationality of the individual and the rationality of the state will be in perfect harmony. Kant makes the distinction between maturity and immaturity to demonstrate this spatio-temporal developmental trajectory of enlightenment. The unenlightened and the immature constitute a threat to those living in a condition of right.

If immaturity is *self-incurred*, Kant writes, it is because the person concerned lacks the requisite resolution and courage to use their own understanding. Returning to the earlier language of this section, those who *could* internalize the laws of moral freedom but do not do so can be held to account. The man of self-incurred immaturity is immoral because he does not obey universalizable maxims, and only by obeying universalizable maxims can one keep the use of one's freedom rationally coherent (by not impinging on the freedom of others). In order for the sovereign, legislative will of a republic to maintain a condition of right and universal freedom, the immature person can be justifiably subject to coercion. This is the same argument as the moral responsibility problem considered above. If a person has an autonomous faculty of understanding, they will know that it is possible to be autonomous and enlightened. It is their responsibility, their fault, if they do not strive to achieve autonomy. For Kant, such a failing stems only from a lack of resolution and courage.

On the other hand, those who are *unable* to use their understanding independently cannot be blamed for their immaturity, because it is not self-incurred. If non-self-incurred immaturity is the inability to use one's own understanding without the guidance of another, then under a republican constitution where autonomous understanding is required, the immature person can only exist in a state of external guidance, dependence or heteronomy. The real political question, therefore, is whether someone's immaturity – which also entails immorality, irrationality and a lack of freedom – is self-incurred or not, and thus whether or not they should be held responsible for it.

The political implications of this question are far-reaching. Whereas self-incurred immaturity justifies the use of punishment and coercion, non-self-incurred immaturity justifies a much greater form of control, not least because the condition already entails dependence on the 'guidance of another'. He who is in a condition of self-incurred immaturity merely requires coercion to prevent him from immorally and irrationally impinging on the freedom of others. However, he who is in a condition of non-self-incurred immaturity can only function in accordance with right if he is guided in his state of heteronomy. *Ergo,* some people in the world need to be looked after like children – they do not and cannot understand the reasoned laws of morality and right, and they can never be truly free and autonomous.

In establishing both an internal-moral and external-political rationale for the meaning of properly qualified freedom, Kant sets up a political dialectic that can be read both positively and negatively. Read positively, the relationship between the immature, the morally irresponsible and the enlightened leads to the liberal discourse of development. What is needed under this rationale is education, institution building, enfranchisement and democratization. Read negatively, however, one reaches a discourse of colonialism. What is needed is the white man's burden of a 'civilizing mission', the rule over those incapable of using their own understanding by those who can, and the spread of the values of the Enlightenment and democracy, by force if necessary. This is a familiar and well-established debate that will run on.

More important for this project is that Kant establishes a basis for *political judgement* based on a progressive, spatio-temporal ontology. Under this basis, moral and political distinctions can be made between different categories of people who are at different stages on the road to enlightenment or development. The distinction between the modern and the non-modern has been established again, echoing that found in Hobbes, but replacing Hobbes's sudden and mythical contractarian moment with an idealized progressive teleology.

Ideal abstract principle constitutes a vital element in the dialectic of this stratified political ontology. Kant's republican constitution is not a simple embodiment of enlightened democratic will. For Kant, we are not yet enlightened, but some people are further along the road to enlightenment than others. An enlightened polity would be a polity of perfectly rational beings. In this way, Kant's concept of enlightenment plays a similar role to that of Augustine's City of God – it is a guiding light, with human existence dwelling in its shadow. It is within that shadow that political distinctions occur, made in relation to the ideal order provided by the concept of enlightenment. So although Kant's politics can be read as a straightforward dualism between the mature and the immature, which plays straight into contemporary developmental/colonial dualisms about democracy versus fundamentalism and so on, it is more revealing to focus on the dialectical elements of Kant's political thought. What is interesting is the interplay between pure reasoned principles and their practical application and function.

Kant writes that 'the problem of setting up a state can be solved even by a nation of devils'.[42] Although in Kant's moral philosophy reasoned moral laws are something by which each individual must learn to govern himself *internally*, in Kant's subsequent political philosophy of right the achievement of living in accordance with universal laws is realized *externally* through constitutional means. It is not necessary for the citizens of a *Rechtsstaat* to be enlightened. As Kant continues, regarding the setting up of a state:

> For such a task does not involve the moral improvement of man; it only means finding out how the mechanism of nature can be applied to men in such a manner that the antagonism of their hostile attitudes will make them compel one another to submit to coercive laws, thereby producing a condition of peace within which the laws can be enforced.[43]

Bearing in mind this external imposition of principle, rather than private moral improvement, it is then revealing to note Kant's thoughts about sovereign or 'legislative' will. For Kant, a legislator need not follow the actual democratic will of a people, but instead merely act in accordance with the universalizing principle of right by following the abstract test of whether a law would be agreeable to a hypothetical united national will:

> It is in fact merely an *idea* of reason, which nonetheless has undoubted practical reality; for it can oblige every legislator to frame his laws in such a way that they could have been produced by the united will of a whole nation, and to regard each subject, in so far as he can claim citizenship, as if he had consented within the general will.[44]

All that is necessary for right government is that it legislates to bring about a condition of right in which the universal use of individual freedom does not contradict itself. Here, the legitimacy of legislative power or sovereignty stems not from its constitutional structure or from the will of the people, but from a commitment to abstract reasoned principles. As Kant intriguingly proclaims:

> A state may well *govern* itself in a republican way, even if its existing constitution provides for a despotic *ruling power*; and it will gradually come to the state where the people can be influenced by the mere idea of law's authority, just as if it were backed up by physical force, so that they will be able to create for themselves a legislation ultimately founded on right.[45]

What is fascinating is the dialectical relationship that forms between the state which governs by imposing and enforcing abstract principles ('*govern* itself in a republican way') and the promise that the people will slowly catch up until the eventual point when they will govern *themselves* autonomously by internalizing the law ('people can be influenced by the mere idea of law's authority').

Put differently, sovereignty guarantees and enforces the minimum conditions for political modernity before political modernity can become a self-realizing fact. This means that unless the ideal of enlightenment has been realized (in which case there would be no more need for an external legislative will), sovereignty is well in excess of freedom. Unless the selfish freedom of a 'nation of devils' has developed to the point where each individual has internalized reasoned moral laws, thus rendering a legislative will unnecessary, sovereign rule will draw its legitimacy not from the free will or consent of the people, but from the ideal notion of a perfectly rational, united national will. The *principle* of properly qualified liberty takes precedence over *actual* political freedom, and, as such, this principle is the chief source of legitimacy for sovereign power. The opposition of liberty to security again gives way to a dialectical resolution in which liberty *is* security.

These considerations lead to three conclusions. First, Kant posits a familiar dualistic transition from philosophical freedom/necessity to political liberty/security, where necessity means being privately subject to the laws of reason, and security means the public enforcement of conditions of right. The temporal and spatial aspects of this transition can be read in both positive and negative ways, which is highly relevant for ongoing debates about globalization, development and imperialism. Second, read dialectically, Kant reveals much about the political relationship between stratified political ontologies – between an imperfect people, on the one hand, and sovereignty as the external expression of the abstract principles of right, on the other. A dialectic of political modernity can be read in Kant which resolves any contradiction between liberty and security firmly in favour of the sovereign enforcement of the latter, as the condition of possibility for the former. Third, sovereign rule draws its legitimacy from the enforcement of the minimum conditions of possibility for political modernity, rather than from the democratic will of a people. This sets up a political imperative for the people to come into conformity and harmony with the sovereign will. Democratic will is only properly qualified when it comes into natural harmony with sovereign will as the expression of right. In this sense, liberty is well and truly subsumed into the problematique of sovereign rule until the hypothetical point when sovereign rule will be rendered superfluous by the complete subjective internalization ('influenced by the mere idea') of the principles of morality and right by truly autonomous citizens of properly qualified civil liberty. Despite their respective reputations, Kant appears far more conservative than Hobbes in terms of either liberty or sovereignty.

The limits of liberalism

The aim of this chapter has been to show how the canonical theorists of liberty can be used to refuse the contradictions of simplistic popular liberal discourse. The first task has been to understand how these theorists can be read to fit into that popular discourse. I have then sought to provide more dialectical readings that address the contradictions involved in these conventional readings, in order to gain a more serious critical purchase on what is at stake in practices of exceptionalism.

The popular discourse is profoundly dualistic. This dualism takes the form of an either/or: either we have liberty or we have tyranny; either we have liberalism or we have tyranny. This is what Foucault calls the 'contract-oppression' model of political theory, which is particularly associated with the seventeenth century and with Hobbes.[46] In this model, political thought works to establish a basis for just government, establishing both the proper rights of sovereign power and the proper limits of sovereign power. The correct basis for sovereign power is founded through a metaphorical contract, in which individuals agree to give up their right to everything they desire in exchange for peace and security. Sovereign power is created to enforce this 'contract'. The purpose of sovereignty is to defend the basic freedom, security and property rights of each individual. If the sovereign acts contrary to these principles, then legitimate government can be considered to have become oppressive government. The basic contradiction is that the sovereign who saves you may also oppress or kill you. Reading Hobbes provides a classic account of this problematique. *Leviathan* elegantly establishes the basic assumptions and principles of a modern liberal subjectivity, extrapolates the problems of conflict that liberal subjectivity may cause, provides an account of the necessity of sovereign government and outlines the limits of legitimate rule. The state may do many things, but it cannot arbitrarily kill an individual, for protection from violent death is the reason for allegiance to a sovereign power in the first place.[47] At stake is either, quite simply, liberty or tyranny.

The idea of this implicit 'contract' permeates the contemporary liberty/security discourse. Many argue that as security threats become greater the state must go further in its most basic duty to provide security. As such, liberty must be compromised in proportion to this increased level of threat. Others argue that when this happens the line separating liberty from tyranny has been crossed.

Kant's presence in the conventional debate is as the expression of a liberal, law-based society. Kant demonstrates the basic principles of a liberal society of individual freedom, which must consist of free individuals who do not take away each other's freedom. The principle of *right* is the embodiment of the principle of universal freedom as a universal law. Ideally, a society will develop in which individuals are influenced by the mere idea of the law, and freedom will become self-perpetuating. As such, Kant's place in the popular discourse is as the expression of government by the rule of law, a government which respects, defends and embodies a free society. He also expresses the hope that all societies will develop towards this self-regulating ideal, with each individual developing their own understanding to the point where they have internalized the principle and law of universal freedom, and so respect the freedom of others.

These Kantian aspirations run into difficulties when confronted with the problem of those who breech the limits of individual freedom or the principles of a free society. If there are individuals who do not respect the freedom of others, it must be because they are incapable of understanding the principle of universal freedom, or, worse, because they understand it but choose not to obey it. In this case, according to this reasoning, sovereign coercion is entirely justified. Coercion is legitimate provided it embodies the law of universal freedom. Yet if coercion is merely the expression of a power interest or a particularistic, dogmatic position, then it is no longer just.[48] Again, it is an either/or dualism of liberty and tyranny. The liberty/security debate poses precisely this problem. If faced with a group of people seemingly bent on following a dogmatic, anti-liberal and violent ideology, sovereign power must defend both the individuals and the principles of a free society. However, if sovereign power ceases to embody the principles of a liberal society, by arbitrarily detaining people for example, then it crosses the line to tyranny and becomes the very thing it sought to reject. This is the great test of liberal government – providing for the security of liberty without destroying liberty. The point of contention is how far this is possible under conditions of existential threat, real or imagined.

The challenge of Schmitt is that there will always be situations in which sovereign power must act exceptionally. The liberal argument is that if this happens sovereign power ceases to be liberal. As such, Schmitt is read as the fascist opposite of liberalism. In the readings of the theory of liberty discussed here, I have sought to counter this conventional dualism.

Exceptionalism is not the opposite of liberty, but the limit of liberty. This is because, read more critically, each of these powerful accounts does not oppose sovereign power to individual freedom, but provides an account of the necessity of sovereign power that derives from an initial problematique of freedom. If the individual is to be understood as free, what are the political consequences? Each account begins with freedom as a problem of conflicting individual desires, as a human condition that inevitably leads to conflict. Each theorist then extrapolates what a politically qualified principle of freedom should look like. Natural freedom thereby becomes 'civil liberty', a form of liberty that is heavily qualified by the sovereign enforcement of the minimum political conditions under which the freedom of every individual is possible. In the political theory of liberty, natural freedom is a dangerous human condition, whereas civil liberty is a political imperative, principle and aspiration. Liberty 'properly so-called' is understood as being tightly subject to the dictates of philosophical and political necessity. Because properly qualified liberty is only possible under these strict conditions, the problem of freedom *from* the state must be reassessed: it is all freedom *under* the state, as the state is the minimum condition of possibility for the socio-political realization of universal freedom. 'Civil liberty' is consequently thrown into a productive dialectic with the spectre of dangerous natural freedom, which always dwells at its limit.

If liberty is to be the original political principle, then all political consequences follow from this starting point. The spectre of dangerous natural freedom – the threat posed by those who do not properly adhere to the universal law of freedom – is a projection of the initial principle of liberty. The principle of liberty is mobilized as a political practice by the invocation of the fear of its own negation. If liberty is what is important, then threats to liberty will take the form of the illiberal. And if the coercive state is the minimum condition of possibility for the realization of a society of political liberty, then enemies of liberty are enemies of the state, and enemies of the state are enemies of liberty. A politics of liberty demands both allegiance to the principle of properly qualified liberty and allegiance to the state which enforces that principle.

Consequently, however, the state as the embodiment of the principle of liberty becomes more important than the actual realization of liberty, because individuals are imperfect and some will invariably stray and revert to (potentially dangerous natural) type. Kant is clear that it is individuals who must come into harmony with the state, not the state that must come into harmony with individuals. Even if the state does not act in accordance with the principle of universal freedom or right, the state is still the minimum condition of possibility for the realization of a society of modern civil liberty. This sets up a more fundamental principle whereby modernity, expressed in the modern ontology of the state, is the minimum condition of possibility for a specifically modern form of liberty.

What conclusions can be drawn for the problem of exceptionalism? Hobbes, read most basically for his mythical account of the progression from dangerous natural freedom to modern liberty 'properly so-called', can be re-read to demonstrate the political consequences of placing a modern ontology at the beginning and centre of politics. As Leo Strauss argues, the harsh political imperatives of the *Leviathan* result, not from problems and threats found in nature, but from problems originating in the subjective will of man, or, in other words, claims originating in a specifically modern subjectivity.[49] Hobbes is therefore not saving us from a natural terror, but saving us from a terror which is a consequence of our own insistence on a specifically modern subjectivity. This terror is produced as a consequence of modern subjectivity and projected onto a modern understanding of space and time, which insists on sharp lines drawn between here and there, now and then, the modern and the barbarous. But since this modern spatio-temporal ontology, manifested in the form of the state, is the minimum condition of possibility for the realization of a modern subject of liberty, Hobbes constructs a dialectic of allegiance, making a distinction between the obedient subject and the seditious subject.

Kant goes furthest in theorizing the principle of universal freedom as a political and philosophical law. He is clear that sovereign state coercion must enforce the limits of both individual liberty and a society of liberty. Kant expresses the liberal aspiration that individuals will come to internalize the mere idea of the universal law of freedom, thus rendering sovereign coercion unnecessary. He thereby sets up a relationship between the principle of properly qualified liberty and the practical failure to realize this. He does not simply establish a natural freedom/civil liberty break as Hobbes does, but rather a progressive teleological hierarchy along which individuals and societies can and should progress towards true autonomous, internalized liberty.

For Kant, true freedom means the autonomy of being one's own lawgiver. The truly liberal subject does not require the imposition of law by sovereign coercion. However, being one's own lawgiver is something of a misnomer. There is only one universal law of freedom that can be derived rationally. This means that there is only one correct way to be autonomous and free. If the modern liberal state is the embodiment of the universal law of freedom and its minimum condition of possibility, then autonomy still means obedience and allegiance to the state. It just so happens, of course, that the spiritual and political home of freedom and enlightenment is Europe, or is that America? From here, the spatio-temporal dialectic of modernity is projected internationally, or, rather, the dialectics of international imperialism/globalization are a direct consequence of the dialectics of modernity. The modern nation-state form may have been bequeathed to the world, but under this understanding most societies have not yet become self-realizing societies of what is actually European or American freedom. Until they do, in the face of the danger posed, sovereign coercion is deemed necessary to ensure that the minimum conditions of modernity and eventually the minimum conditions of liberty properly so-called can be met.

Schmitt and the problem of the exception grow out this tradition, rather than appearing in aberrant opposition to it. Schmitt posits the exception as the contingent threat of violent attack, civil war, unpredictable events, governmental paralysis and impotence, or a descent into the kind of intra-social conflict that is the very negation of political modernity. At the limit of politics is Schmitt's concept of 'the political': the sovereign distinction between friends and enemies made necessary by the inherent threat of political antagonisms becoming mortal conflict. At the limit of constitutionalism, individual rights and the rule of law resides the real possibility of an existentially threatening exception, which due to the overarching principles of political modernity is determined in advance as a threat to the state and thus to the possibility of modern political life. As Chapter 3 will explain, Schmitt's account of sovereignty is based on a Kantian dialectic between the principle of a united and ordered modern polity and the difficulties and tensions in the practical realization of this. For Schmitt, as for Kant, modern nation-state sovereignty is the minimum condition of possibility for the realization and maintenance of political modernity. And for Hobbes, Kant and indeed Schmitt, modernity is the minimum condition of possibility for liberty, even if liberty is imagined in highly restrictive terms. As such, the sovereign speaks for the *principle* of political modernity, not for the democratic will or modern subjects themselves. The principle and practice of modern state sovereignty, as the embodiment of modernity, comes into play as the judgement and decision on who is and is not qualified as properly modern, and where the line and limits should be drawn. When sovereignty is the expression of ideal principles, it becomes the principle and practice by which the line between norm and exception is decided. According to this tradition, the sovereign decision on the exception resides at the limits of politically qualified life.

3   Carl Schmitt and the politics of the exception

This book is about the problem of 'exceptionalism' – 'exceptional' political practices legitimated by claims about 'exceptional' events and 'exceptional' circumstances. The previous chapters dealt with two initial aspects of this problem: first, the contradictions of the popular liberal discourse regarding 'exceptional' politics and questions of liberty and security; and, second, the more sophisticated treatment of these contradictions found in the political theory of Hobbes and Kant.

The aim of this chapter is to explain and critique the workings of Schmitt's exceptionalism. Although many of Schmitt's ideas can be read as unique, the aim here is to show that much of Schmitt grows from an entirely conventional political discourse. Indeed, the aim of the previous two chapters was to try to counter the idea of Schmitt as a political aberration by establishing that he grows out of a tradition rather than simply appearing in opposition to it.

Schmitt

Although by no means the sole theoretical expression of exceptionalism, Carl Schmitt is one of its sharpest articulators. He argues that '[t]he rule proves nothing; the exception proves everything: It confirms not only the rule but also its existence, which derives only from the exception'.[1] Schmitt's challenge is that the exception and exceptionalism carry both a philosophical and political primacy over 'normal' politics. If Schmitt is right, then exceptional political practices cannot simply be wished away with reaffirmations of the 'norms' of due process, human rights and civil liberties. Schmitt argues that no politics can be based solely on sacrosanct formalisms like constitutions, rights and the rule of law, because at their theoretical and political limits resides the contingent and existentially threatening 'real possibility'[2] of an exceptional enemy, event or situation. For Schmitt, such contingency means that at the exceptional limit sovereign decisionism must take philosophical and political primacy over all other considerations. This does not necessarily mean that exceptionalism constitutes the totality of politics (as in Walter Benjamin's permanent state of exception),[3] but that the norm must necessarily and unavoidably give way to exceptionalism in exceptional situations.

The key elements of Schmitt's exceptionalism are contained in his 1922 *Political Theology* and 1932 *The Concept of the Political*.[4] Each presents a subtly different but complementary slant on the concept of exception. *Political Theology* deals with what I will call the *temporal exception*. The temporal exception is 'a case of extreme peril, a danger to the existence of the state, or the like'.[5] It is a contingent event or situation that exposes the limits of normal politics, but law in particular, by falling beyond the realms of pre-dictability or prior codification: 'it cannot be circumscribed factually and made to conform to a preformed law'.[6] Schmitt posits what is basically a metaphysical problem of contingency in order to pose the question of who is responsible for responding to such exceptional events. His answer is that once law has been exceeded, the exigencies of the exceptional event or situation demand a response of unlimited authority that draws legitimacy from a more profound source than law. For Schmitt, existentially threatening contingencies that fall beyond the law necessarily require and justify responses beyond the law. He argues that an exceptional, unlimited authority belongs to the sover-eign, but, moreover, that it is the *capacity* for this kind of authority that actually reveals who is *truly sovereign*; hence the opening line of the book, which reads: 'Sovereign is he who decides on the exception'.[7] In Schmitt's view, the decision on what is extra-legal cannot belong to the law itself; the contingent possibility of exceptional events and situations dictates the neces-sity of extra-legal authority. For Schmitt, sovereignty itself is, and must be, exceptional.

The Concept of the Political pursues the exceptionality of sovereignty itself. Here, Schmitt deals with what I will call the *spatial exception*; that is, he deals with the concept of the exception in terms of the state and state system.[8] The central trope of *The Concept of the Political* is that politics is ultimately the distinction between friends and enemies.[9] This does not mean that Schmitt imagines politics as a state of war or a Hobbesian war of all against all. Rather, it means that at the limit, at the extreme point, the antagonisms of politics always threaten to become a relation of war, and this is what gives politics its fundamental tension. In Schmitt's concept of 'the political', this tension provides the existential imperative for exceptional sovereign power. In order for modern, politically qualified life to be possible, the sovereign state must be able to declare and deal with enemies, both internally or externally. This existential imperative means that in matters of survival the sovereign state must not be constrained by law, domestic or international. The sovereign state is exceptional, and the enemy is an exception. Exceptionalism is both the prerogative of sovereignty and the mark of sovereignty.

Schmitt does not argue that the sovereign capacity to make the friend/ enemy distinction belongs exclusively to the state, but to any political entity that can demonstrate the capacity to declare enemies (thus ceding the possi-bility of a class or religion becoming 'political' if it can successfully make a friend/enemy distinction and mobilize around it). Nevertheless, Schmitt argues that although there is no ontological necessity for this, in empirical terms, sovereignty generally belongs to the state rather than other political groupings, and, importantly, he shrewdly constructs an implicit nation-statist ethic in his work, to which we will return.

Considered in this way, Schmitt comes to represent the problem of exceptionalism in terms of two related challenges. First is the contingent threat of exceptional events or situations, the danger and peril of which are so great as to exceed existing codes of law and government. Second is the exceptionality of sovereignty itself, stemming from the existential imperative to protect against the temporal exception of the contingent event and the spatial exception of the state enemy. Schmitt is not claiming that politics is pure war or pure exceptionalism. He posits a dialectical relationship between law and politics, and politics and war. The possibility of law depends on the exceptional possibility of its suspension; the possibility of politics depends on the exceptional possibility of its transition into violence.

Schmitt posits sources of legitimacy for sovereign political authority beyond the arena of the 'rule' or 'norm'. He argues that beyond the law, beyond everyday political life, there are unavoidably deeper and more fundamental imperatives at work. The challenge of Schmitt's exceptionalism is that it is futile to simply reassert due process, the constitution, the rule of law, civil liberties or human rights in the face of the exigencies of the exception, because all of those principles and practices ultimately exist in a dialectical relationship with the possibility of their own exceptional suspension.

The political

Schmitt's exceptionalism in *The Concept of the Political* is actually very conventional. Here, exceptionalism is *state* exceptionalism. It follows the logic of the intellectual tradition of modern state sovereignty: due to the disenchanted nature of modernity, and because of the human conflict that ensues from the lack of a single, absolute, universally recognized God/truth/way of life, we must have modern state sovereignty. Modern state sovereignty provides and enforces a necessary set of limits that bind our differences within ordered unities, both politically and, in lieu of any higher authority, metaphysically. Within the state, the limits imposed by state sovereignty seek to prevent our conflicts becoming mortal. In the language of the previous chapters, modern state sovereignty imposes the limits within which we can be free. Sovereignty, by its very nature, is exceptional, because it decides on the limit that defines the norm; it *is* the limit, because there is no higher authority.

William Rasch argues that Schmitt's concept of 'the political' derives directly from the post-Nietzschean, Weberian, nihilistic world-view from which he wrote. There are no longer any transcendental grounds from which to derive truth, authority, meaning or ethical ends. Rasch cites the following passage from Weber to demonstrate this link with Schmitt, the key aspects being 'unceasing struggle' and the very Schmittian necessity 'to make a decisive choice':

> So long as life remains immanent and is interpreted in its own terms ... it knows only of an unceasing struggle of these gods with one another. ... The ultimately possible attitudes toward life are irreconcilable, and hence their struggle can never be brought to a final conclusion. Thus it is necessary to make a decisive choice.[10]

From this perspective, because there are no transcendental sources of authority, any political position taken must ultimately constitute its own ground. Competing political positions are warring gods, with no possible final conclusion to their conflict. As long as we remain in this condition of nihilism, we are thrown into a condition of 'unceasing struggle', and it is for this reason that for Schmitt the ultimate political distinction is that between friend and enemy. The irreconcilability of 'attitudes toward life' entails an unceasing political conflict. Schmitt's concept of 'the political' *is* this conflict, in its inherent potential to become, at its most extreme point, a decision on the distinction between friends and enemies.

Schmitt argues that because the potential for the enmity of 'the political' presupposes the potential for combat, the political sphere is elevated in importance above other spheres of human life in light of the mortal danger involved. As Schmitt writes: 'The specific political distinction to which political actions and motives can be reduced is that between friend and enemy', and 'were this distinction to vanish then political life would vanish altogether'.[11] As long as there is the potential for conflict, and consequently a chance, however small, of an exceptional threat to one's existence, then the fundamental friend/enemy tension of 'the political' is alive and well.

There is an important distinction, therefore, between 'politics' and 'the political'. The mortal tension of the latter resides beyond the former, a 'high' politics to the 'low' politics of the mundane norm, and an ever-present possibility. Hence Schmitt's concept of 'the political' – as the distinction between friends and enemies – does not amount to a politics of bellicose vitalism. Civil war is for Schmitt not natural but pathological; it is a sickness of the state. Schmitt does not, contrary to what Richard Wolin argues, 'end up by standing Hobbes on his head, insofar as the prepolitical *bellum omnium* contra *omnes* [war of all against all] is turned into the essence of the political in general'.[12] Rather, for Schmitt, once politics has become war the limit of politics has been exceeded. It is this risk that gives politics its fundamental tension. Consequently, politics is not a war of all against all for Schmitt. Rather, politics must be placed under highly restrictive sovereign limits precisely in order to prevent this happening, because of the ever-present tension of 'the political'. In exactly the same vein as the political and philosophical determinisms of Hobbes and Kant, you can be as free as you like, so long as you obey.

With this in mind, it is important to stress that although Rasch is not wrong to link Schmitt to the specifically late modern world-view of Nietzsche and Weber, Schmitt has a more basic link to the political discourse of modernity. Although Schmitt does not express the classically modern 'scientific' aesthetic of Hobbes and Kant, his invocation of *necessity* links him to their tradition of political theory and the basic categories of modern politics. Schmitt argues that at the exceptional and inherent limit, sovereignty necessarily takes primacy over liberty, law and universalistic concepts like rights. As it was for Hobbes and Kant, Schmitt moves from observations about the innate conflict of human life to an account of the necessity of strong government. Contrary to Rasch, therefore, disenchantment and conflict are not something specific to late modernity, but a common feature in the discourse of political modernity. To become modern, one must leave one's natural state of undetermined, dangerous freedom. From this very conventional account of human conflict, Schmitt argues that civilized, properly qualified, modern political life is only possible under restrictive conditions of sovereign authority. Schmitt's friend/enemy distinction is only an elaboration of the basic tenets of the conventional spatio-temporal narrative of modern politics. The sovereign must enforce the law, but stand outside the law. Law and everyday life would not be possible without the exceptional sovereignty that protects against both internal and external strife, conflict and enemies. The exception resides at the limits of both law and everyday life and, as such, *delimits* both law and everyday life.

Schmitt, liberalism and modern politics

Much of Schmitt's work, and particularly the two texts of concern here – *The Concept of the Political* and *Political Theology* – is written as a polemic against liberalism. This polemic is more complex than many commentators consider. It is in fact two-sided; it hinges on two different faces of liberal politics. On the one hand, Schmitt's objection to liberalism is that it is, or attempts to be, *anti-political*: it seeks a neutralization of the political. It seeks to negate the particularistic sovereign decisionism that fills the theological void of modernity, replacing it with depoliticized edifices such as the 'universal' and 'autonomous' spheres of law, economics and ethics, which deny their own limits and moreover their *political* nature. On the other hand, however, Schmitt considers that liberalism is in fact highly political, and uses its depoliticizing edifices as a means to hide this fact.

Leo Strauss, in his commentary on *The Concept of the Political*, explains that, for Schmitt, 'liberalism … is characterized by the *negation* of the political', but that liberalism nevertheless remains – contradictorily – deeply political, precisely because of its polemical desire to negate the political and depoliticize any field of potential conflict.[13] Strauss puts the problem as follows: 'Liberalism negated the political; yet liberalism has not thereby eliminated the political from the face of the earth but has only hidden it; liberalism has led to politics' being engaged in by means of an antipolitical mode of discourse'.[14]

For Schmitt, liberal attempts to neutralize fields of political contention and conflict through the deployment of seemingly rationalized, inclusive and universal concepts and institutions have, in wars waged in the name of 'humanity' for example, 'an especially intensive political meaning'.[15] Schmitt's two-sided attack on liberalism is on the one hand that it can be weak, compromised and fractious in its depoliticizations, but, on the other, that these depoliticizations are a hypocritical and highly political myth; a claim to apolitical neutrality, inclusivity and universality that hides an underlying *political* position, which entails an inherent potential for enmity.

Schmitt's polemic functions around a tension between liberalism and modern politics. For Schmitt, the mortal tension of 'the political' that resides in all political and social interaction has been contained within the limits enforced by the modern sovereign state. In this way, Schmitt expresses the basic categories of the discourse of political modernity – modernity as a progression from a state of conflict into some kind of qualified, bounded form of modern life. It is both a temporal move and a spatial move that rests firmly on sovereign guarantees and limits. Schmitt considers that the universalizing tendencies of liberalism threaten to undermine the system of limits guaranteed by the particularity of the modern sovereign state. In its fraudulent universalizing depoliticizations, liberal politics is a dangerous, disguised imposition of a politics that exceeds the traditional limits of modern politics and the modern state.

Schmitt specifically critiques the liberal edifice of positive law, which is law constituted from rational, self-contained, immanently valid precepts, rather than deriving from tradition or nature as in the older tradition of 'natural law'. He considers that positive law functions as a reified 'form without content' in three ways: first, as a 'transcendental condition' (i.e. as a 'higher' principle and 'higher' form of cognition); second, as 'a regularity, an evenness' (i.e. considered to have no inherent flaws, grey areas, gaps or lacunae); and, third, as a 'rationalistic' technical refinement (i.e. which derives from and adheres to rational precepts, and as such is a field of technical, rather than political, expertise).[16] Gopal Balakrishnan explains that, for Schmitt, this 'formal' treatment of law amounts to a logical, abstract and gapless totality that is applied as a mere technical problem and pertains to all social action.[17] For Schmitt, legal positivism treats law as a completely self-contained, independent and apparently self-actualizing totality that precludes the possibility of flaws, contestable interpretation and political application by men.[18] These 'formal qualities' of positive law, its gaplessness and professionalization, all contribute to what Schmitt considers to be a typically liberal depoliticized schema that hides the possibility of political conflict beneath a mask of 'neutral' edifices. Law itself cannot operate as the source of authority for law, because the limit of law is not the law itself, but the political. As William Rasch puts it:

> Without the meta-level self-sufficiency of a God-like natural law to provide positive law its groundless ground, all immanent norms must themselves be derived from previous norms, producing the nightmare of a never-ending quest for ultimate normativity. Schmitt therefore concludes that the rule of law is a mere free-floating fiction, 'for no norm … interprets and administers, protects and guards itself; no normative validity validates itself; and there is … no hierarchy of norms, only a hierarchy of concrete people and instances'.[19]

Although Rasch's analysis is incisive, he overplays Schmitt's understanding of the rule of law in a crucial way. It is not the case for Schmitt that law is a complete fiction that is simply the handmaiden of politics. Schmitt is still a jurist. There remains a dialectical relationship between law and politics, norm and exception. If law were to completely give way to a pure politics, then law would have no meaning. Rather, although the everyday purpose of law is to codify the norm/rule, law ultimately derives its strength and vitality from the exception. For Schmitt, it is precisely because law has a limit, both politically (in the unforeseen exceptional circumstance that requires a sovereign political decision) and philosophically (due to the impossibility of a seamless, gapless and flawless totality of law), that the exception exists. And as *limit*, the exception *delimits* the shape of the norm/rule. For Schmitt, the exception serves as limit, guarantee, origin, ground and pure political moment. The sovereign decision on the exception, because it exists on the same exceptional plane, is the definition of sovereignty itself. Sovereignty is by its very nature exceptional.

Schmitt and the international

The corollary of Schmitt's critique of the flaws and contradictions of the liberal tradition is a concern with the deeply political propensities that those flaws and contradictions hide. What concerned Schmitt most of all was the encroachment of the 'depoliticizations' of liberalism into the international sphere. In *The Concept of the Political*, Schmitt had a particular eye on the expansion of Anglo-American liberalism, which he considered an empire by another name. From the position of Germany's post-Versailles emasculation, he identified the international deployment of a liberalism that was highly political in his sense of the term, but which disguised its politics under purportedly apolitical constructions. Schmitt declared that 'this allegedly non-political and apparently even antipolitical system serves existing or newly emerging friend-and-enemy groupings and cannot escape the logic of the political'.[20]

Schmitt identified ethics and economics in particular as the two 'apolitical' poles of the 'neutral' liberal edifice, arguing polemically that '[t]he world will not become depoliticalized with the aid of definitions and constructions, all of which circle the polarity of ethics and economics'.[21] Schmitt considered that the liberal reification of economics, combined with the relentless techno-economic rationalization that Weber identified as characteristic of late modernity, tended toward a depoliticization in the name of the efficacy of the market, technology and bureaucracy.[22] Criticizing the liberalism of Franz Oppenheimer, a contemporary, Schmitt writes:

> The economic way is declared to be reciprocity of production and consumption, therefore mutuality, equality, justice, and freedom, and finally nothing less than the spiritual union of fellowship, brotherliness, and justice. The political way appears on the other hand as a conquering power

outside the domain of economics, namely, thievery, conquest, and crimes of all sorts.[23]

Contrary to this liberal denigration of politics in favour of a 'more civilized' economics, Schmitt argued that an economically oriented entity retains a specifically political dimension that contains the potential for conflict. Economic exchange could, just as easily as military aggression, lead to a situation of conflict, exploitation and repression.[24] Economically rather than militarily oriented policy has its own equally devastating if less openly violent means of waging 'war' or using 'force', such as sanctions, tariff walls, and blockades.[25] Schmitt explains that 'it is ... erroneous to believe that a political position founded on economic superiority is "essentially unwarlike"'.[26] For Schmitt, an economic order that presents itself as depoliticized and neutral is one that is free of political responsibility or accountability, because sovereign responsibility is hidden and dispersed amongst a plethora of diverse economic interests. It would be all too easy to shirk political responsibility by claiming that the market is beyond political control.[27] Schmitt argues that such depoliticizations serve existing power interests well, by removing the means by which they can be legitimately questioned. As he explains: 'When the exploited and the repressed attempt to defend themselves ... they cannot do so by economic means. Evidently the possessor of economic power would consider every attempt to change its power position by extra-economic means as violence and crime'.[28] Hence Schmitt polemically announces that, '[e]conomic antagonisms can become political, and the fact that an economic power position could arise proves that the point of the political may be reached from the economic as well as from any other domain'.[29] For Schmitt, 'the political' is not simply another domain alongside economics, culture, religion and so on, but the extreme *limit* that can be reached from all domains.

In terms of the 'depoliticizations' of ethics, especially in the international sphere, Schmitt considered the defining instance of this as the introduction of 'war guilt' by the Treaty of Versailles. He argued that when an enemy is legally denied the legitimate right to use war as an instrument of policy, any such actions immediately become crimes. The consequence is that the legal and moral equality of opponents enshrined in the institution of the European state system is undone. Due to the 'universal' nature of the criminalization of war (which for Schmitt is anything but universal), enforcement thereof is done in the name of 'humanity'. The result is that '[t]he adversary is thus no longer called an enemy but a disturber of the peace and is thereby designated to be an outlaw of humanity'.[30] This turns the enemy into 'an inhuman monster ... that must not only be fended off but definitively annihilated'.[31]

When war is a crime, Schmitt notes that other names are invented for the enforcement of international law, such as 'peace enforcement', 'police bombing', 'containment' and, particularly, 'humanitarian intervention'.[32] It is no longer enough to simply repel the enemy back to his borders; instead he must be reformed, corrected, punished or even annihilated altogether. Schmitt would retort that the enforcement of such 'universal' values simply creates ever-more morally and legally reinforced reasons to wage war, giving the 'enforcers' just cause and ever-greater destructive licence. Far from ridding the world of war, liberalism gives wars a greater intensity.

Schmitt considered the subjugation of politics to international ethics as the most disturbing of the depoliticizations of liberalism. In the Schmittian understanding, when liberal 'universal' morality enters international politics and becomes allied with the state itself, the state ceases to consider itself limited by the state system. It instead adopts a universalizing, imperialistic self-understanding. For Schmitt, this liberal imperialism disguises the *particular* (the politics of a particular sovereign state) as the *universal* (a politics that claims to transcend particular sovereign states); it attempts to shrug off the in-built limits of the state system.

As such, *The Concept of the Political* is a call to limit international morality by reasserting that under modernity the highest denominator of morality is the sovereign state, and that moral claims can call on no 'higher' authorities such as humanity or universal right. Schmitt instead insisted on state sovereignty and its attendant *jus belli*: 'the real possibility of deciding in a concrete situation upon the enemy and the ability to fight him with the power emanating from the [political] entity'.[33] He is highly critical of the elimination of the sovereign state right and monopoly of legitimate decision regarding the justness of war. His reassertion of state sovereignty is a response to this. Schmitt argues that if the principles of the modern European state system were adhered to, and if the Anglo-American liberal-internationalist perversion of the state system was negated, then war would be tamed, contained and limited. Schmitt's reassertion of the Westphalian ideal serves as a prohibition on wars for any reason other than self-defence in existentially threatening circumstances. For Schmitt, the European modern state system ideally prevents the enemy being made into a heathen to be annihilated.[34]

Today, Schmitt's words provide a cutting critique of 'humanitarian' wars and liberal imperialism. They also serve as a riposte to the demonization and dehumanization of the enemy that is often witnessed in so-called 'humanitarian' wars. The pertinence of Schmitt's critique of liberal imperialism for contemporary global politics is no doubt one of the main reasons for his increasing popularity. Contemporary anti-imperialist sentiment no doubt finds much wisdom in passages found in Schmitt, such as the following:

> There exists no rational purpose, no social ideal no matter how true, no program no matter how exemplary, no social ideal no matter how beautiful, no legitimacy nor legality which could justify men in killing each other for this reason. If such physical destruction of human life is not motivated by an existential threat to one's own way of life, then it cannot be justified. Just as little can war be justified by ethical and juristic norms. If there really are enemies in the existential sense as meant here, then it is justified, but only politically, to repel and fight them physically.[35]

To be clear then, as an *international* theorist Schmitt offers *less* violence than that entailed in universalizing forms of international politics. He offers a sharp critique of a liberal imperialism that hides its violence within 'humanitarian' ideology. Schmitt *does* valorize war, but it is ideally a formally structured war in which the enemy is respected as an equal. This imposes a limitation on war: it should stop short of annihilation. Neither friend nor enemy is to cease to exist as a state, for ultimately the state system must be respected. Many international relations theorists have picked up on this enticing critique of imperialism and humanitarian intervention. As a lesson in cross-cultural tolerance, they tend to seize upon the international pluralism that Schmitt offers.[36] However, it is a grave mistake to end the analysis of Schmitt there. To do so would be to fatally miss the fact that Schmitt's pluralism between states comes at the expense of authoritarianism within states.

State exceptionalism

For the Schmitt of *The Concept of the Political*, the state is the limit *par excellence*. It is not simply limit but ontology. The state is the constitutive material of the human world (and this for Schmitt is a defining element of the centrality of Europe in world history, a centrality which he both valued and considered under threat from new forms of imperialism and hegemony). Any sub-state groupings are of a lower order. They are a danger because they may challenge state sovereignty. 'Politics', as in party politics and so on, is dangerous because it threatens to intensify into the pathological friend/enemy confrontation of 'the political'. Any extra-state groupings, such as an Anglo-American liberal-imperialist alliance or an international class of 'workers of the world', are a challenge to the order of the European state system. In Schmitt, the 'high politics' of the statesman is venerated, while the 'low politics' of the parliament and the party is denigrated.

Understanding Schmitt means understanding the central duality that defines his work and the principle he expresses: international pluralism, domestic unity. The exceptionalism of *The Concept of the Political* is state exceptionalism; it defends the right of each state to be exceptional in the international sphere and to recognize no laws or regulations other than its own, but also the right of each state to be exceptional within its domestic jurisdiction, with the absolute prerogative to act exceptionally with regard to its own laws and people. Hence neither Schmitt as international theorist nor Schmitt as political theorist is an adequate characterization; he must be understood in his duality. The reification of the state, which seems to bring so many pluralistic benefits in the international realm, has the opposite effect in domestic politics. It is a justification of internal repression. The sanctity of the state is paramount. Its necessary unity and coherence require internal peace. As Schmitt writes:

> The endeavour of a normal state consists above all in assuring total peace within the state and its territory. ... As long as the state is a political

entity the requirement for internal peace compels it in critical situations to decide also upon the domestic enemy. Every state provides, therefore, some kind of formula for the declaration of an internal enemy.[37]

In this way, state sovereignty depends on the exception and indeed is the *manifestation* of the exception, as the opening line of his *Political Theology* – 'Sovereign is he who decides on the exception'[38] – makes clear. Behind this idea lies the imperative that the continuing existence of the state must take precedence over all other considerations, especially those regarding the rights and claims of individuals and sub-state groups. No sovereign state would allow itself to be destroyed rather than suspend its laws or values in an emergency or exceptional situation. Hence, for Schmitt, although the sovereign may normally be party to the laws of a polity, 'he' is nevertheless an extra-legal exceptional figure, for it is 'he' (it is ambiguous whether 'he' is an actual or metaphorical figure) who ultimately has the power to suspend laws in the name of survival.

To demonstrate this state exceptionalism, and the socio-political impera-tives it entails, it is worth looking again at his impassioned prohibition on war for reasons other than self-defence: 'If such physical destruction of human life is not motivated by an existential threat to one's own way of life, then it cannot be justified'.[39] There is a cunning sleight of hand at play here. Schmitt does not simply cite 'human life' as sacrosanct, but 'one's own *way of life*'.[40] Conveniently, then, all the attractive prohibitions that Schmitt provides to severely limit justifications for killing do not apply to a state's own citizens if they pose a threat to whatever that state's 'way of life' is considered to be by those in power. Because for Schmitt the declaration of domestic enemies by the state 'is possibly the sign of civil war'[41] that poses an 'existential threat to one's own way of life',[42] the right of self-defence can be invoked. The sover-eign state monopoly on ethical and legal decision at the international level equates to a political monopoly of decision on what a political entity's 'way of life' is and whether it is under threat. The subsumption of national will and national plurality to state sovereignty is a conflation of the political with the social and cultural. At the international level this amounts to a case for nation-state sovereignty and the right to self-determination. At the domestic level it amounts to a justification of internal repression and a demand for socio-cultural as well as political unity.

For Schmitt the *jus belli* – the state's right to declare war – entails a formal limitation on interstate war and mutual respect for state sovereignty on the one hand, and the right of internal repression on the other. The 'way of life' clause means that internal repression is not simply limited to 'security' issues, political violence and so on, but applies to anything that challenges the offi-cial 'way of life' of the nation-state. Despite Schmitt's renunciation of any norm or social ideal as a justification for killing, the defence of an ethical norm is central to his formulations. That ethical norm is the sovereign nation-state itself.

For Schmitt, the legitimate subject of politics is the nation-state, not the individual, company, union, party or class. For Schmitt, politics is high politics; it pertains to the state. Internal state politics pertains to the state only pathologically, insofar as it has the potential to become civil war and destroy the sovereignty of the state. Hence Jacques Derrida argues that, for Schmitt,

> the state presupposes the political, to be sure, hence it is logically distinguished from it; but the analysis of the political, strictly speaking, and its irreducible core, the friend/enemy configuration, can only privilege, from the beginning and as its sole guiding thread, the State form of this configuration – in other words, the friend or enemy qua citizen.[43]

In *The Concept of the Political* exceptionalism is already codified in spatial terms. The exceptional moment will be the emergence of an enemy. This will be either an internal challenge to sovereignty and the cherished national *way of life*, or another state seeking to invade, impose tribute or somehow qualify the sovereign status of that state. In *The Concept of the Political*, the exceptional situation is the point at which the extreme antagonism of 'the political' that resides *in potentia* in all political interaction comes to the surface. It is up to the sovereign political entity, if it is to show that it is truly sovereign, to decide when that moment has arrived and act accordingly. This exceptionalism is already grounded in an ethic of the state. It is less an 'ungrounded' transcendental moment of contingency and more a culturally situated decision on whether there is an existential threat to the national 'way of life'. Because the exceptional situation will no doubt arise at some point in the future, there is an element of temporal uncertainty involved, but here this *temporal* problem is already given as a category of *space*. This is because the exceptional moment will be the emergence of an enemy, and enemies are already codified in spatial terms – they arise either inside or outside as a pathology of the already-given ontology of the spatial state.

Thus the apparent contradiction between Schmitt's anti-imperialist international pluralism on the one hand, and his demand for domestic unity on the other, stem from a single precept about the inherent conflict of modern life. This inherent conflict is expressed through Schmitt's concept of 'the political'. The tension of 'the political' (which derives from its potential to become war) is equally in play in both international and domestic politics, except that the consequences in each sphere are very different. In Schmitt, as Derrida argues, 'there is only one concept of war'.[44] The same account of fundamental conflict applies to both the international and the domestic realm, but the effects are opposite. This is directly because of the reification of the state and, more specifically, the nation-state. Schmitt's account of war privileges war between states, but makes sub-state conflicts into wars over the survival of the (way of life of the) state itself. Derrida explains the apparent contradiction between Schmitt's international and domestic politics as follows:

At once both a paradox and a piece of good sense, this determination establishes war as a war between two States, a war in view of the State, a war between a weakened State and a potential State to be constituted, a war for the seizure or reconstitution of State power.[45]

On the one hand, the formal external enemy is the enemy state, tied up in a system of mutual recognition that entails a commitment to continued co-existence. On the other hand, the internal enemy is a threat to the continued existence of the state. Internal enmity has the potential to become civil war; it is a war over the state itself, a war which challenges the sovereignty of the state by threatening to usurp it, a war between an existing, weakened state and a potential state-in-waiting.

This is why in *The Concept of the Political* there is a single ethical norm, and that is the state. The necessity of the state stems directly from 'the political'. As the book begins: 'The concept of the state presupposes the concept of the political'.[46] For Schmitt, the sovereign state is a theoretical logic (regarding the inherent conflict of everyday human life and freedom), an existential imperative (regarding state survival), an empirical fact (in terms of the historical record of where sovereignty actually resides) and an ethic (as a form of 'high' politics and a 'way of life'). As Schmitt proclaims: 'The high points of politics are simultaneously the moments in which the enemy is, in concrete clarity, recognized as the enemy'.[47] This ethic is affirmed through war in the international sphere and the strong repression of potential civil war in the domestic sphere.

The Concept of the Political is a playing out of the logic of the modern state and modern state system. The remorseless clarity of the text is both captivating and frightening. It demonstrates the logic of state exceptionalism starkly. Yet its overwhelming nation-statist ethic does not capture enough of what is interesting and pressing about the problem of the exception. Schmitt overdetermines the concept of the exception in the course of his polemical political affirmations. That is to say, in *The Concept of the Political* Schmitt invokes but does not fully expand upon the concept of the exception. The metaphysical problem posed by the exception, as a contingent possibility, an unknowable future, a lacuna in totality, a moment of pure sovereign decision, is touched upon but ultimately short-circuited for the sake of an ethico-political vision. We *know* what the exceptional moment will look like, Schmitt effectively argues; it will be the emergence of an internal or external enemy of the state, and because this *will* happen we must continually reaffirm the national sovereignty of the state. Derrida describes Schmitt's metaphysical short-circuit in favour of a vitalist national politics as follows:

As soon as war is possible, it is taking place, Schmitt seems to say; presently, in a society of combat, in a community presently at war, since it can present itself to itself, as such, only in reference to this possible war. Whether the war takes place, whether war is decided upon or declared, is a mere empirical alternative in the face of an essential necessity: war is taking place; it has already begun before it begins, as soon as it is characterized as *eventual* (that is, announced as a non-excluded event in a sort of contingent future). And it is *eventual* as soon as it is *possible*. Schmitt does not wish to dissociate the quasi-transcendental modality of the possible and the historico-factual modality of the eventual.[48]

The Concept of the Political plays out *in extremis* the existential and exceptional logic of the discourse of the modern sovereign nation-state. What it does not do is explore the relation between this statist logic and the problem of the exception understood as a dangerous contingent event.

The temporal, contingent exception

The concept of the exception in Schmitt's *Political Theology* is more profound. Here its form is not already given. In contrast to Derrida's analysis of Schmitt's wars against enemies of the state, the 'quasi-transcendental modality of the possible' *is* dissociated from the 'historico-factual modality of the eventual'. In other words, in *Political Theology* the exceptional situation is not necessarily the *eventual* emergence of a state enemy. Rather, it is a problem of contingency, of a *possible* unknown future; it is a *temporal* exception.

It is true that in *Political Theology* the exception is already conceived as 'an extreme peril, a danger to the existence of the state, or the like',[49] and is thus already conceived in relation to the state, but its form is not yet known. It is characterized, instead, by the fact that it will not fall within the preformed, ideal, 'gapless' codifications of the 'existing legal order'.[50] It will instead fall beyond the 'circumscribed facts' and 'preformed laws' that are designed to anticipate and legislate against the advent of certain contingencies.[51] Before the advent of the exception, its form is unknowable. When it arises, it is characterized by its inability to conform to any prior anticipation of what it might be. The exceptional event or situation is the unforeseen possibility that has not and cannot be predicted. This event, this rupture, unsettles positivistic schemas of codification, prediction and preparation. It undermines political systems, legal institutions and state constitutions by presenting them with contingencies that were not and could not have been anticipated in their design and construction. This idea of the exception is conveyed most clearly by Schmitt in the following passage:

> The exception, which is not codified in the existing legal order, can at best be characterized as a case of extreme peril, a danger to the existence of the state, or the like. But it cannot be circumscribed factually and made to conform to a preformed law ... The precise details of an emergency cannot be anticipated, nor can one spell out what may take place in such a case, especially when it is truly a matter of an extreme emergency and of how it is to be eliminated.[52]

For Schmitt, the exception is the inevitable and potentially deadly eventuality that cannot be foreseen and made subject to laws. When the law has surpassed the limits of its scope, usefulness and authority, what is left is not God, nature or, indeed, a deeper level of law, but the exception and sovereignty. As Schmitt writes: 'The definition of sovereignty must ... be associated with a borderline case and not with routine'.[53] For Schmitt, law is *ultimately* (but not routinely) subordinate to politics. The potential existence of the exception, as an extreme danger that cannot be anticipated by the law, shows the necessity and primacy of sovereign political decision: 'It is precisely the exception that makes relevant the subject of sovereignty, that is, the whole question of sovereignty'.[54]

The concept of this contingent exception confers a transcendental exteriority and autonomy to 'exceptional' events and situations. This kind of event is invoked as, in Schmitt's words, 'a case of extreme peril, a danger to the existence of the state, or the like'.[55] In this way, the concept of the temporal, contingent exception works to constitute and reify a politics of rupture or break. This is both a rupture in the normal passage of national history and a rupture in the normal scope of law and technocratic politics. Representing a moment, event or situation as an exceptional rupture in history or normality serves to legitimate a representation of the present as exceptional. In turn, the invocation of the exception is central to a politics of exceptionalism, in which claims about existential necessities – brought about by exceptional events – are used to legitimate exceptions being made to moral, legal and political norms, both domestically and internationally.

Under this condition of exceptional danger, what I earlier termed the 'excess' of sovereign political authority is brought into sharp focus. For Schmitt, when the limits of liberty and law have been exceeded, there must be some kind of sovereign remainder that serves as a deeper source of authority and legitimacy for the modern sovereign nation-state under exceptional conditions. 'Where does sovereignty ultimately reside?' asks Schmitt: 'The controversy always centered on the question, Who assumes positive authority concerning those matters for which there are no positive stipulations ... ? In other words, Who is responsible for that for which competence has not been anticipated?'[56]

In his invocation of this contingent exception, Schmitt has captured a genuine philosophical problem. It is the 'what if?' that lies beyond the limits of both imagination, representation and experience. This can be put into play as a critique of scientific certainty, against the limits of prediction, against the assurances of positivistic social science, against ethical conviction and against what Foucault would call 'totalizing' schemas of knowledge.[57] What does the liberal state do when the limit of its tolerance is breached? When are political principles to be suspended in the name of security or survival? Under what conditions are exceptional policies and practices considered legitimate? Schmitt is acutely aware of the critical and affective possibilities of invoking conditions of contingent exceptionality. These are the conditions of possibility that must obtain for Schmitt to appear to win the argument on exceptionalism. This is why Schmitt is so relevant and so dangerous.

It is vital, therefore, to be aware of the extremely slippery philosophical and political moves on which Schmitt's exceptionalism rests. Schmitt's political strategy is deeply intertwined with what he presents as philosophical insights. Schmitt is fully aware that there is a profound philosophical problem involved in the idea of the exception. As he writes: 'whether the extreme exception can be banished from the world is not a juristic question. Whether one has the confidence and hope that it can be eliminated depends on philosophical, especially on philosophical-historical or metaphysical convictions'.[58]

However, Schmitt does not pursue this line; instead he turns directly to the problem of sovereignty. He conflates the metaphysical problem with a political co-optation of that problem. He establishes answers to the questions he poses while still in the process of posing them. Schmitt uses the exception as a metaphysical problem of contingency in order to construct a particular vision of politics.

From the beginning, Schmitt's treatment of the 'exception' actually conflates two separate phenomena: the exceptional *event* and the sovereign *response* to that event. Schmitt's problematization of, in Derrida's words, the 'quasi-transcendental modality of the possible' uses the contingency of the exceptional event to establish the existential and juridical necessity of sovereign state absolutism. Hence Schmitt's argument unfolds as follows: 'What characterizes an exception is principally unlimited authority, which means the suspension of the entire existing order. In such a situation it is clear that the state remains, whereas law recedes'.[59]

Schmitt perpetrates a significant conflation between two separate concepts or problems: the exceptional event and the exceptional response. When Schmitt presents 'unlimited authority' as the exception itself, he has very quickly elided the temporal gap between the event and the response. Schmitt does this to establish 'unlimited authority' as the necessary and natural response to the 'extreme peril' of the exceptional event. He swiftly asserts that when an unforeseen event falls outside the codes of law and the jurisdictional competences established in existing institutional and constitutional settlements, '[t]he precondition as well as the content of jurisdictional competence in such a case must necessarily be unlimited'.[60]

The exception is for Schmitt 'a danger to the existence of the state, or the like' and 'truly a matter of an extreme emergency and of how it is to be eliminated'.[61] In the form in which Schmitt relays it, the extreme emergency is from the beginning conflated with the necessary means of its elimination. This overdetermined means of elimination is some form of dictatorship and, more clearly in *Political Theology* than in *The Concept of the Political*, a dictatorship in the form of an individual 'he'. It is quite clear that this political vision is a polemic against liberalism: 'If such action is not subject to controls, if it is not hampered in some way by checks and balances, as is the case in a liberal constitution, then it is clear who the sovereign is'.[62] The exception, when conflated so, is already tied to a particular political norm. Under the dialectic of exceptional politics, the true quality of what politics must necessarily be is revealed.

But Schmitt is even more slippery than this. In his construction, it is not simply a question of who assumes authority in the case of an exception, but who *decides* that there is an exception in the first place. To return to the first line of *Political Theology*: 'Sovereign is he who decides on the exception'.[63] It transpires, once again, that Schmitt's argument depends on a short-circuit, an overdetermination. Schmitt introduces the exceptional event as a contingent possibility and as a critique of the ideal, gapless totality of rationalized positive law and liberal constitutionalism. Schmitt attacks the omniscience regarding the future that is assumed by this model. Aping Machiavelli in *The Prince*, he says that we cannot know what the future may bring. We may build institutions and create procedures, but they will eventually be overcome by the vicissitudes of *fortuna*.[64] Following this line, Schmitt also argues that if the unforeseen event is exceptional and does not conform to any pre-existing idea of normality, there will be no pre-established response that can anticipate its occurrence. 'The most guidance the constitution can provide', he suggests, 'is to indicate who can act in such a case'.[65]

There is a telling flaw in Schmitt's formulations. If the sovereign is to *decide* on the exception, the status of the exceptional event as a contingent and unpredictable eruption of *fortuna* is thrown into doubt. Why does the sovereign need not only to *respond* to the exceptional event, but to *decide* on the exceptional event? What is to say that the sovereign is *telling the truth* when he declares an exception? What is to prevent the sovereign from *falsely* or *arbitrarily* declaring an exception for political gain, especially when unlimited exceptional powers follow from such a declaration?

There is, therefore, a fatal difference between Machiavelli's prince and Schmitt's sovereign. The prince does not decide when *fortuna* has turned. He does not have this power. When *fortuna* turns against the prince it signals the end of his power, the end of his reign, the end of his capacity to be ruler. The reign of the prince is only ever temporary. It is granted to him by *fortuna*, and *fortuna* brings it to an end. He can build defences, and if he is wise, if he learns from history and if he has enough *virtú*, perhaps they will hold, but they will never hold forever.[66]

In contrast, Schmitt's sovereign does not simply respond to the exceptional temporal contingency as best he can, but decides when it has arrived: 'He decides whether there is an extreme emergency as well as what must be done to eliminate it'.[67] Why, it might be asked, must the sovereign decide? This is not the same as asking why the sovereign must respond. If the exceptional event does exist as a possibility, and is indeed a 'case of extreme peril', then why may only the sovereign recognize it? Why is its recognition not merely a technical concern?

The answer is that in *Political Theology* Schmitt employs a similar ethico-political strategy to that of *The Concept of the Political*. Schmitt's treatment of the problem of the exception is already tied up with a particular politics. The concept of the exception is invoked in order to construct political claims about sovereign necessity. Schmitt's sovereign exceptionalism is a political ethic constructed from claims about the metaphysical and politico-philosophical necessity of acting exceptionally; of making exceptions to norms, be they customary, legal or moral. He invokes the notions of limit and exception to attack the prevailing political and legal norm, and from there not only introduces the notion of a more fundamental excess to modern politics, but attempts to determine that excess in a particular way. Schmitt argues that beyond the positivistic norms of the constitution and the law, the true essence of the modern sovereign state can be found. Although the constitution and the law may falter, the sovereign state remains – in a more fundamental, less limited, more authentic way.

Carl Schmitt's politics of the exception is a potentially fascist stitch-up, a brutal suture. We must insist, therefore, that we can still see the joins. Schmitt's stitch-up is to suture together and conflate three different things: (1) the 'real possibility' of the exceptional event; (2) the sovereign decision that the exception exists; and (3) the exceptional sovereign response to the event.

Typically, the idea of an event invokes a temporal sequence of event–response, action–reaction. But the prerogative of Schmitt's sovereign to *decide* on the exception inverts this sequence. In Schmitt, the sovereign prerogative to decide on the exceptional event precedes the event itself, even though sovereign exceptionalism is only justified by the event's 'real possibility'. As Derrida writes in his analysis of Schmitt: 'The realization is not the actualization of a possible but something altogether different: the radicalization of a possible *reality* or a *real* possibility. Here we are no longer in the conventionally Aristotelian opposition of potentiality and act'.[68]

What must be done is to separate the idea of the exceptional *event* from the *response* to the exceptional event. The *exception* must be separated from *exceptionalism*, for they are not the same thing. The *exception* is a philosophical or metaphysical problem. *Exceptionalism* is the *sovereign exception*, the practice by which sovereign authority declares an exception and acts in an exceptional way. Insisting on the separateness of the event and the response allows an appreciation that the exception, whether metaphysically possible or not, need not carry any inherent or prior determination. The possibility of the exceptional event should not be treated as an already-determined political phenomenon. To be sure, the exception poses profound philosophical problems, as Schmitt makes clear. But tied in with Schmitt's sharp philosophical and political insights is a deliberate political determination of those problems.

Schmitt uses the idea of the independently occurring exceptional *event* or *situation* to construct an account of the necessity and primacy of exceptional sovereign *decision*. However, because this sovereign prerogative entails not only the imperative to *respond* to the exception but the prerogative to *decide* whether an exception exists, the independent, causal and contingent existence of the exception is thrown into doubt. What Schmitt constructs as an 'objective' problem of independently occurring exceptional events or situations actually depends on 'subjective' sovereign judgement. Although Schmitt invokes the metaphysical problem of contingency as a rationale for exceptionalism, the primacy of the sovereign prerogative to decide on the exception renders the exceptional event a superfluous part of that rationale. This means that practices and policies of exceptionalism are not brought about by contingent events themselves, as Schmitt tries to assert, but by sovereign declarations of exceptionality. While Schmitt's guileful logic does not itself dissolve the metaphysical problem of the contingent event, within the immanent terms of his political philosophy the invocation of the problem of contingency in the rationale for exceptionalism is undermined by a totalizing sovereign nominalism.

Schmitt is not simply a theorist but a shrewd practitioner of politics. He is an employer of clever textual strategies that operate on the line between concepts and the concrete, the ideal and the real, the norm and the exception. Schmitt knows when to blur that line and when to cut sharply with it. A politics is produced at this line; that is what we must be clear of in both reading Schmitt and reading contemporary politics.

The problem of exceptionalism is no less than the problem of sovereign naming, the sovereign nominalism which Hobbes opposed to the Classical Greek metaphysics he dismantled in the opening chapters of *Leviathan*. Schmitt's sovereign nominalism is massively overdetermined with a particular political ethic. As Derrida puts it: 'As if it were sufficient that an event be possible for it to happen, for it to have already actually taken place in its very perhaps, at the end of the sentence naming its possibility'.[69]

Schmitt's textual strategies are sovereign moves, attempted assertions of authority regarding the exceptionality of events and situations and the political necessities that must ensue. However, the problem of sovereign naming cannot simply be tackled by opposing one political position with another, one attempted sovereign move with another. Although it may be possible to critique Schmitt's politico-theoretical strategy, the problem of sovereign naming reaches further than the imminent logic of Schmitt's texts. The 'flaws' in Schmitt's arguments are in themselves revealing of the problem of the exception. In contemporary terms, declarations of exceptionality have in many ways translated into the kind of politics that Schmitt tried to construct, with enemies declared, agents of sovereign authorities acting outside the law, dissent stifled, society mobilized in warlike ways, and national unity affirmed. So although it is possible to insist that the exceptional event should not be treated as an already-determined political phenomenon (or indeed, already determined as exceptional), this does not tackle the question of the socio-political processes and conditions of possibility under which events and politics can successfully be determined as exceptional.

This discursive and socio-political dimension is why for Schmitt the necessity for strong sovereign decision requires a lack of political challenge to the sovereign capacity to decide. A pluralistic sovereign state is a fractious and unhealthy sovereign state: 'The intensification of internal antagonisms has the effect of weakening the common identity vis-à-vis another state'.[70] Hence in Schmitt's work there is an existential and ethical imperative for national unity and a lack of contestation to sovereign decision. Not only is the very existence of the state under threat if the capacity for exceptional sovereign decision is weak or contested, but, moreover, these decisive moments are when the political life of the strong, unified and healthy nation-state is affirmed: when 'the power of real life breaks through the crust of a mechanism that has become torpid by repetition'.[71]

There is more at stake in the problem of the exception than simply affirming or contesting a monolithic form of authoritarian, exceptional sovereign power. Schmitt's emphasis on the *capacity* for sovereign decision, and his discussion of the possibility of that capacity being weakened, lost or usurped, highlights the dialectical and socio-political aspects of exceptionalism. Exceptionalism is not only a problem of contingency or limit, but also a problem of discourse and socio-political process, and, as such, Schmitt articulates exceptionalism as a relation between politico-legal limits and socio-political conditions. Schmitt argues that in order for the modern nation-statist form of life to be possible, not only must sovereign power have the capacity for exceptionality because of the insoluble problem of exceptional limit and contingency, but politics and society must be organized in such a way as to make this capacity possible. Schmitt's exceptional sovereignty, and the form of ethico-political life it projects and defends, depends on certain socio-political conditions of possibility.

Schmitt comes to represent two continuing problems. The first is the problem of *the exception*, as a problem of contingency and territorial, political and legal limit. The second is the problem of the *politics of exceptionalism*, which in Schmitt's construction is a politics of authoritarian nation-statism. The problem is not one simply of defeating Schmitt at the theoretical level, but of responding to the political conditions and processes that Schmitt represents. A response to Schmitt and the problem of the exception must therefore address, first, the problem of exceptional contingency and limit, its philosophical status and so on, and, second, the politics, discourses and socio-political processes of exceptionalism. Does the problem of the exception necessarily lead to Schmitt's political conclusions? How can the problem of the exception be addressed in a way that resists the move from a problem of limit to an extreme form of nation-statist politics?

4 Giorgio Agamben's exception

'The great historico-transcendental destiny of the Occident'[1]

The last chapter on Schmitt concluded that two main sets of problems need further consideration. The first is 'the exception' as a problem of exceptional contingency and limit. The second is the problem of the politics of exceptional*ism*, particularly its discursive and socio-political processes and conditions of possibility. Schmitt uses the former – the idea of the exception as a metaphysical and philosophical problem of limit and contingent event – to construct a legitimation of the latter – a politics of exceptional policies and practices. His suture of the problem of 'the exception' to a politics of exceptionalism both is overdetermined with an authoritarian nation-statist ethic and rests on some slippery conceptual moves, namely the conflation of the *exceptional event* with both the exceptional sovereign *response* to that event and the sovereign *decision* that the event is exceptional in the first place.

This chapter will focus on the first of these sets of problems – the exception as limit and contingency. The question is whether the exception can be addressed in a way that resists the move to a Schmittian politics. If Schmitt's strategy is to present the problem of the exception in such a way that it appears to carry an inherent set of political determinations, necessities and imperatives, is there a way of addressing the problem of the exception which does not produce or imply these same political effects?

The contemporary Italian philosopher Giorgio Agamben has produced some of the most serious work on these problems. Indeed it would be fair to credit him, at least in part, with the current revival of interest in the exception concept. His work in this area is presented in two books: *Homo Sacer: Sovereign Power and Bare Life*, first published in Italian in 1995 and translated in 1998, and what is described as its sequel, *State of Exception*, first published in Italian in 2003 and translated in 2005. The two books are of a slightly different order. *Homo Sacer* is the longer and more original text. It lays out some rather innovative ideas regarding sovereignty and the figures of man and life. *State of Exception* is a shorter text that is less far-reaching in its ambition, but engages more closely with the debates in the literature concerning the idea of a 'state of exception'.

This chapter is an exposition, analysis and critique of Agamben's work. Through a close reading of these two texts it will establish what Agamben is doing, why it is important, where it is limited or problematic, and what needs to be addressed differently or considered further. It will make reference to contemporary empirical concerns and engage closely with Agamben's readings of key theorists for the problem of the exception, specifically Carl Schmitt, Walter Benjamin and Michel Foucault. The overriding concern is to question the political and methodological implications of Agamben's response to the problem of the exception.

Biopolitics, sacred life and sovereignty as a relation of abandonment

In *Homo Sacer*, Agamben argues that the exception is nothing less than the original relation at the heart of the entire Western paradigm of politics. The Greeks, Agamben argues, made a key distinction between the simple fact of living – *zoē* – and the qualified political life – *bios*. While the mere fact of living in itself had a 'natural sweetness' for Aristotle, the end of politics was not simply this 'bare life'[2] but the politically qualified 'life according to the good'.[3] Agamben claims that this account of politics became canonical for us moderns, centring on competing articulations of the 'good life'.

Agamben then invokes Foucault's distinction between this classical paradigm and the identification of a distinctively modern 'biopolitics', in which biological life (of both the individual and the species) becomes what is at stake in politics. As Foucault writes: 'For millennia, man remained what he was for Aristotle: a living animal with the additional capacity for political existence; modern man is an animal whose politics calls his existence as a living being into question'.[4] For Foucault, biopolitical modernity is marked by political processes, principles and practices which question the very existence of man as a species. Examples might include nuclear deterrence and weapons of mass destruction, environmental degradation and catastrophe, demographic and migratory shifts, epidemiological threats, and the biological sciences.[5]

Agamben argues that in the transition from classical politics to biopolitics, the 'bare life' that was excluded from politics and the polis as the simple unqualified fact of living becomes included in the realm of politics. The concept of biopolitics allows Agamben to claim that this exclusion – which for the Western episteme marked the original distinction between the political and the non-political – in fact marks the 'the fundamental categorical pair of Western politics ... that of bare life/political existence, *zoē/bios*, exclusion/inclusion'.[6] Agamben argues that the original exclusion of 'bare life' from political life has in fact become an 'inclusive exclusion'. In being excluded from properly qualified political life, 'bare life' is thrown into a more basic and fundamental political relationship with the sovereign power that excluded it. As such, 'bare life' is all the more political in being excluded. The exclusion of 'bare life' from properly qualified political life has become, in light of a biopolitics at the level of species existence, a kind of political inclusion.

In this way, Agamben takes the dialectical character of modern Western politics seriously. In contrast to the contradictory dualisms of the contemporary liberty/security discourse discussed in Chapters 1 and 2, Agamben understands that the modern Western subject does not simply exist in opposition to sovereign political authority, but is produced through an originary sovereign relation. For Agamben, sovereign exceptionalism is not simply an oppressive abuse of what should otherwise be a properly balanced relationship between liberty and security, subject and sovereign. Rather, exceptionalism is the very structure of sovereignty itself.

As such, those who are excluded or excepted from liberty and law – perhaps those designated as 'fundamentalists' or 'terrorists' – are not simply placed *outside* modern politics (as those 'over there' or 'back then') but rather brought *into* a more fundamental political relation. As such, Agamben takes seriously Schmitt's axiom that '[t]he rule proves nothing; the exception proves everything: It confirms not only the rule but also its existence, which derives only from the exception'.[7] For Agamben, the exception is not simply an aberration of modern politics but an essential and basic expression of its fundamental structure. Chapters 1 and 2 argued that sovereign exceptionalism cannot be opposed to the principles of modern liberty without the potential contradiction of sovereign power defending liberty by destroying liberty. Agamben avoids the contradictions of this dualistic opposition by considering Western sovereignty as an original, productive, dialectical relation between modern subjectivity and its excluded negation. As such, Agamben argues that

> the inclusion of bare life in the political realm constitutes the original – if concealed – nucleus of sovereign power. *It can even be said that the production of a biopolitical body is the original activity of sovereign power.* In this sense, biopolitics is at least as old as the exception.[8]

For Agamben, the exception is the limit condition in which forms of unqualified or excluded life dwell and are produced, which is in fact the production of a more fundamental biopolitical relation. For Agamben, sovereign power does not affirm its power over life by asserting its dominion, or by presiding over a progression from natural life to politically qualified modern life, but by withdrawing its protection and thus abandoning bare life to a realm of violence and lawlessness. This is the sovereign 'ban', the exclusion which is in fact an inclusion, an inclusive exclusion, because sovereign power applies all the more in withdrawing its protection. As Agamben explains:

> He who has been banned is not, in fact, simply set outside the law and made indifferent to it but rather *abandoned* by it, that is, exposed and threatened on the threshold in which life and law, outside and inside, become indistinguishable. It is literally impossible to say whether the one who has been banned is outside or inside the juridical order.[9]

Agamben brings this originary political exclusion into focus by calling upon the archaic Roman figure of *homo sacer* – sacred man. Here the term sacred means not simply holy but rather the more ambiguous meaning explored in nineteenth-century anthropology by such thinkers as Freud and Durkheim.[10] The sacred is a realm in which the holy and the taboo, the divine and the profane, are ambiguous and often touch. Hence *homo sacer* is one who has been excluded from normal human law and as such is placed in a 'limit condition' between this world and the next, between properly qualified human life and death. This limit condition corresponds to the sphere of the sovereign ban, in which bare life is included through its exclusion. The consequence is that

> The sovereign sphere is the sphere in which it is permitted to kill without committing homicide and without celebrating a sacrifice, and sacred life – that is, life that may be killed but not sacrificed – is the life that has been captured in this sphere.[11]

For Agamben, the sovereign exception is the withdrawal of the law from excluded life, and therefore the exposure of that life to the peril of death. One who kills *homo sacer* will face no sanction. And in being excluded from the normal prohibition on killing, *homo sacer* is also excluded from sacrifice, from the normal ritualized forms of killing and punishment. For example, the bandit, a traditional object of the ban,

> is in a continuous relationship with the power that banished him precisely insofar as he is at every instant exposed to an unconditioned threat of death. He is pure *zoē*, but his *zoē* is as such caught in the sovereign ban and must reckon with it at every moment ... In this sense, no life, as exiles and bandits know well, is more 'political' than his.[12]

Agamben argues that this sovereign sphere in which life 'may be killed but not sacrificed'[13] is made concrete in the site of the concentration camp. Agamben describes the figure of the camp as the absolute biopolitical space, in which 'power confronts nothing but pure life, without any mediation'.[14] The camp, Agamben argues, is the state of exception made permanent in factual basis. It is precisely here that the threshold between law and violence is manifested, in a zone of indistinction in which fact and law become indistinct, and in which every camp guard is effectively sovereign. Agamben raises the spectre of the often deadly scientific experiments that were conducted on both camp inmates in Nazi Germany and death row prisoners in the US, who, because their life was already deemed a life not worthy of being lived and destined for death, could be killed without murder.[15] The camp, Agamben argues, is 'the fundamental biopolitical paradigm of the West'.[16] Provocatively, Agamben claims that the inclusive exclusion of the camp, both as figure and in fact, resides at the heart of every model of citizenship and public space in the West.

Before developing a critique of these ideas, it is worth highlighting the relevance of Agamben's formulations for contemporary political concerns.

Agamben's formulations touch quite incisively on some of the issues raised by contemporary deployments of exceptional sovereign violence. The Guantanamo Bay detention camp is an exemplary site of contemporary exceptionalism that easily demonstrates the application of Agamben's ideas. Guantanamo cannot be explained in the regular terms of law or criminal investigation. The intended purpose of the camp's location outside the regular territory of the United States has been precisely to separate the entire process from normal American legal procedures and constitutional rights. Despite a Supreme Court ruling on 29 June 2006[17] giving the detainees the right to file petitions of *habeas corpus*, the legal status of the detainees remains ambiguous and contested. To apply Agamben's words, it exists in a 'state of exception'. The account of detention given by the 'Tipton Three', three British Muslims held there for over two years, demonstrates this description. As one of them explains: 'we were never given access to legal advice. I asked at various points but they just said that this is not America this is Cuba and you have no rights here'.[18] Similarly, in reference to the countless beatings and abuses the prisoners received, the report explains that 'there was never any redress when they were mistreated or rules were broken'.[19]

Likewise, a letter alleged to be from another British Guantanamo detainee, Moazzam Begg, released by US officials uncensored either 'by mistake or because someone in the US has a conscience',[20] relays details of his detention in both Afghanistan and Cuba. It goes so far as to make allegations of murder committed with impunity:

> I was subjected to pernicious threats of torture, actual vindictive torture and death threats – amongst other coercively employed interrogation techniques ... The said interviews were conducted in an environment of generated fear, resonant with terrifying screams of fellow detainees facing similar methods ... This culminated, in my opinion, with the deaths of two fellow detainees, at the hands of U.S. personnel, to which I myself was partially witness.[21]

The Guantanamo prisoners could be considered as Agamben's *homines sacri*. They have been excepted – etymologically meaning 'taken outside', as Agamben points out[22] – from what might be called the normal rituals of sacrifice. Here these would translate as the American legal processes that can culminate in the death penalty. Instead, the prisoners have been abandoned by the law and are left facing the violence of sovereign power. Seemingly, they can be killed without legal ritual or homicide. As Agamben argues, 'the sovereign is the one with respect to whom all men are potentially *homines sacri*, and *homo sacer* is the one with respect to whom all men act as sovereigns'.[23] Those who deal with the detainees operate outside the law, and, as such, they 'act as sovereigns'.

The politicization of bare life: birth/nation/biopolitics

Agamben's understanding of the sovereign exception is a direct response to the dualistic contradictions in modern liberal politics discussed in Chapters 1

and 2, in which liberties and rights mark not a domain free from sovereign
political authority but precisely the opposite. Agamben begins here by citing
Hannah Arendt's critical observations on the declining fate of the rights of
man. Arendt wrote:

> The conception of human rights, based upon the assumed existence of a
> human being as such, broke down at the very moment when those who
> professed to believe in it were for the first time confronted with people who
> had lost all other qualities and specific relationships – except that they were
> still human.[24]

For Arendt it is the refugee – relieved of citizenship and as a consequence
relieved of the very rights that were supposed to be held on account of being
human alone – that reveals the predicament of the rights of man. Thus liberties and rights only appear to be possible *under* sovereignty, and cannot be
considered in simple dualistic opposition to it. The refugee, no longer a subject of a sovereign power, no longer has rights in any practical sense of the
word, because any rights the refugee holds on account of being merely
human are only realizable through the help or protection of sovereign states.
(Even the humanitarian agencies of the UN are entirely reliant and more
often than not severely constrained by the purse strings tightly held by
states.)[25]

Agamben takes this radical crisis of rights and extends the analysis in terms
of biopolitics. The exclusion of human life deprived of all belonging, citizenship and identity is not simply a paradox, but the 'hidden paradigm of the
political space of modernity'.[26] Agamben tackles the rights of man not as a
founding achievement of the Enlightenment, but as a paradigmatic sign of the
further encroachment of sovereign power:

> It is almost as if, starting from a certain point, every decisive political
> event were double-sided: the spaces, the liberties, and the rights won by
> individuals in their conflicts with central powers always simultaneously
> prepared a tacit but increasing inscription of individuals' lives within the
> state order, thus offering a new and more dreadful foundation for the very
> sovereign power from which they wanted to liberate themselves.[27]

Taking his cue from Foucault, Agamben interprets the crisis of rights as evidence of the increasing confoundedness of classic liberal conceptions of politics. The liberties and rights that are supposed to protect individuals against
sovereign oppression and enshrine the subject as 'sovereign' do quite the
opposite. Liberties and rights cannot be opposed to sovereign exceptionalism
because those liberties and rights are already included in the domain of
sovereign power. For Agamben, as for Foucault, it is not the rights-bearing
citizen that marks the beginning of the modern age, but the entry of the 'bare
life' of the basic human body into political calculations.

Agamben demonstrates this argument with a particularly apt reference to *habeas corpus* – the writ served against the authorities to assert the right against detention without trial – which has of course become a key legal battleground regarding counter-terrorist policies in the US and UK. Agamben inverts the conventional meaning of this 'right' in order to draw attention to its original ambiguity: the ancient writ that preceded *habeas corpus* was originally intended to assure the presence of the accused in a trial, rather than the release of a body held without charge.[28] As such, Agamben considers that *habeas corpus* is a deeply ambiguous extension of biopolitical power: '*Corpus is a two-faced being, the bearer both of subjection to sovereign power and of individual liberties*'.[29]

Thus Agamben invokes Foucault's problematization of the 'sovereign subject' as both 'free' and *made subject to* sovereign power.[30] This double-edged relationship between sovereign power and sovereign subject leads Agamben to posit a reformulation of Schmitt's 'Sovereign is he who decides on the exception',[31] in the claim that

> In modern biopolitics, sovereign is he who decides on the value or the nonvalue of life as such. Life – which, with the declarations of rights, had as such been invested with the principle of sovereignty – now itself becomes the place of a sovereign decision.[32]

Agamben considers that the fact of being born is no longer, if indeed it ever was, a case of being 'born free', but the beginning of the biopolitical relation of subject and sovereign. Natural man is for Agamben the 'immediately vanishing ground … of the citizen',[33] who is included in the nation-state relation of sovereignty by the very fact of being born in its territory. Hence Agamben draws attention to the etymology of the concept of 'nation', from *nascere* – to be born. It is precisely this historical innovation from the French Revolution – that sovereignty should reside in the nation – which 'inscribed this element of birth in the very heart of the political community'.[34] The nation-state comes to include man in its sphere by the very fact of his birth in its territory, and thus comes to decisively establish its dominion over life at precisely the moment when man's liberty was meant to be guaranteed.

Sovereign nominalism

Agamben's take on the problem of the sovereign exception is built around a bold set of claims. Beginning with concepts posited by Carl Schmitt and Michel Foucault in the form of 'the exception' and 'biopolitics' respectively, Agamben erects a productive relation of political/biological life and the sovereign exception as the central pillar of the whole paradigm of Western politics. This move is, quite literally, an illegitimate bastardization of Foucault and Schmitt, and a totalizing projection of the problem of the exception onto the ontology of 'the West' itself. Foucault already offers a rebuke to those who would erect a sovereign consciousness at the centre of philosophy and history: 'What makes you seek beyond all this the great historico-transcendental destiny of the Occident?'[35] What are the political implications of understanding the problem of the exception in this totalizing way? This is the line of critique I will pursue here.

At first glance, there is an immediate advantage to Agamben's totalization of the relation of the sovereign exception. By arguing that the limit condition of the state of exception is *produced* by the originary sovereign relation, Agamben provides a way of resisting Schmitt's slippery textual strategies. To recall Chapter 3, Schmitt justifies sovereign exceptionalism as being necessitated by exceptional events and situations that fall outside the scope of the law. Sovereign power is obliged to step in to fill these unforeseen legal gaps or *lacunae* because of the inherent and contingent dangers posed by them. Schmitt's strategy is to argue that beyond the limits of the law there is a more basic existential imperative – a natural law if you like – for sovereign power to act exceptionally; an imperative which is causally brought about by unforeseen exceptional events or situations.

Chapter 3 argued that this move rests on dubious metaphysical ground because it blurs and conflates three different things: first, the exceptional *event, situation* or *lacuna*; second, the nominalist sovereign *decision* that the event or situation is indeed exceptional; and, third, the exceptional sovereign *response* to the event or situation. Schmitt posits the exceptional event, situation or lacuna as a kind of objective condition that brings about certain exceptional imperatives. Yet if this were the case, why must the sovereign be 'he who decides on the exception'?[36] If there *were* such an *objective* condition as a state of necessity/exception, there would be no need for this exclusive sovereign act of naming; instead, the recognition of a state of necessity/ exception would be obvious and could be reduced to a mere technical procedure rather than a sovereign declaration. What Schmitt does, therefore, is use the idea of an objective necessity to justify a sovereign response that is *more* than a simple response, because it claims the prerogative to declare the existence of the very thing to which it is responding. Schmitt's case for exceptional sovereign power is built on a dubious circular logic: sovereign exceptionalism is justified by conditions that sovereign power itself declares. Thus sovereign exceptionalism is potentially just the arbitrary and unlimited use of power, speciously justified upon the disappearing ground of the exceptional event.

Because Agamben's understanding of sovereignty is as the central relation of the entire Western paradigm, he is able to resist Schmitt's deployment of an 'objective' state of necessity. Agamben understands that sovereignty is from the beginning built upon a relation between norm and exception; it needs no 'objective condition' to bring exceptional sovereignty about. Agamben calls Schmitt's device a 'normative lacuna' – a supposed gap in the law which brings forward its own imperatives, its own demands of what ought to be done. He claims that 'far from occurring as an objective given, necessity clearly entails a subjective judgment, and ... obviously the only circumstances that are necessary and objective are those that are declared to be so'.[37] Because Agamben understands sovereignty as a nominalist and productive relation, he also understands that there is no room for an 'objective necessity' to occur – the 'objective necessity' is only declared as such by a 'subjective judgment'. If the declaration of a state of exception is not a response to an objective 'normative lacuna', then it must have some other purpose. Agamben argues that

> Far from being a response to a normative lacuna, the state of exception appears as the opening of a fictitious lacuna in the order for the purpose of safeguarding the existence of the norm and its applicability to the normal situation.[38]

The point is that under the logic of a totalizing sovereign relation there *cannot* be a gap in the law. Any gap in the law is by default and in effect already filled by sovereign power, especially since in the 'inclusive exclusion' of its relation of abandonment sovereign power applies all the more in not applying:

> In analogy with the principle according to which the law may have lacu-nae, but the juridical order admits none, the state of necessity is thus interpreted as a lacuna in public law, which the executive power is obliged to remedy.[39]

Therefore, Agamben brands the 'normative lacuna' a 'fictitious lacuna' in which sovereignty asserts its totality by demonstrating that even potential gaps are already within its reach and remit. For Agamben these ideas of limits, gaps and lacunae are 'fictions through which the law attempts to encompass its own absence and to appropriate the state of exception, or at least to assure itself a relation with it'.[40]

The importance of these 'fictions' can be understood in the same way that Chapters 1 and 2 critiqued the relationship between freedom, necessity and sovereign power. Ostensibly, Schmitt's understanding of modern politics is founded not on *principle* but on existential *necessity*. Beneath the law there is a more fundamental 'law' of necessity. 'The concept of the state presupposes the concept of the political',[41] Schmitt argues, precisely because 'the political' is the potential for existential conflict inherent in life that necessarily requires the constricting order of the state. Conflict is not a problem provided it is kept within necessary limits. As such, Schmitt often seems fairly open to all the kinds of political and social relations that may take place in a given territory, so long as it is understood that at the exceptional limit the sovereign decision on the enemy or the exception will kick in. '*Argue* as much as you like and about whatever you like, but obey!' he might proclaim, adopting the words of Kant.[42]

In Hobbes and Kant, sovereign political authority exists not in opposition to the principle of the free subject, but *because* of the existential necessities brought about by the free subject. The idea of the terrifying conflict that would occur between free humans outside a relation of political authority serves precisely as a normative limit condition that justifies the existence of a sovereign political order, even though that terrifying limit condition must never be allowed to come about, and indeed never 'really' existed in the first place. In parallel, although the hypothetical danger posed by the lacuna beyond the law is a justification for the existence of exceptional sovereign power, that lacuna must never be allowed to come about. Hence Agamben argues that 'the juridical void at issue in the state of exception seems absolutely unthinkable for the law; ... this unthinkable thing nevertheless has a decisive strategic relevance for the juridical order and must not be allowed to slip away at any cost'.[43]

Although for Agamben there is no objective condition that brings exceptionalism about, he considers that sovereignty is from the beginning built upon a relation between norm and exception, between law and the force of law, the law that applies all the more in not applying. The point is that sovereignty applies both to the norm and the exception from the beginning. Sovereignty produces the exception as a relation of abandonment in which a more fundamental relation of sovereignty is affirmed. The state of exception does not exist as an objective condition beyond the limits of the law, but is produced by sovereign power in order to affirm a more fundamental 'natural law' or 'nomos', which affirms the necessity of sovereignty not simply as the executor of the law, but as the fundamental condition of the Western political paradigm itself – 'the great historico-transcendental destiny of the Occident'.[44]

Law/order/escape: Schmitt and Benjamin

What is really at stake for Agamben is whether or not it is possible to escape from this dialectical relationship of sovereign exceptionalism. Beyond the 'fictitious' state of exception declared by the sovereign, is there a *real* state of exception? These stakes emerge in what is by far the most impressive and valuable element of Agamben's book *State of Exception*: his forensic analysis of the relationship between the work of Schmitt and that of Walter Benjamin. Agamben describes a series of arguments and counter-arguments between the two theorists, with evidence provided through analysis of their correspondence, footnotes that point to common sources, and the likelihood that they would have read each other's work in the same journals. Agamben presents this as a kind of hidden dialogue of text and counter-text.

The first set of arguments in this dialogue is contained in Schmitt's *Die Diktator*, first published in 1921. As Agamben explains, the basic argument of this work revolves around two different kinds of exceptional political authority. The first is 'commissarial dictatorship' – a temporary dictatorship brought about constitutionally, the purpose of which is to defend the constitution by provisionally suspending it in a state of emergency; and second is 'sovereign dictatorship' – an unconstitutional constituent power intended to bring about something new, which as such is legitimated on the basis of an embryonic, future, more just constitution.[45] The crucial point for Schmitt is that both of these figures maintain a relation to a deeper continuation of juridical order, and as such the sovereign relation of norm/exception cannot be escaped.

On the one hand, under 'commissarial dictatorship' the law remains in force, but its *application* is suspended. Agamben describes this as the 'force-of-law'[46]: the residual and more fundamental force of a general juridical will that continues to exist even under the suspension of the law. Even when the law is suspended, 'commissarial dictatorship' continues to act in the *name* of the ~~law~~:

> In this sense, the state of exception is the opening of a space in which application and norm reveal their separation and a pure force-of-~~law~~ realizes (that is, applies by ceasing to apply) a norm whose application has been suspended.[47]

Although the 'commissarial dictatorship' that acts outside the law in the name of the law cannot be included in the constitution without paradox, it maintains a relation to the wider juridical order. It is, according to Agamben's analysis, a fiction 'through which the law attempts to encompass its own absence'.[48]

On the other hand, 'sovereign dictatorship' bears a relationship not to the old constitution but to a constitution-to-come. Sovereign dictatorship is a constituent power that bears the 'minimal form' of the new constitution, and as such 'represents a state of law in which the law is applied, but is not formally in force'[49] – the inverse of the 'force-of-~~law~~'. In both situations, political authority maintains a relation to the law whether law is in force but not applied, or applied but not formally in force. The point is that even a state of exception beyond the law remains in an inescapable relation to a more fundamental form of juridical order.

Agamben argues that it was these Schmittian formulations that Benjamin was responding to in his essay 'Critique of Violence'.[50] In this, similarly to Schmitt, Benjamin posits two figures of authority, which he calls 'lawmaking violence' and 'law-preserving violence'. Law-preserving violence maintains the current constitution, while lawmaking violence posits new laws. These pose a similar all-encompassing relation; as Benjamin writes: '*All violence is either lawmaking or law-preserving. If it lays claim to neither of these predicates, it forfeits all validity*'.[51] These figures closely correspond to Schmitt's commissarial dictatorship and sovereign dictatorship.

Benjamin then attempts to subvert this dual structure – which he considers to encompass the limit possibilities of juridical order – by positing a 'pure violence' placed outside these categories.[52] This 'pure violence' would be (if its form were known) justified neither by an appeal to a *legitimate means* of obtaining a political end, nor by an appeal to *just ends* which justify the illegitimate means needed to obtain them. It would neither make law nor preserve law. Rather, as Agamben describes it, it would simply be a 'pure medium'[53] with no relation other than to itself; perhaps a manifestation of anger with no aim other than expressing itself. As Agamben explains: 'pure violence exposes and severs the nexus between law and violence and thus appears in the end not as violence that governs or executes but as violence that purely acts and manifests'.[54]

Benjamin imagines this 'pure violence' manifested as some kind of post-legal, perhaps messianic, epoch. This works not so much as a substantive political vision but as a symbol of what is at stake in the discourse. Benjamin is trying to proffer an emancipatory line of flight that breaks free of Schmitt's seamless structures of juridical order. He does this by asserting the possibility of a violence beyond any relation to law, and hence beyond the categories of norm and exception which for Schmitt form a seamless and inescapable dialectic. Agamben's quotations from Benjamin reveal these stakes quite clearly; for example: 'If violence is also assured a reality outside the law, as pure immediate violence, this furnishes proof that revolutionary violence – which is the name for the highest manifestation of pure violence by man – is also possible'.[55]

Schmitt's counter-move is, by Agamben's analysis, to neutralize this wayward figure of 'pure violence'.[56] The response is the sovereign *decision*. This subsumes the apparent free-floating, non-relational, undetermined, undecidable quality of 'pure violence' by bringing it back under the aegis of sovereign power. Schmitt ties the undecidability and indeterminacy of 'pure violence' to the extreme circumstances of the exceptional situation, linking it to the necessity of a decision in the state of exception. Precisely because the extreme situation falls outside the legal order, which was Benjamin's deliberate intention in positing his figure of 'pure violence', the sovereign must have the capacity to make a decision where none is possible. This strategic inversion is Schmitt's way of neutralizing Benjamin's anomic and revolutionary line of escape. As Agamben explains, 'the state of exception is the device by means of which Schmitt responds to Benjamin's affirmation of a wholly anomic human action'.[57] Schmitt must at all costs maintain the juridical order, for this is what is at stake. The *anomie* of a pure indeterminate violence outside the law must not be allowed to break free.

Benjamin posits his response in his work on baroque sovereignty, *The Origin of German Tragic Drama*.[58] Unlike Schmitt's sovereign, Benjamin's sovereign is in power but cannot decide. Whereas Schmitt's sovereign is essentially a secularized God and the sovereign exception akin to a miracle,[59] Benjamin's sovereign is a heathen creature, and the exception a catastrophe.[60] The eschatological moment of redemption from the state of exception does not lead to restoration, as it does in Schmitt, but to an 'absolutely empty sky'.[61] Benjamin's sovereign does not occupy the transcendental realm of Schmitt's, but is 'confined to the world of creation; he is the lord of creatures, but he remains a creature'.[62]

There is much at stake in this play of move and counter-move. The most difficult question must be that of which figure, Schmitt or Benjamin, is more dangerous. On the one hand the possibility of a redemptive return to legal order can be seen in Schmitt, while Benjamin brings in a heathen anarchy of fallen creatures. On the other hand Schmitt stands for the tyranny of categories and the impossibility of escaping the dialectical structures of sovereign order, while Benjamin posits the possibility of a violent and wildly uncertain line of flight that breaks free of the dialectic of lawmaking/law-preserving, leading to a previously unthought mode of emancipation. This much is at stake: both see the possibility of redemption at the end of opposing paths – where Schmitt sees miracles Benjamin sees tyranny; where Schmitt sees chaos Benjamin sees escape.

Anomie and bare life

The prize in the battle between Schmitt and Benjamin is anomie. Agamben sets out an analysis of the obscure Roman condition of *iustitium* to illuminate this concept. As he explains, *iustitium* was a period of the complete transgression of all law and structure, often tied to the threat of war or to a period of mourning after the death of the sovereign.[63] In this condition, the authority of public offices became open to all private citizens, and any localization or hierarchy of authority was radically dispersed. In these conditions, 'he who acts … neither executes nor transgress the law … [his actions] will be absolutely undecidable'.[64] From this, Agamben argues that '[t]he state of exception is not a dictatorship … but a space devoid of law, a zone of anomie in which all legal determinations – and above all the very distinction between public and private – are deactivated'.[65] Agamben makes this a direct riposte to Schmitt and all those theories that seek, paradoxically, to tie this condition without law to law itself:

> fallacious … are those theories, like Schmitt's, that seek to inscribe the state of exception indirectly within a juridical context by grounding it in the division between norms of law and norms of the realization of law, between constituent power and constituted power, between norm and decision. The state of necessity is not a 'state of law', but a space without law (even though it is not a state of nature, but presents itself as the anomie that results from the suspension of law).[66]

Agamben is at pains to stress that any idea that anomie is somehow tied to law or a wider juridical order is false. Yet although it is now very clear what is at stake for Agamben, it should be more difficult than it is for him to truly posit a free-floating, non-relational anomie. Is it really possible to conceive of human action in a completely unmediated condition? Agamben wishes to posit anomie as a line of flight that escapes any kind of residual juridical relation, a 'pure medium' in which the dialectic of norm and exception dissolves. The state of exception is for him – as a zone of indistinction – a condition in which life and law, fact and law, coincide. Law ceases to provide a mediation between office and authority, sovereign and subject. As Agamben explains early on in his analysis:

> in the forms of both the state of exception and revolution, the *status necessitatis* appears as an ambiguous and uncertain zone in which de facto proceedings, which are in themselves extra- or antijuridical, pass over into law, and juridical norms blur with mere fact – that is, a threshold where fact and law seem to become undecidable.[67]

Although for Agamben this state of exception may be the end of a distinction or dialectical relation between life and law, contra Agamben, life does not necessarily cease to have relation or mediation. Human action may still bear relation to the memory of the rule, or to less tangible norms such as those expressed by class, culture, family and ethnicity. Recalling *Antigone*, for example, the headstrong heroine steadfastly adheres to an older, more ancient notion of right, even against the emergency decrees issued in a state of war.[68] The theoretical situation of total anomie that Agamben presents effectively subscribes to an early modern, indeed Hobbesian, notion of the individual who is only an abstract figure with no history, subjected only to the immediate forces of violence and desire, who amounts to nothing more than his capacity to kill or be killed.

Instead it should be considered that the subject can never be truly unmediated, least of all when released from the dialectic of law. Even if not mediated by law, the subject is still enmeshed in psychological, cultural, discursive and bodily mediations either in its present relations or in the history of its production as a subject. Even without law, the subject remains within a web of constitutive relations with social forces, institutional discipline, custom, capital, belief, sexuality, memory, trauma, desire and so on. And even in the radical deprivation of these things, the subject is forced into a relation with their absence, legacy and memory, just as Schmitt's sovereign bears a relation to the law even in its absence. It is no more possible to imagine an unmediated, bare, subject-in-itself in anomie than it is possible to access an unmediated thing-in-itself behind the glass wall of perception, representation and interpretation.

With this in mind, it should also be questioned whether life can ever really be 'bare'. Agamben sets much stall by the fact that the Jews were formally stripped of their (at that stage residual) citizenship before being placed in concentration camps.[69] In juridical and biopolitical terms, they were expunged from the national citizenry, and, as such, 'bare life' was produced by sovereignty through a relation of abandonment. However, although the Jews may have been stripped of their political status as citizens, they still continued to have cultural, religious, social and political identities. Although perhaps they were considered 'bare life' by the logic of the Nazi ideology and from the perspective of those convinced by it, the people held in the camps were humans who continued to be mediated not only through their personal degree of affiliation with a Jewish identity, but through their relationships, their origins, their memories, their dialects and their skills.

In fact there *are* examples of what might be called 'bare life' in the two exceptional sites discussed so far, the Nazi concentration camps and Guantanamo Bay. In *If This Is a Man*, Primo Levi's testimony of life in the camps, he describes a figure known only as 'null achtzehn' – zero eighteen, the last three digits of his camp number.[70] This young man had completely lost any sense of identity, the ability to communicate and the ability to offer any resistance to commands. 'I think that even he has forgotten his name, certainly he acts as if this was so', Levi writes.[71] His only quality was absolute passivity and compliance. The 'Tipton Three' describe similarly abject characters in Guantanamo: one man, Michal from Saudi Arabia, tried to hang himself and passed out from asphyxiation. The guards took him down and beat him, and 'now he is basically a cabbage'.[72] They go on to describe that

> For at least 50 of those so far as we are aware their behaviour is so disturbed as to show that they are no longer capable of rational thought or behaviour. We do not describe in detail here the behaviour but it is something that only a small child or an animal might behave like.[73]

These figures could be considered truly abject 'bare life', stripped of all qualities other than the simple fact of being alive. But nonetheless, it is still hard to imagine the total loss of mediation of residual traits like appearance, language and so on. In the concentration camps, certainly, the detainees were reduced to a terrible condition of abjection and prostration, where the limits of their humanity toward themselves and each other were frequently exceeded. Yet there was still politics in the camp, even if not the 'high' sovereign politics that Agamben talks about. Levi wrote about the guilt he felt at having been able to reach a relatively privileged position in the camp hierarchy by working in a chemistry laboratory. There was a politics to his position.

Similarly in Guantanamo, although the physical and psychological breaking points of many of the detainees were often breached, in some cases permanently, the entire structure of the camp seems to have been built around an intense series of political relations or even contests. The structure of physical and environmental manipulation in Guantanamo has been constructed around breaking down the multiplicity of resistances, large and small, offered by the detainees, particularly under interrogation. For example, repeated hunger strikes against camp conditions and the denial of due process were met with a regime of force feeding.[74] One of the Tipton Three describes how 'I scratched "have a nice day" on my Styrofoam cup and this was seen as a disciplinary offence for which I spent another week in isolation'.[75]

Details of these detention regimes suggest quite the opposite of what Agamben argues. The camp is not a state of exception beyond all mediation, but rather, as Fleur Johns argues, a space saturated with norms.[76] These are norms of routine, of discipline, of the 'standard operating procedure' of the US military, of psychological contest, of Byzantine quasi-legal procedures and of violence.[77] There is a proliferation of petty authorities, opaque rules and performative assertions of legitimacy that call for a quite different approach to that of Agamben.

The constitution of sovereignty, the authorization of authority and the historical conditions of possibility for sovereign exceptionalism

The problem with Agamben's work lies in his understanding of sovereignty. For him, sovereignty is pure constitutive nominalism – it produces 'bare life' and the 'fictitious lacuna' of the state of exception in order to maintain a totalizing relation even to the spectre of its own absence. This is why it is so important for Agamben to posit a '*real* state of exception' beyond that totalizing dialectic. Agamben does resist the banal dualisms of the popular liberty/security discourse, in which liberty is opposed to security (and subject is opposed to sovereign) in some kind of 'balance'; instead he understands that in the history of Western political thought the problem of sovereignty grows directly out of the problem of modern subjectivity and does not appear as some kind of oppressive hindrance to it. Agamben understands that in that tradition the modern subject has only ever been seriously considered possible *under* a relation of sovereignty. The subject is thus constituted by that relation, which at the same time brings in the whole problem of limited subjectivity and potentially unlimited sovereign power – the problem of sovereign exceptionalism.

Yet although Agamben understands the constitutive relation of modern sovereignty to the modern subject (in which the subject is both constituted as a properly qualified subject and simultaneously made subject *to* sovereign political authority), he pays no attention to the constitution of modern sovereignty itself. Sovereignty may constitute, but how is it constituted as that which may constitute? Under what conditions of possibility does the sovereign have the capacity to decide on the exception? How must society be constituted in order for sovereignty to have the capacity to decide upon the enemy or the exception? Agamben seems to miss that these are questions of deep concern for Schmitt, who discusses them at length in *The Concept of the Political* with regard to the possibility of the capacity for sovereign decision being lost, weakened, compromised or usurped. This sheds a different light on Schmitt's insistence on the continuation of some kind of residual order or *nomos* beyond the law.

This missing dimension to sovereignty is visible in a quotation Agamben uses but does not fully take up. With regard to the concern that 'constitutional dictatorship, which seeks to safeguard the constitutional order', can easily turn into 'unconstitutional dictatorship, which leads to its overthrow',[78] Agamben quotes the constitutional theorist Carl J. Friedrich, who writes that '[t]here are no ultimate institutional safeguards available for insuring that emergency powers be used for the purpose of preserving the Constitution. Only the people's own determination to see them so used can make sure of that'.[79]

This touches on what is largely missing from Agamben's analysis, which is any consideration of the 'democratic' elements – conceived in the broadest possible way – of the state of exception. Friedrich posits 'the people' as a restraining actor that can prevent emergency powers becoming arbitrary or unlimited. This raises vital questions about the dialectic of sovereign exceptionalism. Are there limits to government action which cannot be encapsulated in constitutional, legal or juridical formulae? How do those limits operate and find expression? Under what conditions is sovereign exceptionalism possible or impossible?

The invocation of 'the people' as an expression of social, cultural and historical conditions and limits, and not simply as a biopolitical object, opens up a vital dimension in the problem of exceptional sovereign power which Agamben neglects. Agamben excludes from his analysis what Rob Walker might call the 'authorization of authority', the deeper historical and discursive conditions that enable authority to be authoritative.[80] Despite Agamben's continual invocation of Schmitt, he does not recognize Schmitt's sustained concern with these problems. For example, in 'The Age of Depoliticizations and Neutralizations' Schmitt is concerned not so much with the singular, totalizing figure of the sovereign, but with questions about how decisive political authority emerges according to the central social and technological conditions of the day.[81] Max Weber explores similar questions in 'The Profession and Vocation of Politics', articulating concerns about the new forms of leadership and political power that will emerge under new historical and social conditions.[82] Although the work of both these theorists ultimately closes down the problem of political authority in different ways (in the rather right-wing reification of charismatic leader figures, for example), Agamben's analysis seems rather unhistorical and undialectical in comparison.

This takes us back to the problem of anomie which is so important for Agamben. If we consider that sovereign exceptionalism is not simply a problem of constitutive sovereign decision at the limit, but a wider problematization of the relation between limits and historical socio-political conditions and processes, then a different light is shed on Schmitt's 'strategic' insistence on the continuation of a form of juridical order, natural law or *nomos* even in relation to an anomic space devoid of law. In Agamben's formulations, the reason for Schmitt's insistence on the impossibility of escape from the sovereign dialectic of norm/exception or law/nomos is because he cannot admit the possibility of an outside to the juridical order. As Agamben argues: 'the juridical void at issue in the state of exception seems absolutely unthinkable for the law; … this unthinkable thing nevertheless has a decisive strategic relevance for the juridical order and must not be allowed to slip away at any cost'.[83] In contrast to Agamben's argument, it should instead be considered that the reason why it is impossible to escape the dialectic of norm/exception is not because of the singular, constitutive totality of sovereign power, but because sovereignty is an effect of the historical and socio-political authorization of authority, an effect of processes which constitute the sovereign as that which can constitute, and a product of the conditions of possibility under which, to paraphrase Schmitt, sovereign is he on whom socio-historical conditions confer the capacity to decide the exception. If we insist on a sceptical stance to the possibility of true anomie, then it is possible to reinterpret Schmitt's insistence on the continuity of a relation between sovereign power and a deeper, extra-legal order. This would note Schmitt's concern with the decisive political outcomes of changing social and historical conditions, rather than only seeing a single-minded obsession with totemic figures of power and authority.

The reason why the dialectic of norm/exception cannot easily be escaped is not because law and sovereign order continue even in their absence, but because the socio-political conditions and processes that mediate and constitute sovereign political authority never cease to bear a relation to social life. This is because they are not simply immediately acting forces that can be switched on or off like an electric current, but constitutive historical processes, the imprint of which cannot simply be erased, suspended or forgotten. To try to imagine the true absence of the mediating and constitutive features of life which constitute and authorize sovereign political authority is to erase the history of the constitution of specifically modern subjects, modern nation-states and modern forms of sovereignty. Life can only be bare and devoid of its historical and socio-political modes of constitution in the abstract formulations of philosophy books. Similarly, the historical and socio-political conditions under which authoritative sovereign decisions are normally possible can never truly cease, except as a normative rhetorical device akin to Hobbes's powerful but mythical state of nature. Although a formal relation of law or juridical power may be suspended, forms of authority in general will continue as long as the history of the constitution of subjects and their socio-political relations remains within both memory and the historically constituted subjectivities of subjects themselves.

It is precisely because Agamben reifies the modern sovereign nation-state and the dialectic between law/exception as an originary and constitutive boundary that the wider historico-political conditions for the constitution of forms of sovereign authority are erased. By projecting a singular dualism of law/life as the structure of the sovereign exception and as 'the great historico-transcendental destiny of the Occident',[84] Agamben erases any consideration of the violent historical and political work that went into making the historically contingent mode of being and sovereign political authority that is central to the political ontology of the West. He erases the long and bloody history of the establishment of the nation-state as the universal unit of political organization. The modern sovereign nation-state has only ever been a historically contingent idealization of what political authority should look like. It is not a timeless principle, but the outcome of often violent historical and socio-political practices.

In contrast, Foucault argues in *'Society Must Be Defended'* that the 'nation' is not simply the originary 'biopolitical' structure of sovereign power, but a principle and practice that emerged through war and violence as a radical political and historical claim.[85] In this account, the nation was an expression of collective identity that served the highly political function of *countering* monarchical sovereign power in a relation of war. Then, through a long history of defeats, victories and co-optations, the nation became synthesized with monarchical sovereignty to constitute a new form of sovereign political authority in the form of the nation-state. The nation worked as a political claim, but also as a claim about the content of history itself; claims about nationhood were claims that the nation was the very subject of history.[86] Through Agamben it is only possible to understand the static position of the body within the sovereign populace, but through Foucault it is possible to understand that claims to nationhood and nation-statehood have been driven by violent practices and powerful accounts of identity, value, aspiration and history. It is only by adding this dimension that it is possible to grasp the way the nation-state has operated as a claim about salvation, belonging, collective aspiration and the realization of universal principles through time in particular spaces. The relation of birth, body and nation should be understood not simply as the originary biopolitical structure of the West, but as a constitutive process which gave rise to a specifically modern form of sovereign political authority.

In contrast to the methods of Agamben, it should not be a question of imagining how things could be otherwise, but of understanding the historico-political reasons why things are not otherwise. It is not a question of imagining lines of flight (or philosophical flights of fancy), but of asking how so many lines of flight were historically closed down in the process of making the modern nation-state the universal organizing political unit of the world. It is a question of asking how today lines of flight are closed down by contemporary expressions of sovereign exceptionalism. What is needed for the problem of the politics of the exception is not *escape* but *critique*, in order to ask: what are the conditions of possibility for sovereign exceptionalism? Considering the array of subject positions implicated and constituted by the problem, the institutional structures of authority at work, the concepts and discourses being deployed, and the strategies being executed, what kind of critique is needed? These are the questions to be pursued in subsequent chapters.

State of exception/permanent state of exception

There is a final criticism to be made about Agamben's treatment of the idea of the state of exception. Agamben's work is valuable in that it allows an understanding of the state of exception as a description of political discourses and structures at their limits. As such, it is a way of situating contemporary political practices at those limits. Agamben explains the use of the idea of the state of exception as follows:

> If, as has been suggested, terminology is the properly poetic moment of thought, then terminological choices can never be neutral. In this sense, the choice of the term *state of exception* implies a position taken on both

the nature of the phenomenon we seek to investigate and the logic most useful for understanding it.[87]

The use of the terminology of the state of exception is both a methodological and political strategy for engaging with a set of political and philosophical problems which find particular expression today. However, both Agamben's 'position' and 'logic' are confused by his frequent invocation of the idea of a *permanent* state of exception.

The value of Agamben's work lies in his theorization of how a politics of the limit works: for example how sovereignty works as a constitutive relation of abandonment. For the most part, the logical operation of the term 'state of exception' is taken to mean a limit condition and a constitutive threshold. It is the potential for sovereignty to actualize itself by withdrawing the protection of the law, abandoning subjects to a state of lawlessness and violence where they can be killed without sanction: 'the sovereign is the one with respect to whom all men are potentially *homines sacri*, and *homo sacer* is the one with respect to whom all men act as sovereigns'.[88]

Agamben's constitutive relation of exceptional sovereignty is undermined by operating in only one direction, with no consideration of how sovereignty is constituted as that which can constitute. He thus reifies a singular relation of norm/exception as the 'great historico-transcendental destiny of the Occident'.[89] Agamben's analysis is not presented as a position on the logic of a historically contingent *discourse* or *ideology* of biopolitical sovereignty. Rather, for Agamben, '[t]he fundamental activity of sovereign power is the production of bare life as originary political element and as threshold of articulation between nature and culture, *zoē* and *bios*'.[90] This is a dualistic, neo-Platonist essentialism; it is a claim about the fundamental nature of sovereign power.

In light of these problems, a more critical mode of analysis is required for dealing with the problem of the exception. What is needed is a more subtle understanding of the way in which particular instances of sovereign exceptionalism emerge according to specific historico-political conditions. The concept of the exception captures the way in which a politics operates at the limits of a given set of historical and socio-political structures and processes. It is not so much that the sovereign decides where political, legal and social limits are, but rather that political authority is constituted in historically contingent ways as 'he' who has the capacity to decide on the exception at the exceptional limit.

When Agamben invokes the idea of a *permanent* state of exception, it is another symptom of these criticisms. With this idea, Agamben undermines the clarity of his analysis of the problem of the exception. For example, in *Homo Sacer* 'the 'juridically empty' space of the state of exception … has transgressed its spatiotemporal boundaries and now, overflowing outside them, is starting to coincide with the normal order, in which everything again becomes possible'.[91] And similarly, in *State of Exception* 'the state of exception has by now become the rule'.[92] These statements do not fit with the complex logic of relationality that Agamben attributes to sovereignty and the state of exception. The idea of a *permanent* state of exception undermines the value of the terminology of the exception: to invoke a permanent state of exception is to collapse the dialectic of norm/exception.

In an extended note on the empirical history of the state of exception, Agamben describes how the exceptional delegation of powers from parliament to the executive – establishing executive rule by decree – became normal practice for all European democracies during, and then frequently after, the First World War. He argues that the passage to executive rule is underway to varying degrees in all the Western democracies, with parliaments becoming only secondary actors in the legislative process. Even more pertinently, he maintains that the 'tendency in all of the Western democracies' is that 'the declaration of the state of exception has gradually been replaced by an unprecedented generalization of the paradigm of security as the normal technique of government'.[93]

While it may be the case that legal states of exception became normalized historically, to describe the present as a permanent state of exception is to undermine the value of the exception as a dialectical concept. If exceptions have become the norm historically, the problem of the dialectic of norm/exception is compounded, not simplified, because the dialectic of norm/exception plays out not just across spatial, legal and political boundaries but through less tangible historical, temporal boundaries too. How does an 'exception' cease to be 'exceptional'? What socio-political or discursive processes are at work in the process of *normalization*? What is the effect of normalized exceptions on new invocations of exceptionality? If the dialectic of norm/exception has a historical dimension, then that process must not be erased with the invocation of a permanent state of exception but described and analysed critically. When Agamben argues that in a permanent state of exception 'everything again becomes possible',[94] it is another attempt at escape, not critique.

Whatever the fate of 'the norm' – whether it is descended from unrepealed emergency powers or coming to resemble what was once considered exceptional – the value of the concept of the 'exception' is that it provides a 'position' and 'logic' regarding the dialectical relationship between contemporary exceptions and the norm. To distinguish contemporary exceptions as the limit and threshold of the norm is to investigate how the one constitutes the other. Put simply, it is a way of characterizing and analysing the 'new' in relation to the 'same'. Even if it is considered that contemporary invocations of exceptionality seem to have no clear end point, both exceptional practices and the victims of that exceptionality who find themselves in a state of legal abandonment are still most incisively understood in terms of an exceptional relation with 'the norm'.

A permanent, generalized state of exception defines the present as a situation in which life in general has become exceptional – we have all had our liberties compromised, power relations are being altered at the biopolitical level and so on. This mirrors the way in which the whole discourse about the 'balance' between liberty and security is wrong, or at least flawed. It is not 'our' liberties that are being exceptionally compromised or suspended, but the liberties of particular target individuals or groups. When 'we' are asked to accept 'necessary compromises' of our liberty for security, it does not mean that 'we' are asked to accept some degree of liberty loss, but that 'we' are asked to accept the exceptional abuse of the liberties of a small minority. It is not a public choice problem, but a legitimation problem. It is the constitution and mobilization of an embattled and unified 'we' in the legitimation of exceptional practices against the exceptional few who will actually suffer. The only liberties 'we' will lose or compromise are those abstract liberties that have only ever been constituted *under* a relation of modern nation-state sovereignty. The real stakes are the violent practices that will be legitimated in the name of those abstract liberties. This is a 'particular' exception – not a generalized state of exception – in which exceptions apply to a few individuals or a specific minority. This needs to be understood in relation to legitimating 'norms', even if those 'norms' are changing in radical ways.

This is why it is important to understand the problem of the exception as dialectical and not dualistic. It is not a case of liberty vs. security, subject vs. sovereign, but a series of problems in the principle, discourse, constitution and practice of liberal forms of modern subjectivity and modern sovereignty. Liberty already implies a relation between those constituted as properly qualified modern subjects with civilized civil liberty and those deemed to be in a condition of dangerous natural freedom. The principle of liberty works to legitimate exceptional practices against exceptional enemies in exceptional circumstances, precisely when liberty is claimed to be 'under threat'. What is needed, therefore, is an appropriate mode of critique for analysing the discourses, structures, principles, objects, concepts and subject positions involved in the deployment and legitimation of practices and discourses of exceptionalism – the entire constellation or discursive formation of the exception and exceptionalism. What should this mode of critique look like, and what are its political and methodological implications?

5   Securitization theory
Practices of sovereign naming

Schmitt's strength stems from his sharp vision of existentially threatening exigencies that reside at the limits of modern politics. For Schmitt, the inherent conflict of political life always bears the possibility of becoming mortal antagonism, hence his argument that '[t]he specific political distinction to which political actions and motives can be reduced is that between friend and enemy'.[1] Similarly, at the limit of politics, law, liberties, rights and technocratic administration resides the 'real possibility' of an existentially threatening 'exceptional event' that falls outside the limits of predictability and the structures of 'normal' politics. For Schmitt, the limit possibilities of political modernity reveal the necessity of exceptional sovereign power, which then becomes the most vital expression of political life. Hence Schmitt argues that '[t]he rule proves nothing; the exception proves everything: It confirms not only the rule but also its existence, which derives only from the exception'.[2]

Under critical analysis, what seem at first to be Schmitt's quite astute assertions about the metaphysics of contingency and the limits of legal and constitutional formalism very quickly reveal some dubious politico-theoretical moves and the affirmation of an ethic of authoritarian national unity. Schmitt uses the idea of the exceptional event or situation to construct an account of the necessity and primacy of exceptional sovereign decision. However, because this sovereign prerogative entails not only the imperative to *respond* to the exception but the prerogative to *decide* whether an exception exists, the independent, causal and contingent existence of the exception is thrown into doubt. What begins as a problem of 'objective necessity' is in fact a problem of 'subjective' or rather 'nominalist' sovereign judgement. The exceptional event becomes the disappearing ground of a circular sovereign logic in which sovereign power declares the existence of the exceptional conditions which justify its own exceptionality.

Furthermore, for Schmitt the necessity for sovereign exceptionalism requires a lack of political challenge to the sovereign capacity to decide on the exception, because a pluralistic sovereign state is a fractious and unhealthy sovereign state: 'The intensification of internal antagonisms has the effect of weakening the common identity vis-à-vis another state'.[3] Thus there is an existential and ethical imperative for national unity and a lack of contestation to sovereign decision. Not only is the very existence of the state under threat if there is not the capacity for a sufficiently decisive response to the exception, but moreover these decisive moments are when the political life of the strong, unified and healthy nation-state is affirmed: when 'the power of real life breaks through the crust of a mechanism that has become torpid by repetition'.[4]

Schmitt does not reify simply a single totemic point of sovereign political authority, but a totalizing dialectic of sovereign political authority. From the problem of the exception Schmitt derives not only an account of the necessity of exceptional sovereign power at the limit, but also an account of the socio-political processes which constitute and mobilize an embattled and ideally unified collective political subjectivity which must be defended. The exception and exceptionalism (which are not the same thing, as argued in Chapter 3) are not simply problems of limit but also of socio-political process.

Securitization theory bears a strong relationship to the problems found in Schmitt. It is an approach that theorizes the sovereign construction of security threats, corresponding invocations of exceptional politics, and the relationship between sovereign authority, societal defence and constitution, and social, political and communicative processes. This chapter will assess whether securitization theory offers a response to the challenge posed earlier: is there a way to critique the problem of exceptionalism which does not reify a Schmittian account of sovereign power?

Securitization theory

Securitization theory, as developed by Ole Wæver, Barry Buzan and their 'Copenhagen School' colleagues, has had a great impact on the field of security studies in the last decade, and has been both extensively lauded and criticized.[5] It is not my aim to provide a comprehensive evaluation of the various positions in this debate. Rather, by focusing mainly on Ole Wæver's seminal paper of 1995, 'Securitization and Desecuritization', which laid out the case for a theory of securitization, this chapter will interrogate the specific relationship between exceptionalism, Carl Schmitt and securitization theory. First, it will describe in more detail the terms of that encounter, noting particular points of contention in Schmitt's theory of exceptionalism. Second, it will analyse the outcome of Michael C. Williams's recent exploration of the link between Schmitt and securitization theory. Third, it will argue that although securitization theory is a promising means of tackling the problem of the exception and the politics of exceptionalism, it does not go nearly far enough. Finally, the chapter will close by invoking the early work of Michel Foucault in a call for a critical response of much further reach.

Securitization theory considers that security is a *process* by which things become 'securitized' through practices of 'securitization'. In this way the theory is a direct response to the problem detected in Schmitt: that the 'objective necessity' of the exceptional event or situation disappears under the 'subjective' character of the sovereign decision on the exception. The approach of Ole

Wæver is to dispense with the 'object' of security altogether. Securitization theory seeks to break with the idea that the word 'security' refers to a 'real thing' that brings about its own imperatives, precisely because of the over-determined primacy of the 'special right' of sovereign naming. Wæver argues that in operational practice it is the state that decides when a security problem is present:

> *In naming a certain development a security problem, the 'state' can claim a special right*, one that will, in the final instance, always be defined by the state and its elites ... By definition, something is a security problem when the elites declare it to be so.[6]

Wæver's concerns about the 'object' of security are actually a response to the problems of earlier progressive approaches, such as those of Johan Galtung and Jan Øberg. Wæver explains that these were characterized by an attempt to widen the referent objects of security in response to the overdetermination of the state in security problems[7] – the latter being precisely the problem I have identified in Schmitt. These progressive approaches sought to widen the security field to include the security concerns of *people* rather than states, expanding into areas such as 'economic welfare, environmental concerns, cultural identity, and political rights'.[8] Wæver argues that these approaches suffered from three problems: first, 'the concept of security becomes all-inclusive and is thereby emptied of meaning'; second, expanding the field of security objects risks contributing to an expansion of state-led security practices; and, third, the approach suffers from 'a lack of political effect on "security", as traditionally defined'.[9]

The overriding problem, as Wæver identifies it, is that when one talks of 'security' one has already entered a field characterized by a privileging of the state. Because the field of 'security' already entails the traditional prerogatives of the state, argues Wæver, an expanded field of security 'objects' may simply result in expanded state prerogatives. Such is the discursive and institutional strength of the 'security' tradition that any attempts to expand the referent objects of security either enlarge the jurisdiction of national security practices or else are simply marginalized by the continuing statist overdetermination of the field. Wæver concedes that other dynamics may be added to the conceptual field of security, such as those at the sub-state and extra-state levels, but the state nevertheless remains at the centre of an hourglass image of the field.[10]

For these reasons, securitization theory forgoes critical or political contestation over the 'objects' of security, and in so doing addresses Schmitt's sleight of hand regarding the advent of existentially threatening exceptional events and the sovereign declaration of the exception. Whereas Schmitt presents the exceptional event as an 'objective' metaphysical imperative, but then renders that problem superfluous to what is actually an affirmation of totalizing nominalist sovereign power, Wæver conceives of security in nominalist terms alone. Instead of trying to locate security problems as objective events that dictate certain necessary responses, Wæver locates security in the linguistic and institutional prerogatives that name security issues as such. Security, argues Wæver, invoking the linguistic theorist John R. Searle, is not a 'real thing' but a 'speech-act'. As he explains:

> What then is security? With the help of language theory, we can regard 'security' as a *speech-act*. In this usage, security is not of interest as a sign that refers to something more real; the utterance *itself* is the act. By saying it, something is done (as in betting, giving a promise, naming a ship). By uttering 'security' a state representative moves a particular development into a specific area, and thereby claims a special right to use whatever means are necessary to block it.[11]

Wæver's arguments about the concept of security are directly transposable to the concept of the exception. In the process, critical focus is shifted away from the exception as a 'real thing' and towards the act and process of declaring exceptions. One might rephrase the Wæver quote above to read: 'we can regard "*the exception*" as a *speech-act* ... *the exception* is not of interest as a sign that refers to something more real; the utterance *itself* is the act'. If 'securitization' is translated into 'exceptionalization', the 'real referent' of the exception is rendered a chimera; there is no 'objective necessity' to the exception, all there is is the *exceptionalizing* speech-act. This would mean that all there is in Schmitt is exceptional sovereign power. In Schmitt's totalizing circularity, exceptional sovereign power is justified as a necessary response to the exceptional event, but only exceptional sovereign power can declare the existence of the exceptional event. Which comes first? The exceptional event or exceptional sovereign power? In fact, exceptional sovereign power comes both first, as declaration, and last, as response, leaving no room for the exceptional event itself. Hence securitization theory would argue that the exception *is* the act of declaring the exception.

Schmitt and the politics of securitization theory

Securitization theory comes to conclusions similar to those of Agamben, in that the exceptional object which is supposed to justify the exceptional prerogatives of state sovereignty is exposed as fictitious. For Agamben, the fiction is the supposed exceptional 'lacuna' at the limit of the law which for Schmitt justifies the necessity of extra-legal sovereign power. Agamben argues that this 'necessity' is in no way an 'objective' occurrence; rather, sovereign power declares a 'fictitious lacuna' in order to affirm its own continuing relation to it, because strategically sovereign power must apply even where it hypothetically does not. For securitization theory, the 'security issue' also loses its objective, imperative qualities; instead of being a 'real referent', it is argued that 'something is a security problem when the elites declare it to be so'.[12] These analyses are directly transposable to the problem of the exception. The exception, as a 'lacuna' in the law, as a limit condition, or as an existentially threatening event or contingent circumstance, is the disappearing ground of exceptionalism.

While the aims of Agamben and Wæver are similar, their methods are different. While Agamben treats the sovereign exception as the central pillar of the entire paradigm of Western politics, Wæver offers not this transcendentalization of the problem of sovereign nominalism, but an acceptance of that practice as a sociological fact, as the 'logic of both our national and international political organizing principles'.[13] While Agamben seeks to work through the *politico-philosophical* implications of sovereign exceptionalism, securitization theory seeks to study and understand sovereign exceptionalism in terms of an intractable *institutional, sociological and discursive tradition.*

Wæver argues that issues are 'securitized' by security elites and state agents through 'speech-acts', whereby they attempt to convince their audience that a particular issue is a security problem and so bring about certain forms of political and social mobilization. The advantage of this methodological innovation is that it treats 'exceptional' security situations as nominalist rather than objectivist problems. This means that the politics of exceptional situations have more to do with discourses and socio-political processes than with any fundamental metaphysical necessity or imperative. Securitization theory thus defuses Schmitt's attempt to seamlessly link the idea of exceptional events with exceptional nation-statist politics by stressing that security is a *discourse* that can be deployed and manipulated through strategies of securitization. As such, there are no events that in themselves dictate particular political responses, but, rather, any event or issue can be turned into a security issue through particular discursive strategies.

Interestingly, however, this argument does not distance securitization theory from Schmitt, but rather brings them closer together. In Schmitt, the 'objective necessity' of the exception is a trick to disguise a totalizing sovereign nominalism. Behind this move lies the fact that for Schmitt sovereign power decides on both the exceptional event and the exceptional response. Schmitt's sovereign also speaks for and thus constitutes the idealized, unified sovereign 'we' of the nation-state. In turn, unity and lack of contestation serve as conditions of possibility for exceptional sovereign decision. Therefore, once the fictitious 'real referent' of the exception is rendered surplus to requirements, Schmitt and securitization theory meet on the same playing field of sovereign nominalism. For both, it is the sovereign state that declares the exception to be so.

Wæver is explicit in his reasons for adopting this approach. Securitization theory does not assume, in his words, 'a classical critical approach to security, whereby the concept is critiqued and then thrown away or redefined according to the wishes of the analyst'.[14] Wæver argues that such approaches have little bearing on the continued operation of the security tradition. Because the security field is so overdetermined with the traditional nominalist prerogatives of the state and its security elites, a critical approach, as Wæver defines it, would have little or no effect. Instead, Wæver describes his task as 'faithfully working *with* the classical meaning of the concept and what is already inherent in it'.[15]

Wæver starts from the position that sovereign state security practices are nominalist, and then asks how those nominalist practices work. This approach raises certain questions. If Schmitt and Wæver are both nominalist, then what does their conceptual closeness mean for the ethico-political implications of securitization theory? If Wæver chooses not to reject the sovereign state nominalism that overdetermines the security field, then how can securitization theory be used to contest Schmitt?

The initial answer is that Wæver claims a specific *political agenda* to securitization theory which is the opposite of Schmitt's. For Wæver, successful acts of 'securitization' are not the 'high points' of politics, as they are for Schmitt, but examples of a process that should, if possible, be avoided or reversed. In Wæver's terms, the explicit avoidance of what he calls a 'critical' agenda is an integral element of this political agenda. In 'working *with* the classical meaning' of security, argues Wæver,

> Such an affirmative reading, not at all aimed at rejecting the concept, may be a more serious challenge to the established discourse than a critical one, for it recognizes that a conservative approach to security is an intrinsic element in the logic of both our national and international political organizing principles.[16]

Wæver's political agenda is one of '*minimizing* security'.[17] Rather than do this through what he calls the 'the classical critical approach to security, whereby the concept is critiqued and then thrown away or redefined according to the wishes of the analyst',[18] Wæver argues that such an agenda would be better served by accepting the resilient organizing principles of security and national/international politics, and then working *away* from them: 'transcending a security problem by politicizing it cannot happen *through* thematization in security terms, only *away* from such terms'.[19] The aim is to establish the workings of the *processes* of securitization as a *knowledge* which can then be used for political ends. If the entrenched and intractable nominalist processes by which security issues are named can be understood, argues Wæver, then it might be possible to use that knowledge to wrest particular issues away from securitizing processes. He terms the political aim of this approach 'desecuritization'.

This is Wæver's response to the statist overdetermination of the concept of security, and thus by corollary his response to Schmitt. Schmitt expresses both a classic and uniquely sharp articulation of this problem, articulated on the basis of legal and socio-political limit, contingency, existential necessity, the nominalist prerogatives of the sovereign state and the construction of a national sovereign 'we' as its constituency. Given that a strong ethic of authoritarian nation-state unity is built into Schmitt's theorization of the existential threat posed by 'the exception', Wæver uses the same nominalist ground to offer an alternative political response. Thus Wæver tries to separate *knowledge* of securitizing processes from any *politics* implicit in that knowledge. His argument is that by accepting the statist nominalism that defines security problems, and instead of wasting time trying to 'throw away' or 'redefine' the concept of security, one can assemble a knowledge of how processes of *securitization* work in order to then use that knowledge for purposes of *desecuritization*. The question is whether or not Wæver is successful in this method. Can Schmitt's authoritarian and anti-pluralist ethic be separated from the nominalist processes of security, or is such an ethic already implied in the very understanding of those processes as nominalist? In this regard, questions must be asked about both Wæver's explicit *politics* and the potentially implicit politics of Wæver's *method*.

Methodological objectivism and communicative ethics

Such concerns have not escaped the attentions of critics. Reflecting upon an array of critical commentaries on securitization theory, Michael C. Williams notes that its division of knowledge and politics has prompted questions about whether the theory is 'implicitly committed to a methodological objectivism'.[20] Even if Wæver does advocate a politics that finds ways to avoid the 'securitization' of issues, or ways to 'desecuritize' issues that have already become 'securitized', the theory itself, as Williams puts it, must be 'at best agnostic in the face of any securitization'.[21] The argument is that because the theory avoids providing a means for critically evaluating the 'securitization' of issues, it must simply accept the 'securitizing' practices of the 'security tradition' as a fact of life. As Williams puts the problem:

> Simply put, if security is nothing more than a specific form of social practice – a speech-act tied to existential threat and a politics of emergency – then does this mean that anything can be treated as a 'security' issue and that, as a consequence, any form of violent, exclusionary, or irrationalist politics must be viewed simply as another form of 'speech-act' and treated 'objectively'? [22]

Even though having knowledge of these practices of 'securitization' may indeed facilitate forms of politics that can avoid or reverse such practices, the theory itself entails a 'basic ambivalence'[23] about these practices. The accusation is that securitization theory cannot judge, only avoid. Williams goes on:

> Questions such as these have led many to ask whether despite its avowedly 'constructivist' view of security practices, securitization theory is implicitly committed to a methodological objectivism that is politically irresponsible and lacking in any basis from which to critically evaluate claims of threat, enmity, and emergency.[24]

The problem is actually much more serious than the 'methodological objectivism' that Williams suggests. There are two main difficulties. First, in terms of Wæver's politics, it is naïve to claim that this critically ambivalent 'methodological objectivism' will be put to the service of 'desecuritization'. In his case for a new approach, Wæver is explicit in his reasons for accepting the nominalist processes of security as a given. It is not a question of whether or not *anything* can be treated as a security issue, but of *how* issues are made into security issues. The politics comes after this understanding is reached. However, at the most basic level, there is no guarantee that the knowledge acquired will be used for that purpose. If the discipline of security studies does as Wæver suggests and builds up a detailed empirical picture of all the successes and failures of 'securitizing' speech-acts, and of all the attempts by other groups to 'desecuritize' certain issues, there is no guarantee that this knowledge will not simply be used by the state or indeed other political actors as a resource for developing more skilful 'securitizing' speech-acts. Foucault has written at great length about state recolonization of strategically important knowledges, especially those that are 'disciplined' in state institutions and funded and promoted by state money.[25] What is the political status, for example, of research into securitization that is funded by, and produced for, government agencies?

Second, in terms of the politics of Wæver's method, it is not simply a question of whether or not securitization theory is 'irresponsible' in its objectivism, but of whether or not there is an implicit politics or ethic already built into the approach. What are the ethico-political implications of simply accepting the statist structures and practices of sovereign nominalism 'uncritically'? Williams notes that the responses of Wæver and his colleague Barry Buzan to these problems remain rather undeveloped: 'it must be admitted that the answers are somewhat less searching than the questioning, and that this remains one of the most underarticulated aspects of securitization theory'.[26]

Williams attempts to come to the rescue of securitization theory by arguing that its reliance on the idea of the 'speech-act' and the communicative processes entailed in such acts provides the basis for an ethic of its own. Williams argues that

> Casting securitization as a speech-act places that act within a framework of communicative action and legitimation that links it to a discursive ethics that seeks to avoid the excesses of a decisionist account of securitization … Communicative action involves a process of argument, the provision of reasons, presentation of evidence, and commitment to convincing others of the validity of one's position.[27]

The argument is that while Schmitt's precepts about politics, security and exceptional situations are used to construct a legitimation of authoritarian decision vested in a single sovereign figure, because securitization theory stresses the communicative *processes* rather than the singular *decisions* involved in making securitizing speech-acts, it entails more openness and possibility for challenge, argument, compromise, collective reasoning, social transformation and democratic legitimation.

There are two problems with Williams's argument. First, and of less importance, Williams admits that this communicative ethic is not something explicitly native to securitization theory, but rather that it is implied in the communicative elements of the theory more generally. Williams notes that this communicative ethic is ultimately derived from Habermas. As such, the usual criticisms apply, in that communicative reason does not adequately take into account the relations of power that permeate discourse, or at least assumes or merely hopes that they can be overcome.[28] In discursive processes some speaking agents are clearly accorded much more authority than others, especially in the field of security, and this is precisely the point. Questions must be asked about the possibility of a communicative ethics under conditions of exceptionalism. Emergency laws, for example, can explicitly suspend the normal deliberative and procedural processes of legislatures and judiciaries. The ideas of communicative ethics and deliberative rationality are precisely what are called into question by the special prerogatives and imperatives of exceptionalism. In fact, Williams notes that the Copenhagen School does not wholly adopt the rosy Habermasian view, in that the acceptance of a speech-act by the audience 'does not necessarily mean in civilized, dominance-free discussion; it only means that an order always rests on coercion as well as on consent'.[29]

Second, and more importantly, Williams's attempt to identify clear blue water between securitization theory and Schmitt is not persuasive. They are conceptually much closer than Williams thinks. While Schmitt clearly does seek to legitimate and valorize the singular sovereign decision, focusing on this alone downplays the important factor of the *capacity* to decide in Schmitt's work, as well as the associated national ethic and ontology he invokes. As Williams explains, in Buzan and Wæver's conceptualization, the possibility of making a successful speech-act is structured first by the capacities of the actors (their position, authority, communicative skill, persuasiveness, resources, etc.) and second by the 'empirical factors or situations to which these actors can make reference', i.e. the facts on the ground of the situation that is the object of possible securitization.[30] Yet the question of the *capacity* to make decisions is equally important for Schmitt.

In *The Concept of the Political*, for example, the ability to recognize and declare the enemy, i.e. to 'securitize', is the essence of sovereignty itself. This ability does not fall to the skill of the sovereign alone, however. Much of the book is concerned with the ability of opposing political groups to hinder or prevent the sovereign declaration of enemies. For example: 'Should ... counterforces be strong enough to hinder a war desired by the state that was contrary to their interests or principles but not sufficiently capable themselves of deciding about war, then a unified political entity would no longer exist'.[31]

Gopal Balakrishnan adds that '[i]n 1914, with the outbreak of the First World War, this is, of course, precisely what did not happen'.[32] The inability of the working classes to prevent the First World War was used by Schmitt as evidence that only the strong sovereign nation-state has genuine sovereign capacities (although it is important to note that for Schmitt this is a historical rather than conceptual answer to Marxism, which he took much more seriously than liberalism). Schmitt's understanding of the healthy sovereign state is one in which these forms of opposition and hindrance are suppressed in favour of national unity, particularly vis-à-vis other states. This suppression is not simply undertaken for the sake of the sovereign leader, however, for the whole schema supports an ethic in which the life of a unified political entity is affirmed precisely at the 'high points'[33] when the enemy is recognized. In other words, Schmitt's ethic is not simply dictatorship from a single sovereign point, but a vitalist and 'democratic' (but certainly not liberal democratic) union of state, leader and people. Schmitt's state is the nation-state and, as such, Schmitt's sovereign decision depends upon, draws upon, expresses and indeed constitutes the collective subjectivity of the nation. In Schmitt, the recognition of an enemy does not simply depend on the decisions of the leader alone, but on a subjective judgement and will that are constituted as national and unified. As he argues, the state has the ability to decide upon the enemy: 'As long as a politically united people is prepared to fight for its existence, independence, and freedom on the basis of a decision emanating from the political entity'.[34]

This aspect of Schmitt's work is foregrounded more fully in 'The Age of Neutralizations and Depoliticizations', a lecture delivered by Schmitt shortly after completing *The Concept of the Political*, in which he presents a more dialectical approach to the question of sovereignty.[35] Here the sovereign is not simply an absolute ruler, but rather one who most successfully understands and expresses the prevailing, dominant and decisive truths and oppositions of the day. This view is much closer to that of Buzan and Wæver regarding the conditions that make successful 'securitizing' acts possible. If Schmitt's view is that the sovereign capacity to successfully declare the enemy and the exception depends upon a decisive understanding of contemporary political, sociological, technological and cultural circumstances, rather than on imposition or coercion alone, then this weakens Williams's distinction between Schmittian *decision* and Copenhagen School *process*.

Returning to the question of communicative ethics, it cannot automatically be assumed that 'securitization' (or 'exceptionalization') is an elite process that can be calmed or quelled through public, communicative processes. Communicative acceptance of a securitizing speech-act may give the act 'democratic' legitimacy, but this does not discount the possibility of a legitimacy derived from a vitalist Schmittian 'democratic' nationalism. The sociological and communicative requirement for the initiator of the speech-act to argue the case in public does not mean that the public will not be convinced by spurious evidence, irrational desires and national, heroic, civilizing or democratizing myths. Being 'public' or 'democratic' does not necessarily equate to being ethically 'good', and what *is* publicly considered ethically 'good', for example democratization or human rights, is all the more amenable to being co-opted into securitizing or exceptionalizing discourses. Moreover, the argument about communicative ethics does not consider the ways in which security threats are used to *constitute* an embattled sovereign 'we' that marginalizes opposition, and this is one of the most important dimensions of Schmitt's political and textual strategy, and one of the most important features of exceptional politics.

The limitations of securitization theory

While it is clear that an appreciation of the nominalist aspects of security problems has been lacking from security studies, Wæver does not go nearly far enough in this direction. Despite the addition of discursive concerns to the classical tradition of security studies, this does not transform our understanding of the field to any great degree. Speech-act theory may be something of a novelty to positivist security analysts, but the merest engagement with Schmitt, or say Max Weber or Walter Benjamin, shows that such concerns about sovereign naming and the legitimating capacities of political actors are not particularly new or radical. If this turn is to be taken seriously, it must be taken much further.

Securitization theory addresses the existence of an overdetermined security field by inserting nominalist process into the analysis. Thus the question is no longer simply whether the facts of a given situation amount to a genuine security problem. It is no longer a question of whether the correct definition of a security problem coincides with a set of concrete facts on the ground. Rather, for securitization theory, it is a question of the political processes by which the word 'security' is successfully *made* to coincide with the facts on the ground. Wæver is constructivist about security issues. The problem is that, despite this, he is not constructivist about where and how securitizing speech-acts occur. To return to the question of 'methodological objectivism', the problem is not simply that securitization theory lacks the means to critically judge which things are securitized, but that securitization theory is selectively constructivist. It may be the case that the 'real referent' of security has been exposed as a construction, but securitization theory does not consider that the security *field* is constructed too. The institutional, social and conceptual practices and structures that name security issues are, for Wæver, concrete and intractable. They are not entirely fixed, but they must be worked with, or around, or away from, in desecuritizing political strategies; they cannot be tackled head on. Wæver wants to accept and work *with* sovereign nominalism without affirming Schmitt's anti-pluralist absolutisms, but in doing so he has already adopted many of the imperatives and necessities that Schmitt's politics hinge upon.

The difference between securitization theory and more traditional approaches to security is that the relationship between the *language* of security and the *reality* of security has been altered. Invoking Foucault's seminal work *Les Mots et les Choses* – published as *The Order of Things* in English but literally translated as 'words and things' – the relationship between the *language* and *reality* of security can be characterized as a relationship between *words* and *things*.[36] The *words* of security are invoked and deployed by securitizing agents, and the *things* of security are the 'real' objects of security issues or the facts on the ground. The novelty of securitization theory is that it is no longer a question of whether the *word* and the *thing* can be said to coincide – i.e. whether an issue *really is* a security issue or whether there is identity or cor-respondence between the security concept and the security object – but a question of how and by whom the word and thing have persuasively been *made* to coincide. Although this may mean that the traditional 'object' of security disappears under the practices that name them, there is still a heavy reliance on the concrete reality of the security situation regarding the posi-tions and capacities of the actors, the security language they can use and so on. Instead of the security issue itself being treated 'objectively', it is now the security *field* that is treated 'objectively'. Rather than analytically establishing the 'reality' of the identity between the words and things of security, it is now a question of analytically establishing the 'reality' of the *processes* and *structures* through which identity between words and things is achieved.

Securitization theory effectively holds that there is a body of linguistic-grammatical rules that both characterize and mobilize the security field, which might include, for example, use of the terms 'enemy', 'threat', 'neces-sity' and 'emergency'. Similarly, securitization theory holds that there are empirical, structural factors that limit or define the securitizing strategies and options available to the actors. In this way, securitization theory fundamentally accepts both the conceptual language and the institutional, structural suppositions of the classic security tradition. For example:

> Conditions for a successful speech-act fall into two categories: (1) the internal, linguistic-grammatical – *to follow the rules of the act* (or, as Austin argues, accepted conventional procedures must exist, and the act has to be executed according to these procedures); and (2) *the external, contextual and social* – to hold a position from which the act can be made ('The particular persons and circumstances in a given case must be appropriate for the invocation of the particular procedure invoked').[37] [my emphasis]

The departure of securitization theory from a more traditional approach is that a discursive element is added between the traditional *words* and *things* of security. The problem is that securitization moves from treating the 'real referent' of security as an 'object' to treating the security *field* as an 'object'. There is still a tight grip between words and things in this understanding. All that has been added is a level of reflection regarding the unity of this tight grip. That is, in treating security as a specific body of rules and structures, securitization theory still treats security as a formal unity, a special category, a model bearing identity. Wæver is explicit in this aim: 'we can identify a specific field of social interaction, with a specific set of actions and codes, known by a set of agents as the security field'.[38]

This 'security field' is not defined by its specific content, but rather by its formal quality. For Wæver, this means that the range of possible security threats is not limited to those of a military type, for example, but can be given a variety of different contents through the securitization process. Diverse content can be moved into the security field if identity with the formal category of security can be achieved through the set of rules, actions, codes and agents that is at hand. This means that although securitization theory is not 'objective' about which issues might become 'security issues', it is 'objective' about the imperatives and principles that will be invoked in the construction of security issues, and 'objective' about the processes by which particular developments are turned into security issues.

In this way, despite adopting a nominalist or constructivist approach, securitization theory ultimately reifies the state in which 'securitization' occurs; it is usually the state that securitizes. Securitization theory waters down its constructivism by treating the discourse, field or tradition of security as a structural, sociological and linguistic *unity* with discernible limits and thresholds that are crossed according to certain formal rules. This understanding of security still entails a characteristic and very Schmittian account of urgency, extraordinary circumstances and exceptional measures which are tied to special state prerogatives and structures. It is possible to recognize when these conditions are moved into and out of, and in this way securitization theory still treats security as a special category: security is still distinguished from politics, and the exception is still distinguished from the norm. This special category – characterized by the basic figurative elements of threat and the statist sovereign prerogative to attach them to particular issues – is already tied to certain social, political and military imperatives. Despite seeking to move away from practices of securitization and exceptionalism, securitization theory in fact reifies them and thus helps perpetuate their 'exceptional' structure. The residual statism of securitization theory is more than a simple empirical position in the ongoing 'whither the state?' debate.[39] For Wæver, whatever the discursive aspects of security problems, the field is still comprised of an urgency that brings forth certain imperatives, tied to exceptional state prerogatives and a mass polity. Wæver writes that the security field is characterized by '[u]rgency; state power claiming the legitimate use of extraordinary means; a threat seen as potentially undercutting sovereignty, thereby preventing the political "we" from dealing with any other questions'.[40]

Wæver's use of discourse is too 'thin'; despite the removal of the security 'object', Wæver's security field is still tied to formal qualities, concrete structures and a certain type of politics. It still betrays the dubious aspects of Schmitt.

It is by no means clear that Wæver can have his sovereign nominalism without Schmitt's attendant absolutisms – the communicative dialectic of sovereign exceptionalism demands and constitutes an idealized, unified national will that stifles dissent and marginalizes opposition. By reifying the basic figurative elements of the security discourse, certain political prerogatives are reified as well, and this is to fall straight into Schmitt's trap in which the exceptional event or situation dictates an exceptional response. This is not simply a dubious ethic, but a dubious metaphysic dictating a dubious ethic. It is no good being constructivist about 'security issues' if one is not sufficiently constructivist about such conditions as 'urgency', 'exception' and the entire constitutive dialectical and structural process that is energized by them.

Discourses of exceptionalism in Schmitt, Agamben and now securitization theory all privilege a sovereign centre. The problem of exceptionalism is successively reduced to, borrowing terms from Foucault, a 'single system of differences' and 'absolute axes of reference':[41] the friend/enemy distinction, the norm and the exception, bare life and political life, politics and security. Each approach remains dualistic to a lesser or greater degree, pursuing clear boundary lines that delimit unities, identities, categories, jurisdictions and limits. If these limits do not attempt to specify the domain of sovereign power, then at least the decision over the shape and location of them is accorded to sovereign power. These approaches ultimately reify what should be problematized. Although each has sought to deal with the political implications of the underlying philosophical and metaphysical problem of the exception, the problem of exceptionalism has been reinforced rather than overcome. While exceptionalism characterizes an array of contemporary events and practices that seem somehow new and disturbing, each successive politico-theoretical approach has sought to reduce the newness and particularity of these events and practices to an underlying theoretical continuity or return. Each approach explains exceptionalism as the expression of a continuous underlying philosophical and political structure, prerogative, imperative or necessity.

The 'archaeological' method of Foucault

In securitization theory, an uncritical acceptance of the structural realities of who is in a position to be an effective agent of security is combined with an invocation, however reflexive, of the canonical tropes and language of the security tradition. Foucault offers a serious rebuke to this kind of approach in *The Archaeology of Knowledge*:

> generally speaking, the analysis of discourse ... substitutes for the diversity of things said a sort of great, uniform text, which has never before been articulated, and which reveals for the first time what men 'really meant' not only in their words and texts, their discourses and their writings, but also in the institutions, practices, techniques, and objects that they

produced. In relation to this implicit, sovereign, communal 'meaning', statements appear in superabundant proliferation, since it is to that meaning alone that they all refer and to it alone that they owe their truth: a plethora of signifying elements in relation to this single 'signified'.[42]

Foucault's criticism can be applied directly to securitization theory, which is built upon a residual statism and a body of formal and figurative rules to the security field. Securitization theory attempts to liberate security studies from the empirical obligation to establish what really is and is not a security issue by arguing that security issues are constituted by nominalist processes. Anything can be made into a security issue, but this great abundance of possibilities must always be channelled through the figurative and affective rules of the security discourse and the institutional structures that dictate how and by whom practices of securitization can be deployed. In this way, the over-determined, statist, exceptional field of security continues to be reified as a 'single signified', despite the addition of discursive considerations. This is Foucault's 'implicit, sovereign, communal "meaning"'. Securitization theory does not travel a great distance from the traditional disciplinary imperative to establish identity between the interpretive concepts of security and the concrete facts on the ground. It adds a layer of reflexivity regarding the constitutive discursive processes at work between concepts and objects, but continues to reify an exceptional field of security, and ultimately fails to escape its determinations. By not taking the question of discourse seriously enough, securitization theory remains within the overdetermined security field, and thus continues to reify the structures and prerogatives of the exceptional state.

Although securitization theory is a step in the right direction, its use and understanding of discursive considerations is too 'thin'. As Foucault proclaims:

> I would like to show that discourse is not a slender surface of contact, or confrontation, between a reality and a language, the intrication of a lexicon and an experience; I would like to show with precise examples that in analyzing discourses themselves, one sees the loosening of an embrace, apparently so tight, of words and things, and the emergence of a group of rules proper to discursive practice. These rules define not the dumb existence of a reality, nor the canonical use of vocabulary, but the ordering of objects.[43]

The distinction between the approach of Wæver and Foucault's more serious discursive departure is not total. Clearly, they are talking about the same concerns when they both seek to describe the 'rules' that define the discursive ordering of objects. Indeed, their approaches are to a great extent similar. For example, in trying to describe the relations, characteristics and instruments that constitute a 'discourse' or 'enunciative modality', Foucault asks questions about speaking subjects, institutional contexts and the constitutive relations between of subject and object. Of the speaking subject he asks: who is speaking? Who is qualified to speak? Who offers the assumption that what the speaker says is true? What hierarchy exists with other individuals? What is required of the speaker? Of the institutional context he asks: what are the institutional sites from which discourses are constituted? What are the legitimate institutional sources and points of application of discursive statements? Of the positioning of subjects in relation to objects and to each other he asks: who are the questioning subjects? The listening subjects? The observing subjects? What are their optimal distances from the object(s) in question? Which positions are privileged? What mediation is there between the nodes of this discursive network?[44]

While Foucault's discursive investigations, as so described, could easily be used as an extension of securitization theory, there is a vital difference between them. While securitization theory posits the unity, identity and formality of discourses, Foucault posits dispersal, difference and specificity. Foucault offers a heavy qualification to his expanding body of descriptive techniques. He asserts that he has not sought to reveal 'formal structures', 'categories', 'rational organization', 'intrinsic necessity', 'a single founding act', 'founding consciousness', a 'horizon of general rationality', a 'freeing from prejudice' towards 'unification and coherence'.[45] Rather, Foucault seeks to establish the problem of discourse as one of 'discontinuity', 'threshold', 'rupture', 'break', 'mutation' and 'transformation'.[46] Foucault demonstrates this difference when he exclaims:

> Take the notion of tradition: it is intended to give a special temporal status to a group of phenomena that are both successive and identical (or at least similar); it makes it possible to rethink the dispersion of history in the form of the same; it allows a reduction of the difference proper to every beginning, in order to pursue without discontinuity the endless search for the origin; tradition enables us to isolate the new against a background of permanence, and to transfer its merit to originality, to genius, to the decisions proper to individuals.[47]

Foucault's critique of the notion of tradition is directly transposable to the problems that beset securitization theory. Despite the theory's interest in the structural and linguistic conditions of possibility for successful securitizing speech-acts, its search for the formalism, continuity and identity of sovereign state nominalism has the effect of perpetuating the notion that there is a kind of special primacy to the realm of security and exceptionalism. By treating security as a formal unity with a repeating, isolable and identifiable threshold, it continues to accord that field a special status and perpetuates the structure of the discourse of exceptionalism. By treating the field of security in terms of an endlessly repeatable discursive and structural *form*, securitization is still seeking to identify a single model of security, or a single model of exceptionalism. In seeking to describe the recurrent identity of the security field, securitization theory bestows an original authority on the whole discourse. The treatment of security as a special category continues to accord 'security' problems and securitizing agents a special status. This is precisely how Schmitt's discourse works: the exception is a problem that occurs at the limits of knowledge and normal politics, it has special qualities that disrupt and threaten the possibility of normality, and hence a special status is required for those who are to operate at its level. Securitization theory repeats this structure in its assumption that the discourse of security is defined by urgency, exceptionality, threat and the need for exceptional sovereign actions, and as such is peopled by special agents, security elites, statesmen and sovereigns.

The political assumption of Wæver is that because security is a special field peopled by a special category of subject, what is needed is ideally a democratization of the field in a move from the elite and secret to the public and communicative, or, more pragmatically, a 'desecuritizing' political counter-discourse that operates counter to the security field. However, this opposition of the special field of security to the 'normal' field of politics perpetuates the dualistic structure of normal/special, everyday/transcendent, politics/security and norm/exception.

In contrast, Foucault's method of 'archaeology' understands discursive formations as dispersed rather than unified, as defined by difference rather than identity, which leads to altogether different implications. For Foucault, discourses are not defined by coherence, unity of style, substance, position, common language or shared assumption, but by plurality, diversity, contradiction and difference. Discourses are at best a problem. This allows a refusal of the discourse of security as a special category with identifiable thresholds, limits, institutional locations and language. It also allows a refusal of the idea that a particular discourse is the manifestation of a historically sedimented relationship of power, which elites continue to enforce and perpetuate. The discourse of exceptionalism *can* be described in such a way, but this does not do justice to the heterogeneous concepts, authorities and subject positions that are in play. Securitization and exceptionalization should not be understood as *a* body of rules and *a* system of entrenched elite prerogatives, but as discursive formations characterized by complex fields of both opposing and complementary positions and concepts. Discourses of security encompass but are not limited by the terrain on which it is possible to oppose the agent of security with the advocate of politics; the chronological space in which argument and counter-argument have occurred and continue to be possible; the historical archive of security statements, anti-security statements, political statements, technical statements, historical statements and philosophical statements which refer to each other, contradict each other, succeed each other and build upon each other. The limits of this terrain are problematic rather than identifiable. It is not a field in which security arguments cohere, a special logic operates, key concepts are invoked, a common grammar is employed and a certain institutional reality functions, but an uncertain expanse in which positions clash, statements contradict each other and disputes occur. There is not an identifiable limit or threshold, a central structure, a field to move in to and out of. There is not a single modality of security, a single model of exceptionalism, a single horizon of sovereignty. Nor is there a security field, a zone of exceptionalism, that unites the peculiarities of historical episodes, dispersed events and contingent happenstances.

In contrast to securitization theory and the previous approaches looked at here, Foucault offers the method of 'archaeology', 'a method that is neither formalizing or interpretive':[48]

> The horizon of archaeology … is not *a* science, *a* rationality, *a* mentality, *a* culture; it is a tangle of interpositivities whose limits and points of intersection cannot be fixed in a single operation. Archaeology is a comparative analysis that is not intended to reduce the diversity of discourses, and to outline the unity that must totalize them, but is intended to divide up their diversity into different figures. Archaeological comparison does not have a unifying, but a diversifying, effect.[49]

The remainder of this book will explore and deploy Foucault's ideas by trying to conceive the discourse of exceptionalism in terms of dispersal rather than unity, specificity rather than continuity, difference rather than sameness, contradiction rather than coherence, and historical positivity rather than conceptual formality.

In *The Archaeology of Knowledge*, Foucault sets out a case for a mode of critique that is both historical and discursive. Chapter 6 will expand upon Foucault's account of an 'archaeological' method that 'describes discourses as practices specified in the element of the archive'.[50] The aim is to establish a mode of critique that can identify and describe the historical and discursive conditions of possibility for principles and practices of contemporary exceptionalism, without reproducing and reifying its exceptional imperatives and determinations.

6 Foucault in Guantanamo

Towards an archaeology of the exception

I began this book by invoking an array of contemporary claims and practices that seemed somehow new. I called this 'exceptionalism'. These claims and practices not only seem new, but they themselves invoke the new. It is claimed that an exceptional event has brought about exceptional times, and exceptional times require exceptional measures. On September 11th 'everything changed'. With the emergence of this constellation of exceptional new circumstances and exceptional new responses, we seem to be faced with a great break in history, the beginning of something new, a sudden irruption. Except that the politics of the exception seems depressingly familiar and predictable. Were we in any doubt, on that fateful day, that the horrors unfolding before our eyes would not be met with an American reign/rain of fire? The terrifying uncertainty of the exceptional event and its interpretation has proved to be a chimera. The meaning and interpretation of the event are now thoroughly incorporated into a regime of legitimation for exceptional sovereign practices. Perhaps the processes and prerogatives that named and interpreted the event had a hold on it before it even happened, awaiting its capture with well-established discourses of threat, urgency, emergency and exception. The 'new' appears to have only reaffirmed the 'same': the permanence of the prerogatives of exceptional sovereign power.

In my analysis so far, these two figures of the new and the same have supported each other. The new has been used to reveal and assert the continuing sameness of sovereign power. Schmitt uses the contingency of the event, the limit inherent in every schema, the 'real possibility'[1] of the exception, to reaffirm a 'single signified'[2]: the metaphysical and political necessity of exceptional nation-statist sovereign power. Similarly, Agamben finds 'the great historico-transcendental destiny of the Occident'[3] in the problem of sovereign exceptionalism. And securitization theory affirms, with its entrenched security discourse, the continued existence of the nominalist prerogatives and practices of sovereign state power under constructed but ultimately formal conditions of 'exceptional' urgency and threat.

Foucault's archaeological method

Foucault's *Archaeology of Knowledge* inspires a riposte to the theorists of exceptionalism, critical or otherwise, taken to task in previous chapters:

theoretical approaches themselves perpetuate the 'sovereign' structures of discourses. Discourses of exceptionalism reify a certain vision of sovereignty: accounts of decision under conditions of contingency; naming, interpretation and representation through authoritative processes; the authorization of authority according to certain conditions of necessity; resolution at the point of contradiction; sovereign judgement at the limit/threshold/border of the normal and the exceptional. It is as if the discourse of exceptionalism contains a 'hidden discourse', a return of the 'same', a 'transcendental act that gives them origin'.[4] Foucault directly opposes all of this. Instead, he offers the method of *archaeology*, which

> is trying to deploy a dispersion that can never be reduced to a single system of differences, a scattering that is not related to absolute axes of reference; it is trying to operate a decentring that leaves no privilege to any centre.[5]

Foucault rejects the dualistic or dialectical opposition of rupture and continuity, the new and the same, the norm and the exception. *Archaeology* is not concerned with the opposition of the original and the banal, the regular and the irregular. This is an invitation to adopt an *archaeological* approach in which all statements (e.g. claims about exceptional events, exceptional times and exceptional measures) are considered not in terms of their sudden irruption, but in terms of their historical conditions of possibility. These conditions, which are dispersed and empirical, and not formal, apply to the exceptional statement and the normal statement alike. This dispersed historicist and discursive approach offers a way to counter the reifying discursive dialectic of norm/exception. Approached in this way, the distinction between norm and exception does not issue from a metaphysical problem of rupture, limit and contingency, but, rather, both norm and exception belong to a particular set of discursive and historical conditions. The exception is not a special metaphysical category, but a problem that is both discursively and historically situated.

Thus it is not a question of identifying the founding moments, the abstract sovereigns and an eternal continuity, as in the permanence of the problem of sovereignty and insecurity. Rather, if one considers that all discursive formations consist of a dispersed and problematic array of objects, statements, concepts and strategies,[6] then the figures of both the 'new' and the 'same' lose their transcendental qualities. *Archaeology* seeks to describe the *historical* rather than formal or ideal conditions of possibility for the appearance of discursive practices and statements. It seeks to describe the specific relations and regularities of object, statement, concept and strategy that constitute the *archive*. The figure of the 'archive' expresses the problem of the *historical conditions of possibility* of discourses: 'the law of what can be said, the system that governs the appearance of statements as unique events'.[7] What 'system' governs the appearance of exceptionalism?

This approach is therefore quite the opposite of those discussed in previous chapters. *Archaeology* would not seek to describe 'exceptionalism' in terms of either originality or continuity. It would not seek to find beneath the appearance of exceptionalism the return of the formal conditions of sovereignty, security or the metaphysical possibility of 'the exception'. It would not describe exceptionalism in transcendental terms. It would not give exceptionalism 'a special temporal status'.[8] Rather than a single analytical and metaphysical horizon of norm and exception, politics and law or politics and security, *archaeology* calls for a *pluralization* of horizons. As we heard in Chapter 5:

> The horizon of archaeology, therefore, is not *a* science, *a* rationality, *a* mentality, *a* culture; it is a tangle of interpositivities whose limits and points of intersection cannot be fixed in a single operation. Archaeology is a comparative analysis that is not intended to reduce the diversity of discourses, and to outline the unity that must totalize them, but is intended to divide up their diversity into different figures. Archaeological comparison does not have a unifying, but a diversifying effect.[9]

Foucault urges a move in the other direction, to resist the move from the particular to the formal, from the dispersed to the unified, from the different to the same. Instead of moving to an 'implicit, sovereign, communal "meaning"'[10], Foucault insists on remaining 'within the dimension of discourse'.[11] 'The enunciative domain is identical with its own surface', writes Foucault; 'There is no subtext'.[12] One can still describe a certain regularity of statements and practices as a discourse, but only one that is dispersed and whose limits are thrown into question and problematized, not unified and formal. 'Exceptionalism' is a broken surface, a dispersed array of appearances drawing upon an archive of the already said, not a metaphysical and existential limit problem traversed by exceptional sovereign authority. The discourse and the archive can be *described*, but to search for hidden meanings, transcendental origins and metaphysical imperatives is to reify. One must move away from the aim of establishing the legitimacy, right or necessity of the discourse of exceptionalism. One must cease to look for the underlying 'truth' or sovereign continuity of the problem of exceptionalism. To engage in critique is not simply to deduce the immanent coherence of a theory or discourse, but to describe its conditions of possibility, and to pursue a Foucauldian *archaeology* is to describe *historical* and *discursive* conditions of possibility.

In Foucault's terms, and contrary to what has been found in the theoretical sites investigated in previous chapters, 'Discourse is not an ideal, timeless form'[13] but, rather,

> it is, from beginning to end, historical – a fragment of history, a unity and discontinuity in history itself, posing the problem of its own limits, its divisions, its transformations, the specific modes of its temporality rather than its sudden irruption in the midst of the complicities of time.[14]

These formulations of Foucault can be distilled into an alternative methodology for tackling the problem of exceptionalism. The aim should be to refuse the metaphysical dialectic between norm and exception, to resist a move towards an implicit sovereign structure, a hidden meaning or a 'single signified'. Instead of moving from empirical instances of exceptionalism to a political theory of exceptional sovereign prerogatives and a mobilized mass polity, the task is to assert the *dispersal* and *historicity* of the *conditions of possibility* of exceptionalism; to stress that successful and mobilizing declarations of exceptions are only possible because of an already-existing discursive formation of objects, enunciative modalities, concepts and strategies.[15] Foucault's notion of the 'discursive formation' does not mean an underlying tradition, a return to the same affirmed by the irruption of the new, but a dispersed archive of historical statements and practices which make contemporary invocations and enactments of exceptionalism possible. When one describes 'exceptionalism', therefore, the aim should not be to describe a special category, but to describe a dispersed regularity, an assemblage of practices, an already-existing archive of statements, an array of competing subject positions, a body of tactics and strategies, a formation of historical conditions of possibility, the limits of which can never be distilled and formalized, only problematized.

'Archaeology' and 'genealogy'

Foucault's *archaeological* approach is not isolated either from the rest of his work or from the huge secondary literature on Foucault. A distinction can be made between his method of 'archaeology', which came first, and 'genealogy', which came later, but it is important to note that the difference is only one of emphasis. As Dreyfus and Rabinow stress, '*[t]here is no pre- and post-archaeology or genealogy in Foucault. However, the weighting and conception of these approaches has changed during the development of his work*'.[16] Archaeology is more concerned with discourse and structure, while the two key departures of genealogy are a greater emphasis on, first, historical power relations and, second, technologies and practices of power that are focused on the body in particular. This chapter draws upon both methodologies, but overall this book places the emphasis on archaeology for four reasons.

First, the language of archaeology is much closer to that used by the theorists who make up much of the subject material tackled here. Schmitt, Agamben and securitization theory all construct their arguments around a structural relationship between objects, subjects and concepts. The 'exception' is constituted as an 'object' of special discourses, imperatives and practices. Principles, processes and practices of sovereign subjectivity play a decisive constitutive role in the naming and designation of 'exceptions'. The concepts of threat, danger, necessity and security are found at the centre of the discourse of exceptionalism, invoking a legitimacy that is supposedly deeper and more profound than that of the law and the 'norm'. The language of archaeology closely correlates with the categories that are in play in the discourse of exceptionalism, but it problematizes, critiques, expands and disperses them.

Second, the emphasis of genealogy on understanding the emergence of historical developments as 'the hazardous play of dominations',[17] a 'stage of forces'[18] and 'the struggle these forces wage against each other'[19] does not play well with the discourse of exceptionalism, because exceptionalism is *already* understood through a modality of violence and force. In the popular liberty/security debate, for example, 'liberty' is subject to a struggle between those who would defend it from the state and those who would defend it from 'terror'. To offer the classic Nietzschean genealogy of liberty as a dominating 'invention of the ruling classes'[20] is not helpful for understanding how liberty has come to play a polyvalent and ambiguous role in the discourse of exceptionalism, contradictorily standing for both individual freedom and state security practices. It is too easy to describe exceptionalism as the domination of the 'ruling classes', manifested as the sovereign decision on the exception (Schmitt), the sovereign decision on bare life and political life (Agamben) or elites declaring issues to be security problems (securitization theory). It would be simple to describe exceptionalism as a special field constructed, bounded and continually reinforced by violent practices of inclusion and exclusion, but this is what is already offered by Schmitt, Agamben and securitization theory. Rather than simply understanding discourses as 'the violent or surreptitious appropriation of a system of rules'[21] or 'the hazardous play of dominations', archaeology places more emphasis on relations between objects, statements, concepts and strategies, the conditions under which each of these categories is constituted, and the way they interact and provide authority to each other. In this sense, in contrast to the Nietzschean slant of genealogy, archaeology is much more of a 'critical' project in the traditional Kantian sense of 'seeking the conditions of possibility and limitations of rational analysis'.[22] The key departure from Kant is the fact that 'Foucault accepts this project but rejects the attempts to find a universal grounding in either thought or Being'.[23] That is, Foucault seeks to describe limits and conditions of possibility which are historical and discursive, rather than found in pure reason or being.

Third, the genealogical idea of history as the imposition of violence and domination is a deeply ambiguous argument that Foucault ultimately steps back from. In the famous essay 'Nietzsche, Genealogy, History' Foucault posits the idea of history as a relation of war and battle: 'The successes of history belong to those who are capable of seizing these rules',[24] he writes. The aim of 'seizing the rules' begs the very question of exceptionalism. Is the way to tackle the problem merely to seize the means of declaring the exception? In an interview conducted in the midst of his 'genealogical phase' (if one can speak of such a thing), Foucault is asked: 'Does the military model seem to you … to be the best one for describing power: is war here simply metaphorical model, or is it the literal, regular, everyday mode of operation of power?' In response, Foucault by no means answers in the affirmative, and instead posits a number of difficult questions about the 'war model', commenting that '[a] whole range of problems emerge here'.[25] In *'Society Must Be Defended'*, a series of lectures delivered around the same time, Foucault thoroughly explores and tests this 'war model', asking: 'if we have to think of power in terms of relations of force, do we therefore have to interpret it in terms of the general form of war? Can war serve as an analyzer of power relations?'[26] Foucault ultimately steps back from the 'war model' of power relations to revert to a more critical, 'archaeological' position.[27] Instead of straightforwardly pursuing 'war' as an 'analyzer of power relations', Foucault critically examines the rise and fall of the 'war model' of power relations in historical and political discourse, describing its conditions of emergence and the multiple inversions, transpositions and syntheses it undergoes. As such, *'Society Must Be Defended'* is not genealogical in the sense described in 'Nietzsche, Genealogy, History', but is more reflective and 'archaeological' in the way it critically describes a discursive terrain upon which multiple historical and political claims are possible. The possibility of these multiple claims and inversions stems not simply from 'the struggle of forces', but from discursive and political synthesis, inversion, co-optation and disciplinarization.

Fourth, although this chapter makes use of a genealogical focus on technologies of the body and 'micro-practices' of power, exceptionalism is a much wider problem than can be explained through technologies of power alone. Beyond the technologies of 'exceptional' practices themselves, such as torture and detention without trial, exceptionalism raises profound questions about the workings of political principles and discourses. How are key political ideas such as liberty and security being used in a discourse of exceptionalism that works to legitimate exceptional practices? How is the problematique of liberty implicated in exceptionalism? How do claims about imperatives and necessities that are more authentic than law find critical purchase? The discourse and practice of exceptionalism cannot and should not be separated into 'levels of analysis', but my particular focus on the widespread failure to find critical purchase on the problem of the exception does call for a slant in emphasis towards archaeology.

It must be made clear, however, that archaeology is *not* concerned exclusively with statements, and genealogy *not* exclusively concerned with practices. Emphasizing archaeology does not exclude genealogy, because they are complementary approaches that largely overlap. As Foucault puts it: 'Archaeology is the method specific to the analysis of local discursivities, and genealogy is the tactic which, once it has described these local discursivities, brings into play the desubjugated knowledges that have been released from them'.[28] The critical focus of this project calls for the analysis of discursivities more than it calls for genealogical tactics.

As a final cautionary point, a focus on discourse does not mean an exclusive focus on language. The argument presented here is that the problem of the exception, and the way it has been treated critically, raises questions about the role and constitution of subject positions, objects, concepts and strategies (although not exclusively in the military sense), and as such the problem is immediately wider than that of discourse understood merely as language. Discourse, as Foucault understands it, is a problem of formations of language and concepts, but also of extra-discursive structures, practices and positions of authority. As he makes clear:

> Of course, discourses are composed of signs; but what they do is more than use these signs to designate things. It is this *more* that renders them irreducible to the language and to speech. It is this 'more' that we must reveal and describe.[29]

Foucault warns that one cannot hope to describe an entire discursive web in a single operation. An aspiration to empirical or theoretical comprehensiveness is an aspiration to a totalizing and sovereign discourse. The remainder of this chapter, therefore, will sketch only a particular corner of the broken surface of contemporary exceptionalism. It will begin to sketch the describable positivity and archive of contemporary American torture.

Torture as historical resemblance/recurrence

It is almost as if Guantanamo Bay were the public face of American torture. There are detailed accounts about the camp and its practices available from former captives. Official pictures of the camp have been disseminated through the media. Although details of the happenings inside Guantanamo are carefully guarded, the very existence of the camp appears to be for domestic and global public consumption. We also know that the US holds thousands more prisoners in less publicized locations across the globe. In 2005 Amnesty International estimated that approximately 70,000 were being held outside the USA. These included: 520 in Guantanamo Bay naval base (plus 234 releases or transfers); 550 in the Bagram and Kandahar air bases in Afghanistan; an unknown number of detainees, estimated at scores, in other US forward operating bases; in Iraq, 6,300 in Camp Bucca, 3,500 in Abu Ghraib prison, 110 in Camp Cropper and 1,300 in other US facilities; 40 estimated to be held at undisclosed CIA locations worldwide; several thousand held by foreign governments at the request of the USA; and 100 to 150 estimated secret transfers ('renditions') of detainees to third countries.[30]

With this global archipelago of exceptionalism in mind, Foucault's commitment to describing discursive formations in their dispersal is productive from the outset. The issue of contemporary American torture exploded into political discourse in the aftermath of 9/11. Although these practices appear profoundly new, there is nothing historically novel about instances of American torture or state torture generally. One should be wary, therefore, of identifying contemporary American torture as the 'sudden irruption' in time of an identifiable unity of practices. But neither should American torture be described as a continuity. It is not possible to identify, without a violent degree of reduction or overdetermination, a single, unified discursive practice of American torture in territorial or political space.

Clearly in some ways the problem of contemporary exceptionalism is new; in its claims to newness, in the rapid proliferation and institutionalization of violent and carceral practices, and in changes in popular legitimacy and political commentary. In other ways exceptionalism is a problem of the same: the problem of sovereign power, the problem of limits, and the problem of symptomatic contradictions between 'liberty' and 'security' in the popular liberal discourse. And on the one hand, the appearance of torture as an instituted practice of power bears resemblance to much earlier times and places. On the other, many aspects of the contemporary array of practices and discourses of exceptionalism deploy more recent technologies and techniques of power.

With this in mind, if the present task is to try to understand contemporary exceptionalism without reproducing sovereign-centred discourses of rupture or origin, then in light of both its apparent newness and its apparent sameness, contemporary exceptionalism should be described and analysed as a novel recombination of already-existing discourses, mechanisms and modalities of power, some in active use already, others reawakened from dormancy. To avoid the pitfalls of other approaches to exceptionalism, the contemporary political problem should be described neither as a full-spectrum break in history in which 'everything changed' nor as a confirmation of the formal sameness of sovereignty, security and modern politics. The *archaeological* response is to describe the discursive formation of contemporary exceptionalism neither as the passage of continuity nor as a great rupture. Both newness and sameness need to be described, in Foucault's terms, at the level of positivity and exteriority, not as transcendental rupture or metaphysical contingency. As Foucault writes, '[t]he idea of a single break suddenly, at a given moment, dividing all discursive formations, interrupting them in a single moment and reconstituting them in accordance with the same rules – such an idea cannot be sustained'.[31] The archaeological approach is, quite clearly then, a critical riposte to the 'ground zeroing' effect of the symbol '9/11'.

The recombination of discursive formations and modalities of power

With these methodological precautions stated, we will now use examples from Foucault's other works to show how it is possible to understand historical and discursive transformations as recombinations of existing and spatio-temporally dispersed regularities, rather than as historical ruptures or breaks. Two of Foucault's works in particular, *Discipline and Punish* and *'Society Must Be Defended'*, are explicitly framed as efforts to move away from 'sovereign-centred' discourses. In *Discipline and Punish*, Foucault uses a genealogical approach to chart and explore various phases and modalities in the historical specificities of forms of power. *'Society Must Be Defended'* takes a similar approach, exploring how collective identities emerged historically as forms of resistant subjectivity to challenge the institution of monarchical sovereign power.

In *Discipline and Punish*, Foucault describes three different assemblages and discourses of power in their historical particularity. First is the 'archaic mechanism' of monarchical sovereign power, characterized by highly symbolic and exemplary vengeance, torture and excess.[32] This is then slowly displaced by a second modality: the rise of discourses of contract and right, in which punishment is enacted not on behalf of the King, but on behalf of society in recompense for the injuries done to it by crime and violence.[33] Foucault describes a third modality of power in addition to these recognizable models, which he calls 'disciplinary power', a less explicit and more meticulously concrete form of power. 'Disciplinary power' derives from the assemblage of multiple new technologies, knowledges, micro-mechanisms and tactics constructed around producing and regulating ever-more utile, efficient and productive forms of life at the individual and in turn social level.[34] (By extension, the final chapter of *'Society Must Be Defended'* returns to 'disciplinary power', broadening it to apply to the level of population and biological life itself in what he calls 'biopower'.[35] Foucault developed the concept of biopower further in his subsequent book, *The History of Sexuality, Volume 1: The Will to Knowledge*.)

How might these different modalities come to be articulated together in contemporary formations? In the closing thoughts of *'Society Must Be Defended'* Foucault describes a particular historical transformation that is especially relevant and illustrative for the problem of describing exceptionalism. Drawing together some of his historical descriptions into explicit arguments about the dangerous turns of twentieth-century politics, Foucault constructs a provocative synthesis and correlation of some of the different modalities of power he previously theorized. Thus in trying to describe the historical transformation of power that was Nazism, Foucault invokes two modalities of power he had previously described quite separately: the archaic sovereign right of life and death described in the first part of *Discipline and Punish*, and the modalities of disciplinary power and biopower that he described as a historically much later formation:

> We have, then, in Nazi society something that is really quite extraordinary: this is a society which has generalized biopower in an absolute sense, but which has also generalized the sovereign right to kill. The two mechanisms – the classic, archaic mechanism that gave the State the right of life and death over its citizens, and the mechanism organized around discipline and regulation, or in other words, the new mechanism of biopower – coincide exactly.[36]

For Foucault, the Nazi state represents a 'paroxysm' of two co-existent and correlating modalities of power, one old and 'archaic', the other a recent innovation. In Nazism, as Foucault describes it, new techniques of power supplemented and transformed existing and revived modalities. As Foucault explains regarding sovereignty and biopower: 'I wouldn't say exactly that sovereignty's old right – to take life or let live – was replaced, but it came to be complemented by a new right which does not erase the old right but which does penetrate it, permeate it'.[37] And again, with regard to the growth of biopower subsequent to disciplinary power:

> This technology of power does not exclude the former, does not exclude disciplinary technology, but it does dovetail into it, integrate it, modify it to some extent, and above all, use it by sort of infiltrating it, embedding itself in existing disciplinary techniques.[38]

Here, Foucault demonstrates what he had expressed many times before: that the emergence of new forms of power does not automatically mean the decline of old forms. Moreover, he is explicitly demonstrating his method of describing historical transformations as neither absolute ruptures nor historical continuities. Foucault's discursive formations and modalities of power have recombinatory qualities. They emerge in novel new combinations, constellations and syntheses in different times and places. In one sense, these innovations and transformations are expressive of the logics already contained within existing modalities of power, old and new. Taken together, however, they express unique political and technological circumstances. Following from Foucault's invocation of the Nazi state as an exceptional 'paroxysm', therefore, it is productive to analyse contemporary transformations of 'exceptional' power as unique recombinations of already-existing and previously existing modalities.

Describing contemporary exceptionalism

What recombinations and syntheses of historically constituted modalities of power are in play in the apparatuses, external points of exercise, circulation, reproduction and infinitesimal mechanisms of contemporary exceptionalism? Here I will draw heavily on Foucault's genealogy of punishment and disciplinary technologies in a descriptive digression into contemporary technologies of exceptionalism in Camp Delta, Guantanamo Bay, Cuba.

The modality of power that Foucault places at the historical and narrative beginning of *Discipline and Punish* is 'The Spectacle of the Scaffold', which is representative of the great panoply of penalties and techniques used in the middle ages, the exemplary and symbolic expression of a terrible sovereign power: 'Corporal punishment, painful to a more or less horrible degree'.[39] Foucault describes this regime of torture not as 'an extreme expression of lawless rage',[40] but as a measured, calculated, compared, hierarchized system of techniques and penalties.

In comparison with today, the litany of actual techniques used in Foucault's description has few parallels with what is known of contemporary American practices. There has been no suggestion of hanging, the cutting off of hands or tongues, the breaking of limbs, burning and so on. There is, however, a different litany of procedures and practices that are 'tantamount to torture', as the International Committee of the Red Cross reported them, breaking its long tradition of silent neutrality.[41] One of the most detailed accounts of Guantanamo available is the report compiled by the 'Tipton Three'. These three British-Asians were captured in Afghanistan before being transported to Guantanamo and held for two and a half years. Eventually they were released and brought back to the UK, where they did not face any criminal charges. Before drawing the historical resemblances more explicitly, let us recount the description of their experiences in detail, which certainly amount to a litany of practices 'tantamount to torture'.

They describe being 'short-shackled', where the hands and feet are shackled together, the shackles cutting into the wrists and ankles, for periods of up to eight hours. This was usually done prior to interrogation, but sometimes this never came. Short-shackling and confined conditions left them with scars and permanent knee and back pain. They were placed in isolation for periods of weeks and months, or over a year in some cases. In isolation cells they were subject to both freezing and extremely hot air-conditioning, strobe lighting, and constant and repetitious loud music. They were systematically deprived of food, water and sleep. Many were subjected to severe beatings, intimidation and attack by dogs. Medical, often surgical, treatment was regularly withheld from those who needed it. The regular cells, or rather cages, were two metres square and exposed to the extreme Cuban sun, heat and cold. Exercise and showers, if any, consisted of a few minutes per week. They were denied knowledge of the date and time, kept 'without hope and starved of information'.[42] There appears to have been a concerted attempt to 'break' the prisoners and many were pushed beyond sanity. They describe several hundred suicide attempts and 'at least a hundred detainees [who] have become observably mentally ill as opposed to just depressed'.[43]

The three prisoners describe being subject to repeated interrogations by a number of different organizations (including MI5, demonstrating British complicity). These interrogations were repetitious and often not subject to any overarching coordination. All three captives eventually gave numerous false confessions. These were only belatedly refuted by MI5 on account of the prisoners' actual location in England at the time of their alleged sighting with Osama bin Laden in Afghanistan.

Many similarities can be drawn with the early economy of power that Foucault describes. First of all there is the opacity of the entire procedure. The Tipton Three were refused all information about their legal status and the fate that awaited them. They only found out from a guard that they were being represented in the UK by the lawyer Gareth Pierce, although British Embassy officials and MI5 refused to confirm this to them. Turning to Foucault's historical account, resemblances can be identified in the opacity and secrecy of the regime:

the entire criminal procedure, right up to the sentence, remained secret: that is to say, opaque, not only to the public but also to the accused himself. It took place without him, or at least without his having any knowledge of the charges or of the evidence. In the order of criminal justice, knowledge was the absolute privilege of the prosecution.[44]

The medieval criminal process, as Foucault describes it, was not simply arbitrary. Rather, it formed part of a 'rigorous model' of truth production. The system depended on a complex and hierarchical economy of truths with an 'operational function'. These rules did not form a seamless modern system of positive law. Rather, their complexity meant that they were flexible, highly arguable, and more or less applicable depending on the specific crime and the status of the accused. As Foucault describes: 'this system of "legal proofs" makes truth in the penal domain the result of a complex art; it obeys rules known only to specialists, and, consequently, it reinforces the principle of secrecy'.[45] The opacity of the investigatory process demonstrates the exclusivity of 'sovereign' ownership of the whole apparatus. The procedures of investigation/punishment relate not to transparent codes of law and scientific truth, but to the symbolic affirmation of 'sovereign' power. As Foucault writes: 'The secret ... form of the procedure reflects the principle that ... the establishment of truth was the absolute right and the exclusive power of the sovereign'.[46] The 'sovereign' ownership of the whole process is the clue to the parallels between contemporary exceptionalism and the archaic economy of truth and power that Foucault describes.

The investigatory procedure in Guantanamo, as described by the Tipton Three, bears some resemblance to these archaic procedures. There is no true/false duality in Guantanamo. The 'truths' pursued by the investigators would not meet any modern legal standard of truth or proof, nor even meet any modern judicial purpose. The former prisoners describe multiple interrogations by investigators from different groups who seemingly did not communicate with each other and were not aware of information that had already been given:

> At some interrogations we were shown photographs of Donald Duck, Mickey Mouse, Tom & Jerry, Rug Rats, Abraham Lincoln, Michael Jackson, Fidel Castro, Che Guevara, Osama Bin Laden and famous people from different countries. Actresses for instance, Sharon Stone, etc. One American interrogator called Mike Jackson, from LA FBI, said that he had been sent by 'the Queen' according to him. He said that MI5 had sent him photographs because they couldn't come and had asked him to ask us about them. These were photographs of British citizens. There was one English woman with blonde hair amongst the photographs. These were all surveillance photographs taken of people as they went shopping in Tescos, etc. or with their friends. Very different people came in fact with the same set of photos (all Americans) and none of them knew that

we had already been asked about the photographs on other occasions. This in fact happened numerous times during the interrogations. We'd be asked the same thing again and again by different sets of interrogators who didn't know the answers. There seemed to be no coordination of the information that they were getting or trying to get. The Army would come and show the pictures to us, then the FBI and then the CIA. They didn't seem to pass information amongst themselves. And from the FBI different people would come from different departments.[47]

In Guantanamo, as it was in the period that Foucault describes, the 'production of truth' forms part of a complex economy of power. The means of investigation and the means of punishment coincide. As then, suspicion is the 'mark of a certain degree of guilt as regards the suspect and a limited form of penalty as regards punishment'.[48] It is the body that constitutes the central object and point of application of both the means of acquiring the truth of guilt and the point of punishment for the guilt that is already presumed:

> The body interrogated in torture constituted the point of application of the punishment and the locus of extortion of truth. And just as presumption was inseparably an element in the investigation and a fragment of guilt, the regulated pain involved in judicial torture was a means of both punishment and of investigation.[49]

The body, marked by torture, bears the imprints of guilt, the marks of retribution that correspond to the terrible acts committed and the reaffirmation of sovereign power. The body is not simply the object of punishment, but the site of the production of sovereign truth and the inscription of the symbolic and material reality of sovereign power:

> The body, several times tortured, provides the synthesis of the reality of the deeds and truth of the investigation, of the documents of the case and the statements of the criminal, of the crime and the punishment. It is an element, therefore, in a penal liturgy, in which it must serve as the partner of a procedure ordered around the formidable rights of the sovereign, the prosecution and secrecy.[50]

Similarly, the body is a key object in the contemporary formation of power in Guantanamo. It is an object constituted by particular forms of enunciative modality (the line of questioning, the status of 'confessions', etc.), particular concepts (exception, 'terrorist', etc.) and strategies (manipulation of the body in order to extract information, 'break' the detainees, quell resistance, etc.). Although this formation of power bears a resemblance to the archaic forms that Foucault describes at the beginning of *Discipline and Punish*, these practices cannot simply be described in terms of the symbolic affirmation of sovereign power alone. Although archaic 'sovereign' elements certainly appear to be vestigial in the contemporary formation being described, the description cannot be reduced to a singular, centred discourse of power. The origins of these discourses and practices are historically dispersed.

Disciplinary power

Although in the practices of Guantanamo there is a resemblance to the spectacular affirmation of sovereign power in terms of the production of truth and the role of the body, the actual mechanisms by which power is exercised resemble the quite different litany of techniques that Foucault describes as *disciplinary power*. Disciplinary power is a 'mechanics of power' built on a 'political anatomy', an elaborate assemblage of techniques and tactics for gaining 'an infinitesimal power over the active body', a power 'of exercising upon it a subtle coercion, of obtaining holds upon it at the level of the [bodily] mechanism itself – movements, gestures, attitudes, rapidity'.[51]

Disciplinary power was to be constructed not around the spectacular rituals of sovereign affirmation, but around an intricate focus on the smallest details of human life.[52] A more detailed knowledge meant a more detailed form of control and a corresponding increase in power and productivity. This knowledge translated into a series of techniques for ordering the utility of the body.

Multiple instances of these techniques of power can be described in Guantanamo Bay. Much of this 'art of the human body' and corresponding 'mechanics of power' is at work in Guantanamo. The organization of the camp closely follows Foucault's rules of distribution. Enclosure goes without saying. Partitioning and cellularization would be expected; here they are taken to extreme levels with the employment of tiny, fully observable mesh cages rather than cells.

In the account given by the Tipton Three we learn that the lives of the prisoners were controlled down the most minute of corporeal details. Every detail of their action and behaviour was observed. This observation was used to build a detailed knowledge of each prisoner to extend further the regime of coercion:

> we were also aware, in Camp X-Ray and later in Delta, that we were being listened to and our conversations were being recorded. On the question of observation I wish to add that being under constant obser- vation was an additional stress ... The observations conducted were not just in relation to what we were saying, but everything we did. They would look to see if we stared at women MPs [military police] or looked down when they walked passed. They looked to see if we used particular comfort items more regularly than others or had any habits that they could clearly identify. As an example, if we were suffering because of the small portions [of food], they would identify this as a weakness or alter- natively if we required medical help, this would depend on our cooperation

in interview. In my view it was clear that they were identifying weaknesses upon which they could play for the purposes of interrogation.[53]

Ostensibly this regime was geared towards the production of truth and intelligence, but it seems that power and coercion themselves became the principle bases of the process. The physical conditions of the captives were tightly tied into a precise tabulation with their behaviour and level of cooperation:

> All three men say that they believe the conditions were designed specifically to assist the interrogators. They were able, with great precision, to control the behaviour of the detainees depending on the type of answers or the level of cooperation they believed they were getting. The interrogators had already made up their mind as to what they wanted and it often became a question of trying to gauge what they wanted to hear and give the right answer.[54]

Power, resistance and politics

Although these examples from Guantanamo have a direct resemblance to the intricacies of disciplinary power that Foucault describes, there are some very obvious differences. Foucault stresses that disciplinary power is not simply negative but productive. The aim is not simply brute repression but utility, efficiency and productivity. Superficially, Guantanamo serves the 'production' of truth and intelligence, but we have heard how uncoordinated and unreliable the 'truth' produced is. In military 'newspeak', Guantanamo has produced very little 'actionable' intelligence. In contrast, the actual regime of corporeal and disciplinary control seems to be much more thorough, yet it is hardly a 'positive' system. There has been no attempt at training, at reform, at shaping the prisoners into something more utile and productive; quite the opposite in fact. The techniques and tactics employed may well be extreme forms of disciplinary power, but the ultimate aims and interests are of a different modality.

Yet there is still a kind of power relationship at work, a 'productive' relation that produces not military intelligence but false confessions, small and petty victories and 'docile bodies'. Nevertheless, and in contrast to Agamben's conceptualization of a 'bare' life that is stripped of its normal social and political qualities in the state of exception, Guantanamo is still permeated by political relations. Many of the prisoners put up resistance in any way they could. Considered in the light of Foucault's understanding of power as circulatory, this resistance provides something for the 'current' of disciplinary power to work against.[55] The particular formation of power in the camp asserts itself through disproportionate responses to these small acts of defiance. As one of the Tipton Three recalls of a rather fitting small act of resistance: 'On another occasion I scratched "have a nice day" on my Styrofoam cup and this was seen as a disciplinary offence for which I spent another week in isolation'.[56]

Contra Agamben, 'bare' life does not constitute the primary object of this formation of power. The 'detainee' is not simply the 'object' of power, but remains a speaking and acting 'subject'. Although power may be affirmed through a display of domination, it still requires a subjective reaction in order to extract what it needs; if not truth and intelligence, then at least cooperation and submission. The dispersed formation of exceptionalism is a tangled network of co-constitutive objects and subjects, the limits of which are never fixed. Nevertheless, the line between vestigial resistance and total domination is not clear either.

In many cases, the regime of disciplinary control went beyond any productive power relation and became absolute mental and corporeal domination. In these cases the disciplinary apparatus produced only bodies reduced to abject animality:

> For at least 50 of those so far as we are aware their behaviour is so disturbed as to show that they are no longer capable of rational thought or behaviour. We do not describe in detail here the behaviour but it is something that only a small child or an animal might behave like.[57]

When Foucault describes disciplinary power in the barracks, the factory, the school, the hospital and the asylum, he is describing very obvious resemblances with the present-day structuring of our work environments, our cities and our complex bureaucratic welfare societies. Although these practices are deployed in the camp, it is in an extreme form, not distinct and excepted from everyday life, but recombined with more 'archaic' modalities of power.

The synthesis of 'archaic' sovereign power with disciplinary power

Returning from this long but necessary descriptive digression, this chapter will conclude by invoking the particular synthesis of modalities and the recombination of historical discourses and techniques of power discussed earlier. In the case of Guantanamo we see a similar synthesis of the 'old' sovereign right of life and death with the 'new' assemblage of disciplinary techniques, but the relation is inverted. Foucault describes how, historically, the archaic institution of sovereignty, with its right of life, death, war and spectacular vengeance was permeated by a network of productive new disciplinary tactics and techniques. Today the transformation has occurred in reverse. A modern regime of disciplinary power has been permeated by a reawakened modality of spectacular sovereign vengeance and war. It is neither an irruption of the new nor a return of the same, but a unique recombination of recurrent and historically dispersed formations of power.

While Foucault describes a historical transformation from archaic sovereignty to discipline that takes place over a few decades, today it is possible to describe a reawakening of the former 'archaic' form in a rare synthesis with the latter modern form. This 'exceptional' synthesis of the modalities of 'archaic' sovereignty and disciplinary power unsettles their historical separation. In the case of Guantanamo, familiar techniques of disciplinary power have been pushed to an exemplary, symbolic, vengeful paroxysm of normality. In practices of contemporary exceptionalism, echoes of the archaic regime of power that Foucault describes are clearly visible. For example, as Foucault writes:

> in monarchical law, punishment is a ceremonial of sovereignty; it uses the ritual marks of the vengeance that it applies to the body of the condemned man; and it deploys before the eyes of the spectators an effect of terror as intense as it is discontinuous, irregular and always above its own laws, the physical presence of the sovereign and of his power.[59]

There is certainly a correlation to be described between the archaic rights and symbolic affirmations of a sovereign power that is 'above its own laws', i.e. exceptional, and the contemporary practices I have called exceptionalism. If the 9/11 attacks were intended as, interpreted as and represented as a symbolic crime against the sovereignty of the United States, then the purpose of the practice of contemporary exceptionalism is not simply to apprehend, investigate, punish and restore law and order, but, rather, the 'terrifying restoration of sovereignty'.[60] A symbolic crime against sovereignty is not simply an affront to the law, but an affront to sovereignty itself: 'It ... requires that the king take revenge for an affront to his very person. The right to punish, therefore, is an aspect of the sovereign's right to make war on his enemies'.[61] In its symbolic import the spectacle of Guantanamo, however shrouded in mystery, resembles the spectacle of public execution in the Middle Ages. The resonances with Foucault's historical descriptions are clear: 'Its aim is not so much to re-establish a balance as to bring into play, at its extreme point, the dissymmetry between the subject who has dared to violate the law and the all-powerful sovereign who displays his strength'.[62]

The 'sovereign right' to make war against declared enemies has come to be expressed through a disciplinary mechanics of power, a particular constellation of subject positions, discursive formations, conceptual and figurative legitimations, political strategies and a detailed political anatomy of the human body. It is not so much an exceptional rupture or a radical departure but a transformation, the conditions of possibility of which reside not in a formal and identifiable unity of sovereign power, but in a dispersed discursive archive of techniques, statements, subject positions and strategies. The exception is not a special category that can be identified according to the formal necessities of abstract political threat and metaphysical contingency, but a unique recombination of historically dispersed regularities that have survived in time and been reawakened in this particular contemporary constellation. It is not a case of a return to origins, a return of the sovereign same, but a unique transformation, correlation and synthesis of everyday practices of disciplinary power with a more distant, reawakened modality of symbolic and spectacular bodily vengeance.

7   The rise and fall of Schmitt at the hands of Foucault and others

It is clear that 'exceptionalism' signifies an array of things which are not the same and do not obey the same logic. Guantanamo does not obey the same logic as the USA PATRIOT Act. Extraordinary rendition does not obey the same logic as the Control Order. The aim of much of this book has been to break the connection between the heterogeneous practices and discursive formation signified by 'exceptionalism' and the philosophical and legal problem of 'the exception', constructed by Carl Schmitt as a 'case of extreme peril'[1] that cannot be known in advance but will require both declaration and extra-legal response from 'he who is sovereign'.[2]

The aim of this chapter is to understand the reasons for Schmitt's rise in popularity amongst critical scholars of security, to make clear the dangers present in that engagement and to discuss alternative approaches to the problem of 'exceptionalism'. In the central chapters of this book I drew a distinction between approaches that do not escape the orbit of Schmitt and an approach inspired by the work of Michel Foucault that does. This chapter will extend that analysis to a wider range of scholarly interventions. Some of these, I contend, risk reifying a Schmittian understanding of 'the exception'. Others demonstrate empirically to great critical effect precisely the kind of dispersed and decentred approach to the problem of exceptionalism that Chapter 6 outlined in theoretical terms. The difference between these two approaches has big political implications for how we understand exceptionalism and the so-called 'war on terror'.

The rise of Schmitt

Schmitt is not a simple thinker, and does not have a stable political position across the range of his works. Gopal Balakrishnan's excellent biography of Schmitt demonstrates a protean intellectual temperament.[3] The German jurist's areas of concern traversed widely disparate registers and seemingly incompatible normative schemas. For example, in *Roman Catholicism and Political Form*, first published in 1923, Schmitt envisaged the Catholic Church as a conservative unifying force for European civilization that could overcome the national and class divisions of the previous century, whereas in the 1922 *Political Theology* he eulogized the extremely unorthodox Catholic eschatological counter-revolutionary thought of Donoso-Cortes.[4] Diverging again in 1926, *The Crisis of Parliamentary Democracy* finally embraced and valorized the political and historical power of the mass as harnessed through the vitalist mythologies of Georges Sorel[5] and György Lukács.[6] By 1927, given the threat of social revolution exported from Russia and the unprecedented juridical, legal and moral transformations being imposed on the international system by the Great War victors through the Paris treaties, Schmitt struggled to articulate what Europe still stood for. *The Concept of the Political* posited the classical European sovereign state as key, even though Schmitt argued that 'the political' preceded and did not presuppose 'the state'.[7]

After the Second World War, however, the Westphalian game was apparently up. With the 2003 translation of the 1950 *Nomos of the Earth*,[8] some international relations thinkers are now looking to this later Schmitt for his abandonment of the Westphalian state form and exploration of the 'post-statist' concepts of the *Grossraum* (literally 'big space', a theory of hegemonic 'spheres of influence' that pre-empted the Cold War) and *Nomos* (a constitutive founding of originary law through territorial appropriation and enclosure).[9] Odysseos and Petito, speaking for the contributors to their edited volume on *The International Political Thought of Carl Schmitt*, argue that Schmitt's later writings 'should be regarded as at least as important for International Relations as the writings of other classical realist scholars such as E.H. Carr, Hans Morgenthau, Raymond Aron, Martin Wight, Hedley Bull or Kenneth Waltz'.[10] These later writings of Schmitt no doubt have much to tell us about international relations, but they have not formed a central part of the exceptionalism debate in the way that *Political Theology* and *The Concept of the Political* have. We also need to be careful about reading Schmitt as a source of political wisdom rather than as a symptomatic figure who must be problematized.

This chapter will expand upon the argument made in Chapter 3: that Schmitt is an especially dangerous thinker who must not always be taken at his word. On the one hand this sets Schmitt apart from other scholars of politics and international relations as someone who cannot be so easily accorded his place in the canon. Yet on the other hand a similar if lesser degree of caution must be applied to the 'classical realist scholars' held up by Odysseos and Petito as greats. Some of the most important work in critical international theory has read these figures not simply as sources of wisdom on international relations, but as *symptoms* of the discipline and *expressions* of its dominant tropes. This move has been especially productive in post-structural and feminist approaches to international relations.[11]

Following this line of thought, the way Schmitt is being read by some contemporary scholars is at odds with the way Schmitt needs to be problematized in the exceptionalism debate. To critique exceptionalism, we need to read Schmitt not as a source of wisdom, analysis or critique, but as a *symptom*. We should consider the rise of Schmitt to be a symptom of the rise of practices of exceptionalism, a symptom of exceptions invoked in political and legal discourse, and a symptom of the attempt by many critical scholars to understand those phenomena. This is the statist Schmitt, the Schmitt of *Political Theology* and *The Concept of the Political*, the Schmitt popularized by Agamben, the Schmitt who inspired securitization theory, whose presence resides in the 'legal black hole' of Guantanamo Bay,[12] in the British government's human rights derogations, in the Bush administration's theory of the unitary executive,[13] and in the use of 'enhanced interrogation techniques' and torture. The rise of Schmitt is a symptom of the recent problematization of exceptionalism, which has some of its roots in the time and place of Schmitt himself, but which is also a novel recombination of other problems and practices, which, as I argued in Chapter 6, have historically dispersed roots.

'The exception' and critical political thought

The concept of 'the exception' is enticing to critical scholars of politics, international relations and security because it is a problem of radical contingency and limit. As Schmitt argues, '[t]he exception confounds the unity and order of the rationalist scheme'.[14] 'The exception' is the limit inherent in every schema. It is a critique of scientific certainty. It is the difficulty if not impossibility of imagining an ethics or politics that does not ultimately suffer from the problem of antagonistic or aporetic limits. It is a question of dynamism at the limit of the static, contingency at the limit of positive knowledge, the unthought at the boundaries of the thought. It is a problem of finitude, beyond which reside the stormy seas of the uncertain and unknowable which Kant attempted to signpost closed: here be dragons.[15]

The compelling limit problems invoked in Schmitt's analysis of 'the exception' are found in many other areas of critical thought. The problem of the limits of knowledge is found in the work of Kant, arguably the first to fully articulate a 'critical' mode of thought aware of its own limits in opposition to uncritical dogmatism.[16] The 'exception' is in some ways akin to Kant's 'noumenon', the thing-in-itself beyond phenomenal appearances which exceeds the human capacity for knowledge.[17] The 'exception' also bears a similarity to Gaston Bachelard's concept of the 'epistemological break'[18] that is disruptive to prior schemas of knowledge. Another close concept is the *clinamen*, an uncaused, unpredictable and undetermined event that brings about turbulence within atomic flows, originally found in the atomistic classical philosophy of Democritus, Lucretius and Epicurus, and taken up by various thinkers of the continental tradition such as Antonio Negri,[19] Louis Althusser[20] and Michel Serres.[21] Going further, Derrida has *différance*,[22] Badiou has the *event*,[23] Lacan and Žižek have the *Real*.[24] All of these thinkers express a concern with epistemological and ontological limits, what might reside at or beyond them, and how they impact on social and political life.

It has been a surprise to many that Schmitt keeps company here. We need to appreciate the reasons why he does. David Chandler has been highly critical of the use of Schmitt by critical international theorists, arguing that they misread him for their own purposes, taking him as a critic of liberal universalism rather than a 'realist' concerned with the 'concrete realities' of conflict and order.[25] Chandler's reading of Schmitt urges more awareness of the differences between the historical circumstances Schmitt was addressing (challenges to nation-state sovereignty and inter-imperialist rivalries) and the quite different contemporary circumstances to which he is often applied (usually forms of liberal imperialism or other liberal universalisms).[26] Nevertheless, Chandler underappreciates the philosophical challenge, indeed enticement, that Schmitt expresses.

This challenge has been taken up most seriously by Sergei Prozorov as a metaphysical problem of constitutive excess. Prozorov's self-declared aim is to rescue the critical content of the concept of 'the exception', which he characterizes as a heterotopic space between order and transgression.[27] As Prozorov writes: 'Conceptually, the Schmittian problematic of the exception as the constitutive principle of the political has arguably made a comeback in the critical discourse, though the full significance of Schmitt's political philosophy still remains underestimated'.[28]

Prozorov's underlying argument, developed in several articles and chapters, is that Schmitt's twin logics of 'the political' (as the ultimate distinction between friends and enemies) and 'the exception' (as the limit inherent in every schema) cannot be overcome.[29] They are the irreducible limits of political life.

Prozorov sees the possibility of an ethic of transgression in Schmitt's irreducible limit problems. In pursing this ethic he seeks to liberate Schmitt from existing interpretations and indeed from Schmitt himself. As he argues, 'we shall venture to recast the most controversial or even scandalous aspects of Schmitt's thought as ethical in their own right'.[30] It is difficult to accept Prozorov's choice here. Schmitt's formal concepts cannot be divorced from his 'scandalous' politics so easily. There are many other ways to reach a critical or ethical treatment of problems of transgression and limit.

I have argued elsewhere (with the c.a.s.e. collective) that 'one may ask how much is left of Schmitt after Prozorov's thorough deconstruction'.[31] If it is a case of Schmitt contra Schmitt or Schmitt *qua* 'not-Schmitt', then Prozorov's approach begs the question of why we need Schmitt to broach this set of philosophical, ethical and political problems in the first place. Since these limit problems are not unfamiliar to a great many continental philosophers, why do we need Schmitt to realize the critical possibilities of the concept of 'the exception', especially when many contemporary thinkers are well aware of the fateful entanglement between Schmitt's metaphysics and Schmitt's 'scandalous' politics? It is a mistake to believe that we can cherry-pick the parts of Schmitt we like and ignore those we do not, because they are inseparable.

We know that Schmitt's exceptional event or situation disappears in a circular logic between sovereign declaration and sovereign response. Chapter 3 of this book demonstrates how Schmitt uses the disappearing ground of 'the exception' to construct an ethic of authoritarian national unity while presenting this as a critique of liberal formalism and legal positivism. Contrary to his exoteric claims, Schmitt's argument is not that we should be mindful of the problem of the exception and its critical potentialities, but that under conditions of modernity the sovereign state claims the prerogative of exceptional decision well in advance of the advent of any exceptional event. Schmitt effectively says that we do not know what the exception will look like, but we know it will be a threat to and imperative for the state.

The critical possibilities of the concept of 'the exception' are thoroughly and irrevocably entangled with Schmitt's politics. This is the inherent danger. The real challenge of Schmitt is not that 'the exception' punctures ethico-political universalisms and legal formalisms, but that the state claims complete domain over this radical contingency irrespective of the advent, content or actual existence of the event itself. This is by no means hidden within Schmitt's arguments, as we can see here: 'The exception is that which cannot be subsumed; it defies general codification, but it simultaneously reveals a specifically juristic element – the decision in absolute purity'.[32]

Giorgio Agamben is right to stress that the dubious circularity of Schmitt's exceptionalism reveals the idea of an exceptional gap in the law to be a 'fictitious lacuna'.[33] Sovereign authority declares and then masters a lacuna in the law in order to demonstrate that sovereign authority applies even where it hypothetically does not. Agamben argues that the 'fictitious lacuna' of the legal exception is of decisive strategic importance if the sovereign is to demonstrate its effectively transcendental sovereign capacities.[34] The idea that exceptional events and situations exceed the capacities of the law is merely a strategic move for the constitution of exceptional, unlimited, sovereign authority. Yet although Agamben gives an incisive account of this move, he does little to critique its validity as a model of sovereign power.

Schmitt's account of 'the exception' may well have critical significance but it is highly normative. This is best demonstrated by returning to the comparison between Schmitt's sovereign and Machiavelli's prince first made in Chapter 3. The prince may conquer the vicissitudes of *fortuna*, imposing dominion over contingency, but his reign will never last forever. *Fortuna* always wins in the end.[35] In comparison, Schmitt's sovereign will conquer contingency *so long as there are no constraints on exceptional sovereign power.* This is a barely concealed normative claim that the sovereign *should* have unlimited exceptional prerogatives in (self-declared) times of exception. If the nominal sovereign fails to demonstrate the capacity for exceptional sovereign decision, then another will emerge who can.[36] This works as a kind of threat (of existential destruction or perhaps revolution) to those who would limit exceptional sovereignty. Schmitt does not demonstrate that there is contingency beyond sovereignty (and therefore the possibility of ethico-political transgression), but that sovereignty is all there is. The bearer of sovereignty may change, but sovereignty never dies.[37] Schmitt's sovereign must colonize the past, present and future of any contingent or transgressive exception.

This is not a descriptive or 'realist' claim that the state is the only game in town. As Prozorov rightly stresses, Schmitt's political philosophy abandons 'any a priori identification of the political with the state or any other positive structure of authority'.[38] Schmitt's claim is that 'the concept of the state pre-supposes the concept of the political'.[39] However, this does not mean that 'the political' is completely divorced from the state and therefore free to be co-opted for transgressive ethical purposes. Although the state and the political are not *necessarily* linked, Schmitt's claim works as a Hobbesian normative warning that if the state is not sovereign (i.e. the decisive political entity), then the alternative is much worse.

Schmitt's feared alternative is not Hobbes's state of nature, but either the spectre of communism or an Anglo-American liberal imperialism. The latter, as Leo Strauss argues in his famous commentary on *The Concept of the Political*, tries to negate the political but actually only hides it.[40] Schmitt's critique of liberal universalism is one of the reasons for his recent rise in popularity,[41] but *The Concept of the Political* is just as much a warning that a non-state grouping such as an economic class could oust the state and become the decisive political grouping, seizing the capacity to decide on enemies and the exception and thereby becoming sovereign. As Schmitt argues,

> a class in the Marxian sense ceases to be something purely economic and becomes a political factor when it reaches this decisive point, for example, when Marxists approach the class struggle seriously and treat the class adversary as a real enemy and fight him within a state.[42]

Schmitt's argument is that if the state is not *a priori* identified with the political, then that is all the more reason why the state *must be* normatively identified with the political. As Foucault argues, '[t]he state is at once that which exists, but which does not yet exist enough'.[43]

As explained in Chapter 3, while *The Concept of the Political* is primarily concerned with the sovereign distinction between friends and enemies as the *ultima ratio* of politics, *Political Theology* has a less determined notion of exception, yet despite its contingency the exception as an event or situation is still 'an extreme danger to the existence of the state, or the like'.[44] The sovereign must 'decide on the exception',[45] and as such the exception as event or rupture disappears in a circular nominalist logic.

For this reason it is a mistake to consider that Schmitt represents the idea of constitutive outsides or transgressive moments. There is no exceptional moment in Schmitt bursting forth from an event horizon of critical potentiality, only an 'exception' declared, manipulated and neutralized by Schmitt's sovereign.

This refutes Andreas Behnke's claim that Schmitt 'rid[s] modernity of its last notions of metaphysical foundations and … point[s] to the radically "secular" nature of order'.[46] In fact the opposite is true. Schmitt rids modernity of any *non*-modern notions of metaphysical foundation, such as heavenly salvation or the contingent river of *fortuna*, and replaces them with an abso-lutely modern sovereign state with metaphysical foundations which foresees the contingency of the exception, heralds its arrival and offers our only salvation from it. *Political Theology* anyone?

The danger is not, as Behnke argues, that we fail to appreciate the creative role of limits and the impossibility of an order without a constitutive outside, but that we completely miss Schmitt's sleight of hand that makes the exceptional sovereign state everything and the exceptional moment nothing. The exception as moment, event or limit is not important for Schmitt; it does not in fact exist, except through the decision of the sovereign. The whole purpose of Schmitt's work on the exception is not to make us aware of the problem of limits and outsides, but to use the problem of limits and outsides to construct a normative account of state sovereignty as necessarily unified, unlimited, irrepressible, transcendent and God-like. As Schmitt argues here: 'The existence of the state is undoubted proof of its superiority over the validity of the legal norm. The decision frees itself from all normative ties and becomes in the true sense absolute'.[47] Despite Schmitt's claim that the decision is free from normative ties, the sovereign state and its capacity for decision are the essence of Schmitt's normative and metaphysical argument.

Schmitt's absolutist nation-state is by no means a fleeting necessity, reluctantly called for in times of emergency to suspend the normal order for the sake of security. Rather, for Schmitt, it is something highly desirable. It is naïve for Behnke to argue that, 'for Schmitt, this suspension is always temporary, and in defence of order'.[48] Schmitt is uncompromising in his valorization of the exception and his disdain for the rule or norm:

> The exception is more interesting than the rule. The rule proves nothing; the exception proves everything: It confirms not only the rule but also its existence, which derives only from the exception. In the exception the power of real life breaks through the crust of a mechanism that has become torpid by repetition.[49]

Behnke argues that the critical attractiveness of Schmitt is that he signals the 'impossibility of any "self-immanence" of order',[50] and that there is always a constitutive and transgressive exceptional outside. But this fails to consider that while Schmitt may deconstruct the self-immanence of order, he does this in order to construct a simultaneously self-immanent and transcendent form of state sovereignty.

A critique of exceptionalism is not possible on Schmitt's terms, only a valorization. How, then, can we address the question posed throughout this book? Can we critique exceptionalism in such a way that does not reify sovereign state power? How can we win the argument with Schmitt?

Prozorov's work presents several different avenues for taking on Schmitt, but none of these is ultimately satisfactory. We have heard how Prozorov's work on the possibility of a Schmittian ethics turns Schmitt into something unrecognizable.[51] Prozorov's previous article, 'X/Xs: Toward a General Theory of the Exception',[52] deals with Schmitt so formally and deconstructs him so thoroughly that there is nothing much left.[53] In 2007, following these pieces, Prozorov presented an as yet unpublished paper entitled 'The World Community and the Closure of the Political: How to Overcome Carl Schmitt'.[54] In this paper, Prozorov muses on two decades of contemporary debate on Schmitt, arguing that both Schmitt and his concept of the political have yet to be overcome in attempts to rethink the political:[55]

> It is as if Schmitt's political theory functions as a negative foundation of the current discourse on rethinking the political, i.e. something that must be presupposed and traversed as a precondition of the very act of its transcendence, which ironically appears to lead us nowhere than back to Schmitt.[56]

Prozorov's observation, or perhaps complaint, is that there are very few, if any, self-declared Schmittians. Prozorov claims that scholars get into Schmitt only in order to get out of him, but they fail: antagonism cannot be reduced to agonism (Mouffe),[57] enmity cannot be bracketed and contained on common ground (Žižek),[58] and the decision cannot be destroyed through deconstruction (Derrida).[59] Prozorov argues that Schmitt's dualistic political logic is *immutable*. His suggestion, his way to overcome Schmitt is 'to invent a conceptual constellation ... in which the logic of the political is no longer operative'.[60] Prozorov's eventual answer, via Badiou and Agamben, is 'love'. As he explains, citing Agamben in places:

> love contains all the prerequisites of 'happy life' as 'an absolutely profane "sufficient life" that has reached the perfection of its own power and of its own communicability – a life over which sovereignty and right no longer have any hold'. In this manner, love indeed begins (only) when the logic of the political arrives at its end.[61]

Although it is philosophically sound, there is clearly a strong dose of irony in Prozorov's argument. He refers to Agamben's idea of 'a "happy life" of love' only 'half-jokingly'.[62] For Prozorov, the only way to overcome Schmitt is either through irony or by making him into something else. Is the underlying argument that we cannot really overcome Schmitt at all?

Prozorov understands better than anyone why it is so difficult to escape the orbit of Schmitt. Yet he does not entertain the key move which *can* win the argument with Schmitt. This is the Foucauldian move to the *empirical*. The move to the empirical does not destroy Schmitt's immutable logic like Prozorov's ironic move to love, but instead disperses it and confounds it. It disrupts the reification of both the metaphysical rupture of exception and the God-like sovereign who would declare it. The move to the empirical is both a philosophical and political move which directly challenges the symptomatic Schmittian understanding of exceptionalism and the 'war on terror'.

The Foucauldian alternative

Foucault is the necessary antidote to Schmitt. He understands the seriousness of the problem and offers an alternative. As he claims in *'Society Must be Defended'*: 'This theory of sovereignty ... is the great trap we are in danger of falling into when we try to analyze power'.[63] Schmitt may well point to the 'impossibility of any "self-immanence" of order',[64] but Foucault reveals the impossibility of any self-immanence of sovereignty. What we need in response to the politics of the exception is precisely what Foucault famously called for: 'a political philosophy that isn't erected around the problem of sovereignty ... We need to cut off the King's head'.[65]

This is exactly what has been done by numerous scholars who take up this Foucauldian challenge and successfully break free of the orbit of Schmitt in their analysis of exceptionalism. For them the problem of exceptionalism is not located in the metaphysical rupture of the 'exceptional' event, in structural flaws in liberal politics and positive law, or in the sovereign decision. Rather, exceptionalism is a problem of, in Didier Bigo's words, a 'multiplicity of practices of government'.[66]

It is Paul Veyne, in 'Foucault Revolutionizes History' (first published in 1978), who most clearly recognizes the innovation of Foucault's approach. It stresses *practice* over objects, ideology and agency. As Veyne argues:

> Foucault has not discovered a previously unknown new agency, called practice; he has made the effort to see people's practices *as they really are*; what he is talking about is the same thing every historian is talking about, what people do. The difference is simply that Foucault undertakes to speak about practice *precisely*, to describe its convoluted forms, instead of referring to it in vague and noble terms.[67]

From this Foucauldian perspective there is no 'vague and noble' idealist metaphysical object called the 'exception' that determines political behaviour, there is no special form of sovereign agency that decides on the exception, and there is no dialectical motor of history manifest in the structural limits of liberal politics and law. There is merely practice: *what people do.*

Foucault's method is to refuse to begin his analysis with given concepts like the state or sovereignty. Rather than start with avowedly timeless political objects and try to establish how concrete practices derive from them, Foucault wishes to understand how practices are rationalized and formed into these timeless political objects. As he puts it in his opening methodological comments in the lecture series *The Birth of Biopolitics*:

> I would like to point out straightaway that choosing to talk about or to start from governmental practice is obviously and explicitly a way of not taking as a primary, original, and already given object, notions such as the sovereign, sovereignty, the people, subjects, the state, and civil society,

that is to say, all those universals employed by sociological analysis, historical analysis, and political philosophy in order to account for real governmental practice. For my part, I would like to do exactly the opposite and, starting from this practice as it is given, but at the same time as it reflects on itself and is rationalized, show how certain things – state and society, sovereign and subjects, etcetera – were actually able to be formed, and the status of which should obviously be questioned.[68]

Schmitt posits the existence of a 'universal' problem, that of 'the exception', to account for, rationalize and legitimate governmental practices of exceptionalism. Agamben goes even further when he locates the exception in the politics of the Greeks and Romans, treating it as a timeless problem that has always impinged on politics even if we did not previously realize it. Instead of beginning with 'the exception', Foucault would begin with *practices* of exceptionalism. The Foucaudian approach is to ask how a whole series of practices came to be articulated around a supposedly universal concept which did not previously exist. Referring to this method as used in his previous studies, Foucault explains that,

It was a matter of showing by what conjunctions a whole set of practices – from the moment they become coordinated with a regime of truth – was able to make what does not exist (madness, disease, delinquency, sexuality, etcetera), nonetheless become something, something however that continues not to exist.[69]

With this method in mind we can ask: how have a whole series of quite different practices, which I do not need to list again, come to be articulated around the problem of the exception? How have a whole series of governmental technologies coalesced and been given legitimacy by the recent 'truth' of the notion that exceptional times call for exceptional measures? The aim, according to Foucault,

is to show how the coupling of a set of practices and a regime of truth form an apparatus (dispositif) of knowledge-power that effectively marks out in reality that which does not exist and legitimately submits it to the division between true and false.[70]

Contrary to Schmitt's claim that the objective 'exception' reveals the necessity of the decision, we can deploy Veyne's Foucauldian argument that '[o]bjects seem to determine our behaviour, but our practice determines its own objects in the first place'.[71] The exception does not determine practices of exceptionalism, but the other way around. And the practice of exceptionalism that determines the exceptional object is not the transcendent sovereign decision that Schmitt constructs, repeated in Agamben and securitization theory, but only the 'crooked and dissimilar contours of the real practices that succeed one another in history'.[72] In other words, it amounts to a multiplicity of heterogeneous practices of government, the origins of which are historically dispersed.

Scholarly approaches to exceptionalism that break free of the orbit of Schmitt describe practices of exceptionalism in all their dispersed, non-sovereign-centred heterogeneity. They show that 'exceptions' are constructed through practices of exceptionalism, not through a transcendental sovereign nominalism built around an original and timeless exception. As Bigo succinctly puts it, '[d]ecisionism is an illusion'.[73]

Common to these approaches is an understanding that exceptionalism is not where it is supposed to be.[74] Heterogeneous practices of exceptionalism do not reside in the transcendent sovereign decision, but in the practices of 'petty sovereigns'[75] merely following procedures, in the machinery of dispersed forms of government and in the unexpected margins of social life. The individuals, operatives, agents and practitioners engaged in these practices are not automatons; they are aware of what they are doing, they follow rules and procedures which they rationalize and represent to themselves as necessary, which they perhaps depart from at times and rationalize again, but there is nothing transcendent in their practices that, as Schmitt puts it, 'breaks through the crust of a mechanism that has become torpid by repetition'.[76] Veyne argues that those involved in the Foucauldian notion of 'practice'

> must not be sleepwalkers; they must have their own representations of certain technical or social rules, and they have to have the requisite mentality or ideology. All of this constitutes a practice. But the people involved do not know what this practice is: it 'goes without saying' for them.[77]

This meticulously empirical and material approach to history does not deny agency, but it does not reify a special sovereign agency that transcends, traverses or transgresses exceptional limits. The move to practice is not deterministic, but understands agency within historical conditions of possibility and the limited self-understanding of any agent. For example, Veyne's understanding of the agency of a political governor is quite different to the quasi-theological sovereign of Schmitt:

> the governor who gives his flock free bread or denies it gladiators believes he is doing what every governor has to do ... he is not aware that his practice, observed in and of itself, conforms to a specific grammar, that it embodies a specific politics.[78]

And similarly, Veyne argues with regard to a king that

> he is aware only of his own reactions, that is, he knows what he is doing, when he reacts to events by making decisions. But he does not understand that these particular decisions are a function of a certain royal practice, just as a lion's decisions are a function of being a lion.[79]

The Foucauldian method does not deny the existence of policy decisions or the choices of political leaders. It is not as simple as a bottom-up approach as opposed to a top-down one. For example, the lawyer Philippe Sands has identified and explored at length the effects of the infamous 'Rumsfeld memo' which authorized 'enhanced interrogation techniques', but this does not turn Rumsfeld into Schmitt's exceptional sovereign.[80] Decisions are merely a function of practice. The Foucauldian approach aims to undermine the special status of such decisions, to destroy Schmitt's attempt to give them a transcendental, theological quality, to remove them from the special realm of contingency, limit, uncertainty, threat and necessity that Schmitt constructs, and to account for their apparent truth and legitimacy in empirical, not metaphysical, terms. The aim is to explain how the truth and legitimacy of exceptionalism, the *dispositif* of exceptionalism, came to exist under present conditions.

As Foucault explains of his method:

> this does not mean showing how it was possible for an error to be constructed – or how an illusion could be born, but how a particular regime of truth, and therefore not an error, makes something that does not exist able to become something. It is not an illusion since it is precisely a set of practices, real practices, which established it and thus imperiously marks it out in reality.[81]

As we will see, empirical research projects on practices of 'exceptionalism' demonstrate that 'exceptionalism' is not a legal, philosophical or political category. It is merely a grouping of practices that have been articulated around a newly legitimate discourse of exception. Their naming as exceptional is not their point of origin, and the practices themselves are not often recent inventions. Even though their current form and configuration may be original, they are often only variations of practices that already exist and have historical precedent. Chapter 6 made this argument about the peculiar combination of archaic and modern modalities of power over the body and truth found in Guantanamo Bay. As Veyne argues: 'everything is historical, and everything depends on everything else'.[82] Empirical investigations into practices of exceptionalism undermine the idealized decisionism of Schmitt and the Schmittian literature along these lines. The Foucauldian move to practice eliminates the spectre of a transcendental sovereign agency that inhabits the arena of the exceptional.

Examples of the Foucauldian alternative

Let us now look at some examples of this kind of work. In her article 'Guantánamo Bay and the Annihilation of the Exception', Fleur Johns argues that the practices of the camp are designed to avoid precisely the kind of contingent decisionism valorized by Schmitt. This is by no means a defence of the camp, but a call to re-examine the politics of its practices as part of any critique. Her research documents the self-proclaimed strenuous efforts of camp officials and military legal staff to follow procedures and regulations. Taking these claims seriously, Johns argues that although the category of unlawful combatant 'implies an extra-legal status, these detainees have, since the outset, been the focus of painstaking work of legal classification'.[83] Instead of a space of exception, Johns's interpretation is that the detention camp 'may be read as a profoundly anti-exceptional legal artefact'.[84]

Far from finding the camp a space of 'utter lawlessness', Johns finds in Guantanamo Bay a space 'filled to the brim with expertise, procedure, scrutiny and analysis'.[85] The creation of an entire regime of military tribunals, quasi-legal procedural categories and standard operating procedures, not to mention their frequent revision in response to judicial rulings,[86] has clearly occupied the administrative structures of the US executive and military for many thousands of hours of labour. This is not sovereign decision in the realm of contingent emergency, but quite the opposite. Johns shows that the '*experience* of decision-making' of the operatives involved is in general one of 'deferral and disavowal' to established processes and procedures.[87] The categories and administrative prose of the camp explicitly seek to avoid the exceptional nominalism represented by Schmitt's 'decision'. Far from the idealized exceptionalism found in Schmitt, the practices of the camp seem strenuously geared towards their own regularization and normalization.

In another example, Louise Amoore uses Derrida to argue that the deferral of practitioners to procedures is no decision at all, but 'simply the application of a body of knowledge of, at the very least, a rule or norm'.[88] For operatives in the complex apparatus of the sprawling 'homeland security' project, 'decisions' amount to nothing more than following established procedures and applying the calculations of knowledge-based systems. As Amoore argues: 'From the algorithmic "decision trees" that appear on the screens of the anti-terror hotline operator, to the pre-screened visualizations of the border guard, in fact no decisions are taken at all, they are only deferred into a pre-programmed calculation'.[89] The agency of Amoore's research subjects is not that of Schmitt's exceptional sovereign mastering the stormy seas of contingency, but precisely what Veyne describes: a conjunction of the 'requisite mentality', representations of 'technical and social rules', and the bringing 'into material reality [of] the potentialities of his historical period' that constitute a practice.[90]

Amoore's research supports Judith Butler's analysis of the so-called 'war on terror', which similarly displaces the grand sovereign decision. In the practices of the 'war on terror', judgement is devolved to unspecified individuals within dispersed governmental machineries, whom Butler characterizes as 'petty sovereigns'.[91] Contra Schmitt, and in a clearly Foucauldian vein, Butler argues against the temptation to attribute these practices to 'something called the "state," imagined as a powerful unity'. Butler contends that '[t]his description doubtless misdescribes the situation … since governmentality designates a field of political power in which tactics and aims have become diffuse, and in which political power fails to take on a unitary and causal form'.[92] Her analysis makes the vital move to an empirically dispersed understanding of power in its many forms.

We can see Veyne's limited form of practice-based agency in Butler's 'petty sovereigns' too, subjectified by their functions and responsibilities, but subject to the specific grammar of their practices, believing they are 'doing what every governor has to do'.[93] Butler argues thus:

> Of course, they are not true sovereigns; their power is delegated, and they do not fully control the aims that animate their actions. Power precedes them, and constitutes them as "sovereigns," a fact that already gives the lie to sovereignty.[94]

Butler ties the Foucauldian concept of governmentality to her own concept of performativity in order to describe the effect of these practices. Their repeated performance by operatives serves to constitute them as normal, to regularize practices of exceptionalism as ordinary functions of governmental practice.[95] This supports Johns's analysis that many of the supposedly 'exceptional' practices of the 'war on terror' work *away from* Schmitt's transcendental sovereign decision towards their own normalization. Practices of 'exceptionalism', a notion now very much in scare quotes, have at their heart the aim of, in Johns's words, 'the annihilation of the exception'.[96] This is an exception which never existed in the first place. To repeat Foucault's words, 'a whole set of practices was able to make what does not exist … nonetheless become something, something however that continues not to exist'.[97] And not only does the exception continue not to exist, but practices of exceptionalism work towards their own annihilation. The exception is indeed the rapidly disappearing ground of exceptionalism.

All of this runs contra to Schmitt and Schmittian understandings of security, particularly their construction and reification of a space of transgression or exception beyond the realm of order or the norm. The direction of travel of practices of exceptionalism is in precisely the opposition direction; not constructing the exceptional, but constructing the normal, fleeing from Schmitt's space of emergency and contingency. This 'norm' is the product not of Schmitt's decision on the exception, but merely of the performative repetition of practices.

These Foucault-inspired empirical researches challenge not only the imagined metaphysical realm of emergency, but also the location of exceptionalism. Johns, Amoore and Butler all locate exceptionalism away from the sovereign centre, instead locating it in dispersed officialdom. Going further, a remarkable article by Roxanne Lynn Doty locates exceptionalism away from the field of government entirely.[98]

Doty's article explores the rise of volunteer groups in the southern border states of the US who patrol the US/Mexican border without official sanction. The best known of these is the 'Minutemen', whose discourses invariably make strong and often counter-intuitive links between 9/11, terrorism, security and (Mexican) immigration.[99]

For Doty, the decisions of volunteers to take matters into their own hands in response to their perception of cross-border migration as a security threat challenges the nominalist assumptions of Schmittian exceptionalism and securitization theory. As she asks, '[w]hat if "the state" is not the only site of the "sovereign decision" on the exception, the enemy, and the political? What if securitization is a widely dispersed and at times amorphous phenomenon not controlled or even initiated by elites?'[100] Going against Schmitt's version of sovereignty, which presupposes that the sovereign speaks for society and is co-existent with society,[101] Doty's case study undermines this social–sovereign unity by highlighting dispersed and marginal forms of decision that nevertheless seek to decide on the exception:

> Border vigilantes and the anti-immigration movement call attention to the possibility that perhaps there is no sovereign or elite voice, in all cases, which definitively utters security. Rather, widely dispersed utterances constitute a myriad of decisions and can come from what, on first glance, may seem irrelevant or peripheral, perhaps even fringe.[102]

Doty's conclusions go in the same direction as those of Johns, Amoore and Butler: we need to account for practices of exceptionalism without recourse to idealized notions of unitary sovereign decision. As she writes, 'we must be sensitive to the possibility that "on the ground" practices ... often disrupt the concepts and theoretical systems that would seek to illuminate them'.[103]

Conclusions

Practices disrupt concepts, that is the key lesson for critical theorists of security. Practices do not occur in idealized locations like the exceptional limits or zones of transgression that enamour thinkers like Schmitt, Agamben and Prozorov. Exceptionalism occurs elsewhere, away from the centre, away from the limit, away from the concept. It occurs in the dispersed fingers of government, in quiet agencies often away from the public spectacle of politics, in everyday life and at the fringes of society.

Exceptionalism is not where it is supposed to be; not in conceptual terms, not in socio-political terms, not in historical terms. Exceptionalism is supposed to be in the zero-time of now, the time of clear and present danger, in response to a contingent future of threat that erupts into the present.[104] The exception and its attendant decision is supposed to cut through the torpor of everyday life and the banal mechanisms of the administration of things. Except that the exception is only made to exist through the conjunction of a set of practices with a regime of truth that we might call the 'war on terror'. Even then, the exception is the disappearing ground of these practices, 'something ... that continues not to exist'.[105]

The reason why Schmitt appeals to some critical thinkers is that his concepts work as a sharp critique of liberal and rationalistic universalisms. It is ironic that these thinkers allow the exception, a supposedly anti-universalistic concept, to become an ahistorical, 'primary, original, and already given object',[106] a universalism without content that for Schmitt is, indeed *must be*, the absolute domain and prerogative of the state. It is also ironic that Schmitt's writings were polemics against 'politics as technology'[107] but as far as exceptionalism is concerned politics as technology effectively wins out over Schmitt's idealized sovereign decision.

Although this is not quite true. Foucault is not a sociologist. It is not simply a question of the governmental over the political. Although there may be a tendency in some Foucault-inspired literatures to move exclusively to the empirical, Foucault does not abandon a concern with *politics*, although he does not specify *a politics* for us. It is through this refusal or at least abstinence from specifying a politics that Foucault remains open politically.

In Foucault the imperative is always to problematize, always to historicize. How did a particular problem come to be articulated as a problem historically? How did a problem which did not previously exist come to exist as a problem? What practices came to be organized around that problem? What regime of truth came to articulate that problem and give legitimacy to its practices? What regime of truth did those practices legitimize? These are the questions we must ask of the problem of exceptionalism. The exception is not an original political object, but a problem that has a history, both a very recent history and a longer history from other dark times and places that resonate with our own. Foucault's historicism does not test universals against history, but assumes *a priori* that universals or idealized concepts do not exist.[108]

Why has Schmitt risen to prominence? Not because the concept of the exception has always existed, with Schmitt as its twentieth-century prophet, but because the exception has become a problem of government through the conjunction of a series of practices with a certain regime of truth. Simultaneously the exception has become a problem of critique for those who wish to understand 'the art of governing'[109] and the conditions of possibility for a *dispositif* of exceptionalism that has somehow come to be understood by some as 'the reasoned way of governing best'.[110]

The exception is not an originary object. It can be historicized. It does not exist, but it has a history through which it has been made into *something*, a *problem*. It is not brought into being by the exceptional sovereign decision. The exception is only the correlate of a heterogeneous array of practices looking for legitimacy. The exceptional decision is only a function of that *dispositif*.

Schmitt does not win this argument, nor should we help him do so.

Notes

1 Introduction

1 For examples of this debate, see Joanna Apap, *Justice and Home Affairs in the EU: Liberty and Security Issues after Enlargement* (Cheltenham: Edward Elgar, 2004); Didier Bigo and Anastassia Tsoukala, *Terror, Insecurity and Liberty: Illiberal Practices of Liberal Regimes after 9/11*, Routledge Studies in Liberty and Security (London: Routledge, 2008); Nancy Chang, *Silencing Political Dissent: How Post-September 11 Anti-Terrorism Measures Threaten Our Civil Liberties* (New York: Seven Stories; London: Turnaround, 2002); David B. Cohen and John Wilson Wells, *American National Security and Civil Liberties in an Era of Terrorism*, 1st edn (New York: Palgrave Macmillan, 2004); David Cole and James X. Dempsey, *Terrorism and the Constitution: Sacrificing Civil Liberties in the Name of National Security*, 3rd edn (New York: New Press, 2006); M. Katherine B. Darmer, Robert M. Baird, and Stuart E. Rosenbaum, *Civil Liberties vs. National Security: In a Post-9/11 World* (Amherst, N.Y.: Prometheus Books, 2004); Laura K. Donohue, *The Cost of Counterterrorism: Power, Politics, and Liberty* (Cambridge; New York: Cambridge University Press, 2008); Richard M. Ebeling and Jacob G. Hornberger, eds, *Liberty, Security, and the War on Terrorism* (Fairfax, Virg.: Future of Freedom Foundation, 2002); Danny Goldberg, Victor Goldberg and Robert Greenwald, *It's a Free Country: Personal Freedom in America after September 11* (New York: RDV Books, 2002); Richard C. Leone and Greg Anrig, *The War on Our Freedoms: Civil Liberties in an Age of Terrorism*, 1st edn (New York: BBS Public Affairs, 2003); Tamar Meisels, *The Trouble with Terror: Liberty, Security, and the Response to Terrorism* (Cambridge: Cambridge University Press, 2008); Eric A. Posner and Adrian Vermeule, *Terror in the Balance: Security, Liberty, and the Courts* (New York: Oxford University Press, 2007); Stephen J. Schulhofer, *The Enemy Within: Intelligence Gathering, Law Enforcement, and Civil Liberties in the Wake of September 11* (New York: Century Foundation Press, 2002).

2 Carl Schmitt, *Political Theology: Four Chapters on the Concept of Sovereignty*, trans. George Schwab (Cambridge, Mass.; London: MIT Press, 1985), p. 5.

3 See, for example, Giorgio Agamben, *Homo Sacer: Sovereign Power and Bare Life*, trans. Daniel Heller-Roazen (Stanford, Calif.: Stanford University Press, 1998); Giorgio Agamben, *State of Exception*, trans. Kevin Attell (Chicago, Ill.; London: University of Chicago Press, 2005); Jef Huysmans, 'Minding Exceptions. Politics of Insecurity and Liberal Democracy', *Contemporary Political Theory*, vol. 3, no. 3 (2004); Chantal Mouffe, *The Challenge of Carl Schmitt* (London: Verso, 1999); Louize Odysseos and Fabio Petito, eds, *The International Political Thought of Carl Schmitt: Terror, Liberal War and the Crisis of Global Order* (London; New York: Routledge, 2007); Sergei Prozorov, 'The Ethos of Insecure Life: Reading Carl

Schmitt's Existential Decisionism as a Foucauldian Ethics' in *The International Political Thought of Carl Schmitt: Terror, Liberal War and the Crisis of Global Order,* ed. Louize Odysseos and Fabio Petito (London; New York: Routledge, 2007); Sergei Prozorov, 'X/Xs: Toward a General Theory of the Exception', *Alternatives: Global, Local, Political,* no. 30 (2005); William Rasch, 'Conflict as a Vocation: Carl Schmitt and the Possibility of Politics', *Theory, Culture & Society,* vol. 17, no. 6 (2000); Michael C. Williams, 'Words, Images, Enemies: Securitization and International Politics', *International Studies Quarterly,* vol. 47 (2003).

4 Agamben, *Homo Sacer*; Agamben, *State of Exception.*

5 Barry Buzan and Ole Wæver, *Regions and Powers: The Structure of International Security,* Cambridge Studies in International Relations, 91 (Cambridge: Cambridge University Press, 2003); Barry Buzan, Ole Wæver and Jaap de Wilde, *Security: A New Framework for Analysis* (Boulder, Colo.: Lynne Rienner, 1998); Ole Wæver, 'Securitization and Desecuritization' in *On Security,* ed. Ronnie D. Lipschutz (New York; Chichester: Columbia University Press, 1995).

6 Michel Foucault, 'Truth and Power' in *Power/Knowledge: Selected Interviews and Other Writings 1972–1977,* ed. Colin Gordon (New York: Harvester Wheatsheaf, 1980), p. 121.

7 Gilles Deleuze, *Foucault* (London: Continuum, 2006), p. 51; Beatrice Han, *Foucault's Critical Project: Between the Transcendental and the Historical, Atopia* (Stanford, Calif.: Stanford University Press, 2002); Christina Hendricks, 'Foucault's Kantian Critique: Philosophy and the Present', *Philosophy & Social Criticism,* vol. 34, no. 4 (2008); K. Robinson, 'An Immanent Transcendental: Foucault, Kant and Critical Philosophy', *Radical Philosophy,* no. 141 (2007); Jon Simons, *Foucault and the Political* (London; New York: Routledge, 1994), p. 13.

8 Michel Foucault, *The Order of Things: An Archaeology of the Human Sciences* (London: Routledge, 2001), pp. 351–55.

1 The liberty/security discourse and the problem of the exception

1 See Richard A. Falk, *The Costs of War: International Law, the UN, and World Order after Iraq* (New York; London: Routledge, 2008); Philippe Sands, *Lawless World: Making and Breaking Global Rules* (London: Penguin, 2006); Phil Shiner and Andrew Williams, *The Iraq War and International Law* (Oxford: Hart Publishing, 2008).

2 Giorgio Agamben et al., *Arxipèlag d'excepcions: Sobiranies de l'extraterritorialitat (Archipelago of Exceptions: Sovereignties of Extraterritoriality)* (Barcelona: CCCB, 2005).

3 See *All Party Parliamentary Group on Extraordinary Rendition* (cited 3 April 2009); available from http://www.extraordinaryrendition.org/; Stephen Grey, *Ghost Plane: The Inside Story of the CIA's Secret Rendition Programme* (London: Hurst, 2006); Trevor Paglen and A. C. Thompson, *Torture Taxi: On the Trail of the CIA's Rendition Flights* (Hoboken, N.J.: Melville House, 2006).

4 See, for example, Moazzam Begg and Victoria Brittain, *Enemy Combatant: A British Muslim's Journey to Guantanamo and Back* (London: Free Press, 2006); Marc Falkoff, *Poems from Guantánamo: The Detainees Speak* (Iowa City, IA.: University of Iowa Press, 2007); Shafiq Rasul, Asif Iqbal and Rhuhel Ahmed, 'Report of Former Guantanamo Detainees. Composite Statement: Detention in Afghanistan and Guantanamo Bay' (New York: Center for Constitutional Rights, 2004).

5 See, for example, CHALLENGE, *The Changing Landscape of European Liberty and Security* (research project and online observatory); available from www.libertysecurity.org; Bülent Diken and Carsten B. Laustsen, *The Culture of Exception:*

Sociology Facing the Camp, International Library of Sociology (London; New York: Routledge, 2005).

6 See Thomas Hobbes, *Leviathan*, ed. Richard Tuck (Cambridge: Cambridge University Press, 1996), p. 89.

7 See, for example, Mark Neocleous, 'Security, Liberty and the Myth of Balance: Towards a Critique of Security Politics', *Contemporary Political Theory*, vol. 6, no. 2 (2007); Jeremy Waldron, 'Security and Liberty: The Image of Balance', *Journal of Political Philosophy*, vol. 11, no. 2 (2003).

8 Chang, *Silencing Political Dissent*.

9 Schulhofer, *The Enemy Within: Intelligence Gathering, Law Enforcement, and Civil Liberties in the Wake of September 11*.

10 Goldberg, Goldberg and Greenwald, *It's a Free Country: Personal Freedom in America after September 11*.

11 Chang, *Silencing Political Dissent*, pp. 19–42.

12 Donohue, *The Cost of Counterterrorism: Power, Politics, and Liberty*, pp. 1–2; Kam C. Wong, 'The Making of the USA Patriot Act I: The Legislative Process and Dynamics', *International Journal of the Sociology of Law*, vol. 34, no. 3 (2006); Kam C. Wong, 'The USA Patriot Act: Some Unanswered Questions', *International Journal of the Sociology of Law*, vol. 34, no. 1 (2006).

13 Chang, *Silencing Political Dissent*, pp. 67–68.

14 Ibid., pp. 69–87.

15 Schulhofer, *The Enemy Within: Intelligence Gathering, Law Enforcement, and Civil Liberties in the Wake of September 11*, p. 65.

16 Ibid.

17 Ibid., p. 66.

18 Ibid., p. 17.

19 See also Fox Butterfield, 'A Nation Challenged: The Interviews; a Police Force Rebuffs F.B.I. on Querying Mideast Men', *New York Times*, 21 November 2001. Ted Gottfried, *Homeland Security versus Constitutional Rights* (Brookfield, Conn.: 21st Century Books, 2003), p. 43.

20 Andrew Kirkland, 'The Weight of a Nation' in *It's a Free Country: Personal Freedom in America after September 11*, ed. Danny Goldberg, Victor Goldberg and Robert Greenwald (New York: RDV Books, 2002), p. 309.

21 Ibid., p. 310.

22 Chantal Mouffe, *The Democratic Paradox* (London: Verso, 2000).

23 See, for example, BBC News, *BBC Breakfast with Frost Interview: David Blunkett, Home Secretary* (18 November 2001), available from http://news.bbc.co.uk/1/hi/programmes/breakfast_with_frost/1662785.stm.

24 E.U. Network of Independent Experts in Fundamental Rights (cfr-cdf), 'The Balance between Freedom and Security in the Response by the European Union and Its Member States to the Terrorist Threats' (European Commission, Unit A5, 'Citizenship, Charter of fundamental rights, Racism, Xenophobia, Daphne program', of DG Justice and Home Affairs., 2003), p. 6.

25 Ibid.

26 Ibid., p. 11.

27 Ibid., p. 10.

28 See, for example, Council of Europe, 'Council of Europe Convention on Action against Trafficking in Human Beings (Cets No. 197)' (2005); Council of Europe, 'Council of Europe Convention on Laundering, Search, Seizure and Confiscation of the Proceeds from Crime and on the Financing of Terrorism' (2005).

29 Agamben, *Homo Sacer*, p. 106.

30 E.U. Network of Independent Experts in Fundamental Rights (cfr-cdf), 'The Balance between Freedom and Security in the Response by the European Union and Its Member States to the Terrorist Threats', p. 36.

154   *Notes*

31 Ibid.
32 Ibid.
33 Ibid., p. 37.
34 Ibid.
35 'A Bill with Huge Powers', *Guardian*, 20 June 2003.
36 Joint Committee on the Draft Civil Contingencies Bill, 'Draft Civil Contingencies Bill, Report and Evidence' (London: The Stationery Office, 2003), p. 12.
37 Ibid., p. 16.
38 Ibid., p. 17.
39 Ibid., p. 16.
40 Ibid., p. 19.
41 Ibid., p. 13.
42 See UK Government, 'The Government's Response to the Report of the Joint Committee on the Draft Civil Contingencies Bill' (London: The Stationery Office, 2004).
43 Liberty, 'Liberty Response to the Draft Civil Contingency Bill' (2003), p. 9.
44 Ibid., p. 10.
45 See, for example, Eunan O'Halpin, 'British Intelligence and the Case for Confronting Iraq: Evidence from the Butler and Hutton Reports', *Irish Studies in International Affairs*, vol. 16 (2005).
46 '[T]he operation of government is carried on to a large extent not directly through laws made by Parliament, but by means of rules made by members of the executive under powers delegated to them by Parliament. This body of rules is known as delegated legislation, but it may also be described as secondary (or subordinate) legislation', A. W. Bradley and K. D. Ewing, *Constitutional and Administrative Law*, 14th edn (Harlow: Pearson Longman, 2007), p. 675.
47 See ibid., pp. 73, 688, 759.
48 Liberty, 'Liberty Response to the Draft Civil Contingency Bill', p. 13.
49 E.g. Joint Committee on the Draft Civil Contingencies Bill, 'Draft Civil Contingencies Bill, Report and Evidence', p. 52; Liberty, 'Liberty Response to the Draft Civil Contingency Bill', p. 13.
50 Liberty, 'Liberty Response to the Draft Civil Contingency Bill', p. 13.
51 Ibid.
52 See Annelise Riles, *Rethinking the Masters of Comparative Law* (Oxford: Hart, 2001), p. 80. Riles explains that 'the Nazi legal of theory of *Führerprinzip* [held] that all law emanated from the state, as embodied by the *Führer*'.
53 UK Government, 'The Government's Response to the Report of the Joint Committee on the Draft Civil Contingencies Bill', pp. 14–15.
54 Cabinet Office, 'Civil Contingencies Act 2004: A Short Guide' (2004), p. 6.
55 'Civil Contingencies Act' (2004), p. 27.
56 Joint Committee on the Draft Civil Contingencies Bill, 'Draft Civil Contingencies Bill, Report and Evidence', p. 50.
57 UK Government, 'The Government's Response to the Report of the Joint Committee on the Draft Civil Contingencies Bill', p. 17.
58 See Nevil Johnson, *Reshaping the British Constitution: Essays in Political Interpretation* (Basingstoke: Palgrave, 2004), pp. 7–20; Anthony Stephen King, *The British Constitution* (Oxford: Oxford University Press, 2007), pp. 19–23.
59 See Isaiah Berlin, *Liberty: Incorporating Four Essays on Liberty* (Oxford: Oxford University Press, 2002), pp. 166–217.
60 R. B. J. Walker, 'Sovereignties, Exceptions, Worlds' in *Sovereign Lives: Power in Global Politics*, ed. Jenny Edkins, Véronique Pin-Fat and Michael J. Shapiro (New York; London: Routledge, 2004), p. 243.
61 See, for example, Nadine Gurr and Benjamin Cole, *The New Face of Terrorism: Threats from Weapons of Mass Destruction* (London: I. B. Tauris, 2000); Charles W.

Kegley, *The New Global Terrorism: Characteristics, Causes, Controls* (Upper Saddle River, N.J.: Prentice Hall; London: Pearson Education, 2003); Walter Laqueur, *The New Terrorism: Fanaticism and the Arms of Mass Destruction* (London: Phoenix, 1999).

62 See, for example, Mabel Berezin and Martin Schain, *Europe without Borders: Remapping Territory, Citizenship, and Identity in a Transnational Age* (Baltimore: Johns Hopkins University Press, 2003); Nick Vaughan-Williams, *Border Politics: The Limits of Sovereign Power* (Edinburgh: Edinburgh University Press, 2009); R. B. J. Walker, *After the Globe, before the World* (London; New York: Routledge, 2009).

63 Philippe Bonditti, 'L'Organisation de la lutte anti-terroriste aux Etats-Unis', *Cultures & conflits*, no. 44 (2001).

64 Schmitt, *Political Theology*, p. 5.

65 Gaston Bachelard, *The Formation of the Scientific Mind: A Contribution to a Psychoanalysis of Objective Knowledge*, trans. Mary MacAllester Jones (Manchester: Clinamen, 2002), p. 24.

66 Ibid.

67 Maja Zehfuss, 'Forget September 11', *Third World Quarterly: Journal of Emerging Areas*, vol. 24, no. 3 (2003).

68 Michel Foucault, *The Archaeology of Knowledge*, trans. A. M. Sheridan Smith (London: Routledge, 2002).

69 Beatrice Hanssen, *Critique of Violence: Between Poststructuralism and Critical Theory*, Warwick Studies in European Philosophy (London: Routledge, 2000), p. 162.

70 See, for example, Michel Foucault, *Discipline and Punish: The Birth of the Prison*, trans. Alan Sheridan (London: Penguin, 1999); Michel Foucault, *The History of Sexuality, Vol. 1*, trans. Robert Hurley (London: Penguin, 1990); Michel Foucault, *Madness and Civilization: A History of Insanity in the Age of Reason*, trans. Richard Howard, Routledge Classics (London: Routledge, 2001).

71 Foucault, 'Truth and Power'.

72 Foucault, *The Order of Things*, p. 333.

73 Schmitt, *Political Theology*, p. 5.

74 Walker, 'Sovereignties, Exceptions, Worlds', pp. 240–41.

75 R. B. J. Walker, *Inside/Outside: International Relations as Political Theory* (Cambridge: Cambridge University Press, 1993), p. 4.

76 Walker, 'Sovereignties, Exceptions, Worlds', p. 242.

77 Michel Foucault, *'Society Must Be Defended': Lectures at the Collège de France, 1975–76*, trans. David Macey (New York: Picador, 2002), p. 6.

78 Foucault, 'Truth and Power', p. 133.

2 Freedom and liberty in classic political theory: Hobbes and Kant

1 See, for example, Jürgen Habermas, 'The Horrors of Autonomy: Carl Schmitt in English' in *The New Conservatism: Cultural Criticism and the Historians' Debate*, ed. Shierry Weber Nicholsen (Cambridge, Mass.: MIT Press, 1989); Stephen Holmes, 'Schmitt: The Debility of Liberalism' in *The Anatomy of Antiliberalism* (Cambridge, Mass.; London: Harvard University Press, 1993); Richard Wolin, 'Carl Schmitt: The Conservative Revolutionary Habitus and the Aesthetics of Horror', *Political Theory*, vol. 20, no. 3 (1992).

2 Hobbes, *Leviathan*, p. 11.

3 Ibid., p. 86.

4 William E. Connolly, *The Augustinian Imperative: A Reflection on the Politics of Morality* (Newbury Park, Calif.; London; New Delhi: Sage, 1993), pp. 38–40; Alasdair C. MacIntyre, *A Short History of Ethics: A History of Moral Philosophy*

from the Homeric Age to the Twentieth Century, 2nd edn (London: Routledge, 2002), p. 111; Christopher Morris, *Western Political Thought, Volume One: Plato to Augustine* (London: Longmans, 1967), p. 237.

5 Samuel Isaiah Mintz, *The Hunting of Leviathan: Seventeenth-Century Reactions to the Materialism and Moral Philosophy of Thomas Hobbes* (Bristol: Thoemmes Press, 1997), p. 127.

6 Ibid.

7 Hobbes, *Leviathan*, p. 9.

8 Ibid., p. 147.

9 Ibid., p. 146.

10 Ibid., p. 147.

11 Ibid.

12 Ibid., p. 53.

13 Ibid.

14 Ibid., p. 87.

15 Ibid.

16 Ibid.

17 Ibid.

18 Ibid., p. 89.

19 Ibid., p. 117.

20 Ibid., p. 120.

21 Ibid.

22 Ibid., p. 9.

23 Leo Strauss, *The Political Philosophy of Hobbes, Its Basis and Its Genesis* (Chicago, Ill.: Chicago University Press, 1963), p. viii.

24 Hobbes, *Leviathan*, p. 9.

25 Walker, *Inside/Outside*, p. 20.

26 Hobbes, *Leviathan*, p. 89.

27 J. B. Schneewind, 'Autonomy, Obligation, and Virtue: An Overview of Kant's Moral Philosophy' in *The Cambridge Companion to Kant*, ed. Paul Guyer (Cambridge: Cambridge University Press, 1992), p. 314.

28 Ibid. citing Jean-Jacques Rousseau, *On the Social Contract*, ed. Roger D. Masters, trans. Judith R. Masters (New York: St Martin's Press, 1978), p. 56.

29 Henry E. Allison, *Kant's Theory of Freedom* (Cambridge: Cambridge University Press, 1990), p. 2.

30 Immanuel Kant, *Groundwork for the Metaphysics of Morals*, ed. Allen W. Wood (New Haven, Conn.; London: Yale University Press, 2003). Cited in Schneewind, 'Autonomy, Obligation, and Virtue', p. 320.

31 Allison, *Kant's Theory of Freedom*, p. 2.

32 Schneewind, 'Autonomy, Obligation, and Virtue', p. 330.

33 Mintz, *The Hunting of Leviathan*, p. 119.

34 Ibid.

35 Allison, *Kant's Theory of Freedom*, p. 3.

36 Wolfgang Kersting, 'Politics, Freedom, and Order: Kant's Political Philosophy' in *The Cambridge Companion to Kant*, ed. Paul Guyer (Cambridge: Cambridge University Press, 1992), p. 344.

37 Immanuel Kant, *The Metaphysics of Morals*, ed. Mary J. Gregor, trans. Mary J. Gregor (Cambridge: Cambridge University Press, 1996), p. 24.

38 Kersting, 'Politics, Freedom, and Order', p. 345.

39 Immanuel Kant, 'The Metaphysics of Morals' in *Kant: Political Writings*, ed. Hans Reiss (Cambridge: Cambridge University Press, 1990), p. 134.

40 Mark Timmons, *Kant's Metaphysics of Morals: Interpretative Essays* (Oxford: Oxford University Press, 2002), pp. 46–54.

41 Immanuel Kant, 'An Answer to the Question: "What Is Enlightenment?"' in *Kant: Political Writings*, ed. Hans Reiss (Cambridge: Cambridge University Press, 1990), p. 54.
42 Immanuel Kant, 'Perpetual Peace: A Philosophical Sketch' in *Kant: Political Writings*, ed. Hans Reiss (Cambridge: Cambridge University Press, 1990), p. 112.
43 Ibid., p. 113.
44 Immanuel Kant, 'On the Common Saying: "This May Be True in Theory, but It Does Not Apply in Practice"' in *Kant: Political Writings*, ed. Hans Reiss (Cambridge: Cambridge University Press, 1990), p. 79.
45 Kant, 'Perpetual Peace: A Philosophical Sketch', p. 118.
46 Foucault, *'Society Must Be Defended'*, pp. 16–17.
47 Hobbes, *Leviathan*, p. 98.
48 Kant, 'On the Common Saying: "This May Be True in Theory, but It Does Not Apply in Practice"', p. 79.
49 Strauss, *The Political Philosophy of Hobbes*, p. viii.

3 Carl Schmitt and the politics of the exception

1 Schmitt, *Political Theology*, p. 15.
2 Carl Schmitt, *The Concept of the Political*, trans. George Schwab (Chicago, Ill.: University of Chicago Press, 1996), pp. 28, 35, 36–37, 45, 55.
3 Walter Benjamin, 'Theses on the Philosophy of History' in *Illuminations*, ed. Hannah Arendt (New York: Schocken Books, 1968).
4 There are 1927, 1932 and 1933 versions of *The Concept of the Political*, with subtle changes in each. The currently available English version is translated from the 1932 edition. For more on these changes in relation to Schmitt's personal biography and relationship with the Nazi party, see Gopal Balakrishnan, *The Enemy: An Intellectual Portrait of Carl Schmitt* (London; New York: Verso, 2000).
5 Schmitt, *Political Theology*, p. 6.
6 Ibid.
7 Ibid., p. 5.
8 Concepts which are not without their temporal dimensions. See Walker, *Inside/Outside*, p. 17.
9 Schmitt, *The Concept of the Political*, p. 26.
10 Max Weber, 'Science as a Vocation' in *From Max Weber: Essays in Sociology*, ed. H. H. Gerth and C. Wright Mills (New York: Oxford University Press, 1946), p. 152. Cited in Rasch, 'Conflict as a Vocation', p. 7.
11 Schmitt, *The Concept of the Political*, p. 26.
12 Wolin, 'Carl Schmitt: The Conservative Revolutionary Habitus and the Aesthetics of Horror', p. 442.
13 Leo Strauss, 'Notes on Carl Schmitt, the Concept of the Political' in *Carl Schmitt: The Concept of the Political* (Chicago, Ill.: University of Chicago Press, 1996), p. 84.
14 Ibid.
15 Schmitt, *The Concept of the Political*, p. 54.
16 Schmitt, *Political Theology*, p. 28.
17 Balakrishnan, *The Enemy*, p. 45.
18 Ibid., p. 47.
19 Rasch, 'Conflict as a Vocation'. Citing Carl Schmitt, *Legalität und Legitimität* (Berlin: Duncker and Humblot, 1993), p. 53.
20 Schmitt, *The Concept of the Political*, p. 79.
21 Ibid., p. 78.
22 This is the subject of John McCormick, *Carl Schmitt's Critique of Liberalism: Against Politics as Technology* (Cambridge: Cambridge University Press, 1997).
23 Schmitt, *The Concept of the Political*, pp. 76–77.

24 Ibid., p. 77.
25 Ibid., p. 79.
26 Ibid., p. 78.
27 Frederick von Hayek, although undoubtedly a disciple of Schmitt, is interestingly one of the most polemical and influential exponents of the neo-liberal laissez-faire approach to the market, and gained great influence amongst the resurgent right of the Reagan administration. McCormick argues that Hayek can be considered the result of Schmittian claims about the 'irreducibility' of conflict being applied to the economic rather than political sphere, and hence Hayek similarly advocates its recognition rather than its subjugation/concealment, McCormick, *Carl Schmitt's Critique of Liberalism*, pp. 303–04.
28 Schmitt, *The Concept of the Political*, pp. 77–78.
29 Ibid., p. 78.
30 Ibid., p. 79.
31 Schmitt quoted by Strauss, 'Notes on Carl Schmitt, the Concept of the Political', p. 95.
32 Schmitt, *The Concept of the Political*, p. 79.
33 Ibid., p. 45.
34 Grigoris Ananiadis, 'Carl Schmitt on Kosovo, or, Taking War Seriously' in *Balkan as Metaphor: Between Globalization and Fragmentation*, ed. Dušan I. Bjelic and Obrad Savic (Cambridge, Mass.; London: MIT Press, 2002).
35 Schmitt, *The Concept of the Political*, p. 49.
36 For example, see Andreas Behnke and Linda Bashai, 'War, Violence and the Displacement of the Political' in *The International Political Thought of Carl Schmitt: Terror, Liberal War and the Crisis of Global Order*, eds Louiza Odysseos and Fabio Petito (London; New York: Routledge, 2007); Chantal Mouffe, 'Carl Schmitt's Warning on the Dangers of a Unipolar World' in *The International Political Thought of Carl Schmitt: Terror, Liberal War and the Crisis of Global Order*, eds Louiza Odysseos and Fabio Petito (London; New York: Routledge, 2007).
37 Schmitt, *The Concept of the Political*, p. 46.
38 Schmitt, *Political Theology*, p. 5.
39 Schmitt, *The Concept of the Political*, p. 49.
40 Ibid.
41 Ibid., p. 47.
42 Ibid., p. 49.
43 Jacques Derrida, *Politics of Friendship*, trans. George Collins, *Phronesis* (London: Verso, 1997), p. 120.
44 Ibid., p. 121.
45 Ibid.
46 Schmitt, *The Concept of the Political*, p. 19.
47 Ibid., p. 67.
48 Derrida, *Politics of Friendship*, p. 86.
49 Schmitt, *Political Theology*, p. 6.
50 Ibid.
51 Ibid.
52 Ibid.
53 Ibid., p. 5.
54 Ibid., p. 6.
55 Ibid.
56 Ibid., p. 10.
57 Michel Foucault, Donald Fernand Bouchard and Sherry Simon, *Language, Counter-Memory, Practice: Selected Essays and Interviews* (Oxford: Blackwell, 1977), p. 231.
58 Schmitt, *Political Theology*, p. 7.

59 Ibid., p. 12.
60 Ibid., p. 7.
61 Ibid., p. 6.
62 Ibid., p. 7.
63 Ibid., p. 5.
64 See Niccolo Machiavelli, *The Prince*, trans. Peter E. Bondanella (Oxford; New York: Oxford University Press, 2005), p. 84.
65 Schmitt, *Political Theology*, p. 7.
66 Machiavelli, *The Prince*, pp. 85–86.
67 Schmitt, *Political Theology*, p. 7.
68 Derrida, *Politics of Friendship*, p. 124.
69 Ibid., p. 129.
70 Schmitt, *The Concept of the Political*, p. 32.
71 Schmitt, *Political Theology*, p. 15.

4 Giorgio Agamben's exception: 'the great historico-transcendental destiny of the Occident'

1 Foucault, *The Archaeology of Knowledge*, p. 231.
2 Agamben, *Homo Sacer*, p. 4.
3 Ibid., pp. 1–2.
4 Michel Foucault, *The History of Sexuality, the Will to Knowledge*, trans. Robert Hurley, vol. 1 (New York: Random House, 1978). Cited in Agamben, *Homo Sacer*, p. 3.
5 See Michael Dillon, *Biopolitics of Security in the 21st Century: The Political Economy of Security after Foucault* (London: Routledge, 2010); Michael Dillon and Luis Lobo-Guerrero, 'The Biopolitical Imaginary of Species-Being', *Theory, Culture and Society*, vol. 26, no. 1 (2009); Michael Dillon and Julian Reid, *The Liberal Way of War: The Martial Face of Global Biopolitics* (London: Routledge, 2007); Julian Reid, *The Biopolitics of the War on Terror: Life Struggles, Liberal Modernity and the Defence of Logistical Societies*, *Reappraising the Political* (Manchester: Manchester University Press, 2007).
6 Agamben, *Homo Sacer*, p. 8.
7 Schmitt, *Political Theology*, p. 15.
8 Agamben, *Homo Sacer*, p. 6.
9 Ibid., pp. 28–29.
10 Emile Durkheim, *The Elementary Forms of the Religious Life. A Study in Religious Sociology*, trans. Joseph Ward Swain (London: George Allen & Unwin, 1915); Sigmund Freud, *Totem and Taboo: Resemblances between the Psychic Lives of Savages and Neurotics*, trans. Abraham Arden Brill (London: George Routledge & Sons, 1919).
11 Agamben, *Homo Sacer*, p. 83.
12 Ibid., pp. 183–84.
13 Ibid., p. 83.
14 Ibid., pp. 170–71.
15 Ibid., pp. 154–59.
16 Ibid., p. 181.
17 'Hamdan V. Rumsfeld, 126 Supreme Court 2749' (2006).
18 Rasul, Iqbal, and Ahmed, 'Report of Former Guantanamo Detainees', p. 252.
19 Ibid., p. 155.
20 Clive Stafford Smith, legal counsel to Moazzam Begg, quoted in George Wright and agencies, 'Guantánamo Briton "Tortured in US Custody"', *Guardian*, 1 October 2004.
21 Moazzam Begg, 'Letter from Moazzam Begg' (2004).

22 Agamben, *Homo Sacer*, p. 18.
23 Ibid., p. 84.
24 Hannah Arendt, *The Origins of Totalitarianism* (New York: Harcourt Brace Jova-
    novich, 1979), p. 299. Cited in Agamben, *Homo Sacer*, p. 126.
25 United Nations Department of Public Information, *Basic Facts About the United
    Nations* (New York: UN, 2000), pp. 19–20.
26 Agamben, *Homo Sacer*, p. 123.
27 Ibid., p. 121.
28 Ibid., p. 125.
29 Ibid.
30 Ibid., p. 124.
31 Schmitt, *Political Theology*, p. 5.
32 Agamben, *Homo Sacer*, p. 142.
33 Ibid., p. 128.
34 Ibid.
35 Foucault, *The Archaeology of Knowledge*, p. 231.
36 Schmitt, *Political Theology*, p. 5.
37 Agamben, *State of Exception*, p. 30.
38 Ibid., p. 31.
39 Ibid.
40 Ibid., p. 51.
41 Schmitt, *The Concept of the Political*, p. 19.
42 Kant, 'An Answer to the Question: "What Is Enlightenment?"', p. 55.
43 Agamben, *State of Exception*, p. 51.
44 Foucault, *The Archaeology of Knowledge*, p. 231.
45 Agamben, *State of Exception*, pp. 32–40.
46 Ibid., p. 39.
47 Ibid., p. 40.
48 Ibid., p. 51.
49 Ibid., p. 36.
50 Ibid., pp. 52–53.
51 Walter Benjamin, 'Critique of Violence' in *Walter Benjamin: Selected Writings,
    Vol. 1 1913–1926*, ed. Marcus Bullock and Michael Jennings (Cambridge, Mass.;
    London: The Belknap Press of Harvard University Press, 1996), p. 63.
52 Ibid., p. 69.
53 Agamben, *State of Exception*, p. 62.
54 Ibid.
55 Benjamin, 'Critique of Violence'. Cited in Agamben, *State of Exception*, p. 53.
56 Agamben, *State of Exception*, p. 54.
57 Ibid.
58 Ibid., pp. 55–57.
59 See Schmitt, *Political Theology*, pp. 36–54.
60 Agamben, *State of Exception*, pp. 55–57.
61 Ibid., pp. 56–57.
62 Walter Benjamin, *The Origin of German Tragic Drama*, trans. John Osborne
    (London: Verso, 1998). Cited in Agamben, *State of Exception*, p. 57.
63 Agamben, *State of Exception*, p. 41.
64 Ibid., p. 50.
65 Ibid.
66 Ibid., pp. 50–51.
67 Ibid., p. 29.
68 Blake Morrison, 'Femme Fatale', *Guardian*, 4 October 2003; Tom Paulin, 'Whose
    Side Are You On?', *Independent on Sunday*, 28 September 2003; Sophocles, 'Anti-
    gone' in *The Three Theban Plays* (Harmondsworth: Penguin, 1984).

69 Agamben, *Homo Sacer*, p. 132.
70 Primo Levi, *If This Is a Man: The Truce*, trans. Stuart Woolf (London: Vintage, 1996), p. 48.
71 Ibid. See also Jenny Edkins and Véronique Pin-Fat, 'Through the Wire: Relations of Power and Relations of Violence', *Millennium: Journal of International Studies*, vol. 34, no. 1 (2005), p. 10.
72 Rasul, Iqbal, and Ahmed, 'Report of Former Guantanamo Detainees', p. 266.
73 Ibid., p. 267.
74 Foreign Affairs Committee, House of Commons, *Visit to Guantanamo Bay: Hc 44, Second Report of Session 2006–07-Report, Together with Formal Minutes and Written Evidence* (London: The Stationery Office, 2007), p. 23.
75 Rasul, Iqbal, and Ahmed, 'Report of Former Guantanamo Detainees', p. 149.
76 Fleur Johns, 'Guantanamo Bay and the Annihilation of the Exception', *The European Journal of International Law*, vol. 16, no. 4 (2005).
77 For a sophisticated analysis of these quasi-legal structures and discourses, see Judith Butler, *Precarious Life: The Powers of Mourning and Violence* (London: Verso, 2004).
78 Agamben, *State of Exception*, p. 8.
79 Carl J. Friedrich, *Constitutional Government and Democracy*, 2nd edn (Boston: Ginn, 1950), p. 584. Cited in Agamben, *State of Exception*, p. 8.
80 R. B. J. Walker, 'After the Future: Enclosures, Connections, Politics' in *Re-Framing the International: Law, Culture, Politics*, ed. Richard A. Falk, Lester Edwin J. Ruiz and R. B. J. Walker (New York; London: Routledge, 2002), p. 23; R. B. J. Walker, 'Lines of Insecurity: International, Imperial, Exceptional', *Security Dialogue*, vol. 37, no. 1 (2006), p. 66.
81 Carl Schmitt, 'The Age of Neutralizations and Depoliticizations', *Telos*, no. 96 (1993).
82 Max Weber, 'The Profession and Vocation of Politics' in *Weber: Political Writings*, ed. Peter Lassman and Ronald Speirs (Cambridge: Cambridge University Press, 1994).
83 Agamben, *State of Exception*, p. 51.
84 Foucault, *The Archaeology of Knowledge*, p. 231.
85 Foucault, *'Society Must Be Defended'*, pp. 69, 134, 236; Andrew W. Neal, 'Cutting Off the King's Head: Foucault's *"Society Must Be Defended"* and the Problem of Sovereignty', *Alternatives: Global, Local, Political*, no. 29 (2004).
86 Foucault, *'Society Must Be Defended'*, p. 137.
87 Agamben, *State of Exception*, p. 4.
88 Agamben, *Homo Sacer*, p. 84.
89 Foucault, *The Archaeology of Knowledge*, p. 231.
90 Agamben, *Homo Sacer*, p. 181.
91 Ibid., p. 38.
92 Agamben, *State of Exception*, p. 9.
93 Ibid., p. 14.
94 Agamben, *Homo Sacer*, p. 38.

5 Securitization theory: practices of sovereign naming

1 Schmitt, *The Concept of the Political*, p. 26.
2 Schmitt, *Political Theology*, p. 15.
3 Schmitt, *The Concept of the Political*, p. 32.
4 Schmitt, *Political Theology*, p. 15.
5 See for example Claudia Aradau, 'Security and the Democratic Scene: Desecuritization and Emancipation', *Journal of International Relations and Development*, no. 7 (2004); Thierry Balzacq, 'The Three Faces of Securitization: Political Agency,

Audience and Context', *European Journal of International Relations*, vol. 11, no. 2 (2005); Andreas Behnke, 'No Way Out: Desecuritization, Emancipation and the Eternal Return of the Political – A Reply to Aradau', *Journal of International Relations and Development*, no. 9 (2006); Maria Green Cowles, James A. Caporaso and Thomas Risse-Kappen, eds, *Transforming Europe: Europeanization and Domestic Change*, Cornell Studies in Political Economy (Ithaca, NY; London: Cornell University Press, 2001); L. Hansen, 'The Little Mermaid's Silent Security Dilemma and the Absence of Gender in the Copenhagen School', *Millennium: Journal of International Studies*, vol. 29, no. 2 (2000); Jef Huysmans, *The Politics of Insecurity: Fear, Migration and Asylum in the EU* (London: Routledge, 2006); Williams, 'Words, Images, Enemies'.

6 Wæver, 'Securitization and Desecuritization', p. 54.
7 Ibid., p. 48.
8 Ibid., p. 47.
9 Ibid., p. 48.
10 Ibid., p. 49.
11 Ibid., p. 55.
12 Ibid., p. 54.
13 Ibid., pp. 56–57.
14 Ibid., p. 56.
15 Ibid.
16 Ibid., pp. 56–57.
17 Ibid., p. 56.
18 Ibid.
19 Ibid.
20 Williams, 'Words, Images, Enemies', p. 521.
21 Ibid., p. 522.
22 Ibid., p. 521.
23 Ibid., p. 522.
24 Ibid., p. 521.
25 See, for example, Foucault, *The Archaeology of Knowledge*; Foucault, *Discipline and Punish*; Foucault, *'Society Must Be Defended'*.
26 Williams, 'Words, Images, Enemies', p. 521.
27 Ibid., p. 522.
28 See Michael J. Shapiro, *Reading the Postmodern Polity: Political Theory as Textual Practice* (Minneapolis: University of Minnesota Press, 1992), pp. 1–17; Simons, *Foucault and the Political*, pp. 110–16.
29 Buzan, Wæver and Wilde, *Security: A New Framework for Analysis*, p. 23. Cited in Williams, 'Words, Images, Enemies', p. 523.
30 Williams, 'Words, Images, Enemies', p. 514. See also Ole Wæver, 'The EU as a Security Actor: Reflections from a Pessimistic Constructivist on Post-Sovereign Security Orders' in *International Relations Theory and the Politics of European Integration: Power, Security, and Community*, ed. Michael C. Williams and Morten Kelstrup (London: Routledge, 2000), pp. 252–53.
31 Schmitt, *The Concept of the Political*, p. 39.
32 Balakrishnan, *The Enemy*, p. 111.
33 Schmitt, *The Concept of the Political*, p. 67.
34 Ibid., pp. 45–46.
35 Schmitt, 'The Age of Neutralizations and Depoliticizations'.
36 Foucault, *The Order of Things*.
37 Buzan, Wæver and Wilde, *Security: A New Framework for Analysis*, p. 32. Cited in Williams, 'Words, Images, Enemies', p. 514.
38 Wæver, 'Securitization and Desecuritization', p. 51.

39 See, for example, John M. Hobson, *The State and International Relations* (Cambridge: Cambridge University Press, 2000); Robert. O. Keohane and Joseph. S. Nye, *Power and Interdependence: World Politics in Transition* (New York: Little Brown, 1977); James N. Rosenau, *The Study of Global Interdependence: Essays on the Transnationalization of World Affairs, Essays on the Analysis of World Politics* (London: Pinter, 1980).
40 Wæver, 'Securitization and Desecuritization', p. 51.
41 Foucault, *The Archaeology of Knowledge*, p. 226.
42 Ibid., p. 133.
43 Ibid., p. 54.
44 Ibid., pp. 55–58.
45 Ibid., pp. 59–60.
46 Ibid., p. 6.
47 Ibid., p. 23.
48 Ibid., p. 151.
49 Ibid., p. 177.
50 Ibid., p. 148.

6 Foucault in Guantanamo: towards an archaeology of the exception

1 Schmitt, *The Concept of the Political*, p. 45.
2 Foucault, *The Archaeology of Knowledge*, p. 133.
3 Ibid., p. 231.
4 Ibid., p. 226.
5 Ibid.
6 Ibid., pp. 34–43.
7 Ibid., pp. 145–46.
8 Ibid., p. 23.
9 Ibid., p. 177.
10 Ibid., p. 133.
11 Ibid., p. 85.
12 Ibid., p. 135.
13 Ibid., p. 131.
14 Ibid.
15 Ibid., pp. 34–43.
16 Hubert L. Dreyfus and Paul Rabinow, *Michel Foucault: Beyond Structuralism and Hermeneutics* (Brighton: Harvester, 1982), p. 104.
17 Michel Foucault, 'Nietzsche, Genealogy, History' in *The Foucault Reader*, ed. Paul Rabinow (London: Penguin, 1991), p. 83.
18 Ibid.
19 Ibid.
20 Friedrich Nietzsche, 'The Wanderer and His Shadow (1880)' in *Complete Works* (New York: Gordon Press, 1974). As cited by Foucault, 'Nietzsche, Genealogy, History', p. 78.
21 Foucault, 'Nietzsche, Genealogy, History', p. 86.
22 Dreyfus and Rabinow, *Michel Foucault: Beyond Structuralism and Hermeneutics*, p. 122.
23 Ibid.
24 Foucault, 'Nietzsche, Genealogy, History', p. 86.
25 Foucault, 'Truth and Power', p. 123.
26 Foucault, *'Society Must Be Defended'*, p. 266.
27 Neal, 'Cutting Off the King's Head: Foucault's *"Society Must Be Defended"* and the Problem of Sovereignty'.
28 Foucault, *'Society Must Be Defended'*, pp. 10–11.

29 Foucault, *The Archaeology of Knowledge*, p. 54.
30 Amnesty International, 'Guantánamo and Beyond: The Continuing Pursuit of Unchecked Executive Power' (2005), p. 4.
31 Foucault, *The Archaeology of Knowledge*, p. 193.
32 Foucault, *Discipline and Punish*, p. 33.
33 Ibid., p. 109.
34 Ibid., p. 137.
35 The term first appears in Foucault, *'Society Must Be Defended'*, p. 243.
36 Ibid., p. 260.
37 Ibid., p. 241.
38 Ibid., p. 242.
39 Foucault, *Discipline and Punish*, p. 33.
40 Ibid.
41 International Committee of the Red Cross, 'Report of the International Committee of the Red Cross (ICRC) on the Treatment by the Coalition Forces of Prisoners of War and Other Protected Persons by the Geneva Conventions in Iraq During Arrest, Internment and Interrogation' (2004).
42 Rasul, Iqbal and Ahmed, 'Report of Former Guantanamo Detainees', p. 253.
43 Ibid., p. 267.
44 Foucault, *Discipline and Punish*, p. 35.
45 Ibid., p. 37.
46 Ibid., p. 35.
47 Rasul, Iqbal and Ahmed, 'Report of Former Guantanamo Detainees', p. 173.
48 Foucault, *Discipline and Punish*, p. 42.
49 Ibid.
50 Ibid., p. 47.
51 Ibid., p. 137.
52 Ibid., p. 141.
53 Rasul, Iqbal and Ahmed, 'Report of Former Guantanamo Detainees', p. 121.
54 Ibid., p. 131.
55 See Michel Foucault, 'The Subject and Power' in *Power: Essential Works of Foucault, 1954–1984; Vol. 3*, ed. James D. Faubion (London: Penguin, 2002).
56 Rasul, Iqbal and Ahmed, 'Report of Former Guantanamo Detainees', p. 149.
57 Ibid., p. 267.
58 Foucault, *'Society Must Be Defended'*, p. 241.
59 Foucault, *Discipline and Punish*, p. 130.
60 Ibid., p. 110.
61 Ibid., p. 48.
62 Ibid., pp. 48–49.

7 The rise and fall of Schmitt at the hands of Foucault and others

1 Schmitt, *Political Theology*, p. 6.
2 Ibid., p. 5.
3 Balakrishnan, *The Enemy*.
4 Ibid., p. 43.
5 Georges Sorel, *Reflections on Violence*, trans. T. E. Hulme (London: G. Allen & Unwin, 1916).
6 György Lukács, *History and Class Consciousness: Studies in Marxist Dialectics*, trans. Rodney Livingstone, 2nd edn (London: Merlin Press, 1971).
7 Schmitt, *The Concept of the Political*, p. 19.
8 Carl Schmitt, *The Nomos of the Earth in the International Law of the Jus Publicum Europaeum*, trans. G. L. Ulmen (New York: Telos Press, 2003).

9 Odysseos and Petito, eds, *The International Political Thought of Carl Schmitt: Terror, Liberal War and the Crisis of Global Order* (London; New York: Routledge, 2007).

10 Ibid., p. 2.

11 See, for example, Véronique Pin-Fat, 'The Metaphysics of the National Interest and the "Mysticism" of the Nation-State: Reading Hans J. Morgenthau', *Millennium: Journal of International Studies*, vol. 31, no. 2 (2005); Christine Sylvester, *Feminist Theory and International Relations in a Postmodern Era* (Cambridge: Cambridge University Press, 1994); Walker, *Inside/Outside*; Cynthia Weber, *International Relations Theory: A Critical Introduction*, 2nd edn (London; New York: Routledge, 2005).

12 Johan Steyn, 'Guantanamo Bay: The Legal Black Hole', *International and Comparative Law Quarterly*, vol. 53 (2004).

13 Steven G. Calabresi and Christopher S. Yoo, *The Unitary Executive: Presidential Power from Washington to Bush* (New Haven, Conn.; London: Yale University Press, 2008).

14 Schmitt, *Political Theology*, p. 14.

15 Diana H. Coole, *Negativity and Politics: Dionysus and Dialectics from Kant to Poststructuralism* (London; New York: Routledge, 2000), p. 28.

16 Jens Bartelson, *The Critique of the State* (Cambridge: Cambridge University Press, 2001); Gilles Deleuze, *Kant's Critical Philosophy: The Doctrine of the Faculties* (London: Athlone, 1995); Kimberly Hutchings, *Kant, Critique, and Politics* (London; New York: Routledge, 1995), p. 5.

17 Coole, *Negativity and Politics: Dionysus and Dialectics from Kant to Poststructuralism*, p. 15.

18 Gaston Bachelard, 'The Epistemological Break: Beyond Subject and Object in Modern Science', translated excerpt in *Gaston Bachelard, Subversive Humanist*, Mary MacAllester Jones (Wisconsin; London: University of Wisconsin Press, 1991), pp. 46–54.

19 Antonio Negri, *Time for Revolution*, trans. Matteo Mandarini (New York; London: Continuum, 2003), p. 44.

20 Louis Althusser, 'The Underground Current of the Materialism of the Encounter' in *Philosophy of the Encounter, Later Writings, 1978–87*, ed. Francois Matheron and Oliver Corpet (London; New York: Verso, 2006), p. 174.

21 Michel Serres, *The Birth of Physics* (Manchester: Clinamen, 2000), p. 3.

22 Jacques Derrida, 'Différance' in *Margins of Philosophy* (Chicago, Ill.: University of Chicago Press, 1982).

23 Alain Badiou, *Being and Event* (London: Continuum, 2005).

24 Slavoj Žižek, Rex Butler and Scott Stephens, *Interrogating the Real: Selected Writings* (New York; London: Continuum, 2005).

25 David Chandler, 'The Revival of Carl Schmitt in International Relations: The Last Refuge of Critical Theorists?' *Millennium: Journal of International Studies*, vol. 37, no. 1 (2008).

26 See Louiza Odysseos and Fabio Petito, 'Vagaries of Interpretation: A Rejoinder to David Chandler's Reductionist Reading of Carl Schmitt', *Millennium: Journal of International Studies*, vol. 37, no. 2 (2008); Odysseos and Petito, eds, *The International Political Thought of Carl Schmitt: Terror, Liberal War and the Crisis of Global Order*.

27 Prozorov, 'X/Xs: Toward a General Theory of the Exception', p. 106.

28 Ibid., p. 82.

29 Prozorov, 'The Ethos of Insecure Life. Reading Carl Schmitt's Existential Decisionism as a Foucauldian Ethics'; Sergei Prozorov, 'The World Community and the Closure of the Political: How to Overcome Carl Schmitt', paper presented at Making Sense of a Pluralist World: Sixth Pan-European Conference on

International Relations, Turin, 2007; Prozorov, 'X/Xs: Toward a General Theory of the Exception'.

30 Prozorov, 'The Ethos of Insecure Life. Reading Carl Schmitt's Existential Decisionism as a Foucauldian Ethics', p. 222.

31 c.a.s.e. collective, 'Europe, Knowledge, Politics Engaging with the Limits: The c.a.s.e. Collective Responds', *Security Dialogue*, vol. 38, no. 4 (2007), p. 572.

32 Schmitt, *Political Theology*, p. 13.

33 Agamben, *State of Exception*, p. 31.

34 Ibid., p. 51.

35 Machiavelli, *The Prince*, p. 84. See also Walker, *Inside/Outside*, pp. 38–41.

36 Schmitt, 'The Age of Neutralizations and Depoliticizations'.

37 Ernst Hartwig Kantorowicz, *The King's Two Bodies: A Study in Mediaeval Political Theology* (Princeton; Chichester: Princeton University Press, 1997).

38 Prozorov, 'The Ethos of Insecure Life. Reading Carl Schmitt's Existential Decisionism as a Foucauldian Ethics', p. 223.

39 Schmitt, *The Concept of the Political*, p. 19.

40 Strauss, 'Notes on Carl Schmitt, the Concept of the Political', p. 84.

41 See Ananiadis, 'Carl Schmitt on Kosovo, or, Taking War Seriously'; Mouffe, *The Challenge of Carl Schmitt*; Mouffe, *The Democratic Paradox*; Odysseos and Petito, eds, *The International Political Thought of Carl Schmitt: Terror, Liberal War and the Crisis of Global Order*; Rasch, 'Conflict as a Vocation'; William Rasch, 'Introduction: Carl Schmitt and the New World Order', *South Atlantic Quarterly*, vol. 104, no. 2 (2005).

42 Schmitt, *The Concept of the Political*, p. 37.

43 Michel Foucault, *The Birth of Biopolitics: Lectures at the Collège de France, 1978–1979*, ed. Arnold Davidson, trans. Graham Burchell (Basingstoke: Palgrave Macmillan, 2008), p. 21.

44 Schmitt, *Political Theology*, p. 6.

45 Ibid., p. 5.

46 Andreas Behnke, 'Presence and Creation: A Few (Meta-)Critical Comments on the c.a.s.e. Manifesto', *Security Dialogue*, vol. 38, no. 1 (2007), p. 108.

47 Schmitt, *Political Theology*, p. 12.

48 Behnke, 'Presence and Creation: A Few (Meta-)Critical Comments on the c.a.s.e. Manifesto', p. 108.

49 Schmitt, *Political Theology*, p. 18.

50 Behnke, 'Presence and Creation: A Few (Meta-)Critical Comments on the c.a.s.e. Manifesto', p. 108.

51 Prozorov, 'The Ethos of Insecure Life. Reading Carl Schmitt's Existential Decisionism as a Foucauldian Ethics'.

52 Prozorov, 'X/Xs: Toward a General Theory of the Exception'.

53 c.a.s.e. collective, 'Europe, Knowledge, Politics Engaging with the Limits: The c.a.s.e. Collective Responds', p. 572.

54 Prozorov, 'The World Community and the Closure of the Political: How to Overcome Carl Schmitt'.

55 Ibid., p. 1.

56 Ibid., p. 2.

57 Ibid., p. 4.

58 Ibid., p. 6.

59 Ibid., p. 7.

60 Ibid., p. 2.

61 Giorgio Agamben, *Means without End: Notes on Politics* (Minneapolis; London: University of Minnesota Press, 2000), p. 114. Cited in Prozorov, 'The World Community and the Closure of the Political: How to Overcome Carl Schmitt', p. 27.

62 Prozorov, 'The World Community and the Closure of the Political: How to Overcome Carl Schmitt', p. 30.
63 Foucault, *'Society Must Be Defended'*, p. 36.
64 Behnke, 'Presence and Creation: A Few (Meta-)Critical Comments on the c.a.s.e. Manifesto', p. 108.
65 Foucault, 'Truth and Power', p. 121.
66 Didier Bigo, 'Security: A Field Left Fallow' in *Foucault on Politics, Security and War*, ed. Michael Dillon and Andrew W. Neal (Basingstoke: Palgrave Macmillan, 2008), p. 102.
67 Paul Veyne, 'Foucault Revolutionizes History' in *Foucault and His Interlocutors*, ed. Arnold I. Davidson (Chicago, Ill.; London: University of Chicago Press, 1997), p. 156.
68 Foucault, *The Birth of Biopolitics: Lectures at the Collège de France, 1978–1979*, p. 20.
69 Ibid., pp. 40–41.
70 Ibid., p. 41.
71 Veyne, 'Foucault Revolutionizes History', p. 155.
72 Ibid., p. 156.
73 Didier Bigo, 'Frontier Controls in the European Union: Who Is in Control?' in *Controlling Frontiers: Free Movement into and within Europe*, ed. Didier Bigo and Elspeth Guild (Aldershot: Ashgate, 2005), p. 75.
74 Here I am paraphrasing R. B. J. Walker, 'Europe Is Not Where It Is Supposed to Be' in *International Relations Theory and the Politics of European Integration: Power, Security, and Community*, ed. Michael C. Williams and Morten Kelstrup (London: Routledge, 2000).
75 Butler, *Precarious Life: The Powers of Mourning and Violence*, p. 56.
76 Schmitt, *Political Theology*, p. 15.
77 Veyne, 'Foucault Revolutionizes History', p. 158.
78 Ibid., p. 154.
79 Ibid., p. 158.
80 Philippe Sands, *Torture Team: Deception, Cruelty and the Compromise of Law* (London: Allen Lane, 2008).
81 Foucault, *The Birth of Biopolitics: Lectures at the Collège de France, 1978–1979*, p. 41.
82 Veyne, 'Foucault Revolutionizes History', p. 171.
83 Johns, 'Guantanamo Bay and the Annihilation of the Exception', p. 617.
84 Ibid., p. 614.
85 Ibid., p. 618.
86 E.g. 'Hamdan V. Rumsfeld, 126 Supreme Court 2749'. For a detailed legal analysis, see Donohue, *The Cost of Counterterrorism: Power, Politics, and Liberty*, pp. 71–91.
87 Johns, 'Guantanamo Bay and the Annihilation of the Exception', p. 631.
88 Louise Amoore, 'On Forgetting the War on Terror' in *Terrorism and the Politics of Response*, ed. Angharad Closs Stephens and Nick Vaughan-Williams, Routledge Critical Terrorism Studies (London; New York: Routledge, 2009), p. 136; Jacques Derrida, 'Nietzsche and the Machine (in Conversation with Richard Beardsworth)', *Journal of Nietzsche Studies*, no. 7 (1994).
89 Amoore, 'On Forgetting the War on Terror', p. 136.
90 Veyne, 'Foucault Revolutionizes History', p. 158.
91 Butler, *Precarious Life: The Powers of Mourning and Violence*, p. 56.
92 Ibid.
93 Veyne, 'Foucault Revolutionizes History', p. 154.
94 Butler, *Precarious Life: The Powers of Mourning and Violence*, p. 62.

95 For a longer analysis of Butler's intervention, see Andrew W. Neal, 'Goodbye War on Terror? Foucault and Butler on Law, War and Exceptionalism' in *Foucault on Politics, Security and War*, ed. Michael Dillon and Andrew W. Neal (Basingstoke: Palgrave Macmillan, 2008).

96 Johns, 'Guantanamo Bay and the Annihilation of the Exception'.

97 Foucault, *The Birth of Biopolitics: Lectures at the Collège de France, 1978–1979*, pp. 40–41.

98 Roxanne Lynn Doty, 'States of Exception on the Mexico–U.S. Border, Colo.: Security, "Decisions," and Civilian Border Patrols', *International Political Sociology*, vol. 1, no. 2 (2007).

99 Ibid., pp. 120–21.

100 Ibid., p. 116.

101 Ibid., p. 129.

102 Ibid., p. 130.

103 Ibid., p. 133.

104 On the relationship between zero-time and nationalism, see Angharad Closs Stephens, 'Oppressed by Our Utopias: The Politics of Communities, Origins and Temporality' (unpublished doctoral thesis, Keele University, 2007).

105 Foucault, *The Birth of Biopolitics: Lectures at the Collège de France, 1978–1979*, pp. 40–41.

106 Ibid., p. 20.

107 McCormick, *Carl Schmitt's Critique of Liberalism*.

108 Foucault, *The Birth of Biopolitics: Lectures at the Collège de France, 1978–1979*, p. 20.

109 Ibid., p. 19.

110 Ibid.

Bibliography

Agamben, Giorgio. *Homo Sacer: Sovereign Power and Bare Life*. Translated by Daniel Heller-Roazen. Stanford, Calif.: Stanford University Press, 1998.

—— *Means without End: Notes on Politics*. Minneapolis; London: University of Minnesota Press, 2000.

—— *State of Exception*. Translated by Kevin Attell. Chicago, Ill.; London: University of Chicago Press, 2005.

Agamben, Giorgio, Tariq Ali, Zygmunt Bauman, Teddy Cruz, Keller Easterling, Anselm Franke, Stephen Graham, Thomas Keenan, Shimon Naveh, Lluís Ortega, José Luis Pardo, Josep Ramoneda, Eyal Sivan, Rafael Vilasanjuan and Eyal Weizman. *Arxipèlag d'excepcions: Sobiranies de l'extraterritorialitat (Archipelago of Exceptions: Sovereignties of Extraterritoriality)*. Barcelona: CCCB, 2005.

All Party Parliamentary Group on Extraordinary Rendition [accessed 3 April 2009]. Available from: http://www.extraordinaryrendition.org/.

Allison, Henry E. *Kant's Theory of Freedom*. Cambridge: Cambridge University Press, 1990.

Althusser, Louis. 'The Underground Current of the Materialism of the Encounter'. In *Philosophy of the Encounter, Later Writings, 1978–87*, edited by Francois Matheron and Oliver Corpet. London; New York: Verso, 2006: 163–207.

Amnesty International. 'Guantánamo and Beyond: The Continuing Pursuit of Unchecked Executive Power'. 2005. Available from: http://www.amnesty.org/en/library/info/AMR51/063/2005.

Amoore, Louise. 'On Forgetting the War on Terror'. In *Terrorism and the Politics of Response*, edited by Angharad Closs Stephens and Nick Vaughan-Williams, Routledge Critical Terrorism Studies. London; New York: Routledge, 2009: 130–43.

Ananiadis, Grigoris. 'Carl Schmitt on Kosovo, or, Taking War Seriously'. In *Balkan as Metaphor: Between Globalization and Fragmentation*, edited by Dušan I. Bjelic and Obrad Savic. Cambridge, Mass.; London: MIT Press, 2002: 117–62.

Apap, Joanna. *Justice and Home Affairs in the EU: Liberty and Security Issues after Enlargement*. Cheltenham: Edward Elgar, 2004.

Aradau, Claudia. 'Security and the Democratic Scene: Desecuritization and Emancipation'. *Journal of International Relations and Development*, no. 7, 2004: 388–413.

Arendt, Hannah. *The Origins of Totalitarianism*. New York: Harcourt Brace Jovanovich, 1979.

Bachelard, Gaston. 'The Epistemological Break: Beyond Subject and Object in Modern Science.' Translated excerpt in *Gaston Bachelard, Subversive Humanist*,

Mary MacAllester Jones. Wisconsin; London: University of Wisconsin Press, 1991, pp. 46–54.

——— *The Formation of the Scientific Mind: A Contribution to a Psychoanalysis of Objective Knowledge*. Translated by Mary MacAllester Jones. Manchester: Clinamen, 2002.

Badiou, Alain. *Being and Event*. London: Continuum, 2005.

Balakrishnan, Gopal. *The Enemy: An Intellectual Portrait of Carl Schmitt*. London; New York: Verso, 2000.

Balzacq, Thierry. 'The Three Faces of Securitization: Political Agency, Audience and Context'. *European Journal of International Relations*, vol. 11, no. 2, 2005: 171–201.

Bartelson, Jens. *The Critique of the State*. Cambridge: Cambridge University Press, 2001.

BBC News. *BBC Breakfast with Frost Interview: David Blunkett, Home Secretary*. 18 November 2001. Available from: http://news.bbc.co.uk/1/hi/programmes/breakfast_with_frost/1662785.stm.

Begg, Moazzam. 'Letter from Moazzam Begg'. 2004. Available from: http://image.guardian.co.uk/sys-files/Guardian/documents/2004/10/01/guan_letters.pdf.

Begg, Moazzam and Victoria Brittain. *Enemy Combatant: A British Muslim's Journey to Guantanamo and Back*. London: Free Press, 2006.

Behnke, Andreas. 'No Way Out: Desecuritization, Emancipation and the Eternal Return of the Political – A Reply to Aradau'. *Journal of International Relations and Development*, no. 9, 2006: 62–69.

———. 'Presence and Creation: A Few (Meta-)Critical Comments on the c.a.s.e. Manifesto'. *Security Dialogue*, vol. 38, no. 1, 2007: 105–11.

Behnke, Andreas and Linda Bashai. 'War, Violence and the Displacement of the Political'. In *The International Political Thought of Carl Schmitt: Terror, Liberal War and the Crisis of Global Order*, edited by Louisa Odysseos and Fabio Petito. London; New York: Routledge, 2007: 107–23.

Benjamin, Walter. 'Theses on the Philosophy of History'. In *Illuminations*, edited by Hannah Arendt. New York: Schocken Books, 1968: 253–64.

———. 'Critique of Violence'. In *Walter Benjamin: Selected Writings, Vol. 1 1913–1926*, edited by Marcus Bullock and Michael Jennings. Cambridge, Mass.; London: The Belknap Press of Harvard University Press, 1996.

———. *The Origin of German Tragic Drama*. Translated by John Osborne. London: Verso, 1998.

Berezin, Mabel and Martin Schain. *Europe without Borders: Remapping Territory, Citizenship, and Identity in a Transnational Age*. Baltimore: Johns Hopkins University Press, 2003.

Berlin, Isaiah. *Liberty: Incorporating Four Essays on Liberty*. Oxford: Oxford University Press, 2002.

Bigo, Didier. 'Frontier Controls in the European Union: Who Is in Control?' In *Controlling Frontiers: Free Movement into and within Europe*, edited by Didier Bigo and Elspeth Guild. Aldershot: Ashgate, 2005: 49–99.

———. 'Security: A Field Left Fallow'. In *Foucault on Politics, Security and War*, edited by Michael Dillon and Andrew W. Neal. Basingstoke: Palgrave Macmillan, 2008: 93–114.

Bigo, Didier and Anastassia Tsoukala. *Terror, Insecurity and Liberty: Illiberal Practices of Liberal Regimes after 9/11*, Routledge Studies in Liberty and Security. London: Routledge, 2008.

Bonditti, Philippe. 'L'Organisation de la lutte anti-terroriste aux Etats-Unis'. *Cultures & Conflits*, no. 44, 2001.

Bradley, A. W. and K. D. Ewing. *Constitutional and Administrative Law*. 14th edn. Harlow: Pearson Longman, 2007.

Butler, Judith. *Precarious Life: The Powers of Mourning and Violence*. London: Verso, 2004.

Butterfield, Fox. 'A Nation Challenged: The Interviews; a Police Force Rebuffs F.B.I. on Querying Mideast Men'. *New York Times*, 21 November 2001.

Buzan, Barry and Ole Wæver. *Regions and Powers: The Structure of International Security*, Cambridge Studies in International Relations, 91. Cambridge: Cambridge University Press, 2003.

Buzan, Barry, Ole Wæver and Jaap de Wilde. *Security: A New Framework for Analysis*. Boulder, Colo.: Lynne Rienner, 1998.

Cabinet Office. 'Civil Contingencies Act 2004: A Short Guide'. 2004. Available from: http://www.ukresilience.info/ccact/1decshortguide.pdf.

Calabresi, Steven G. and Christopher S. Yoo. *The Unitary Executive: Presidential Power from Washington to Bush*. New Haven, Conn.; London: Yale University Press, 2008.

c.a.s.e. collective. 'Europe, Knowledge, Politics Engaging with the Limits: The c.a.s.e. Collective Responds'. *Security Dialogue*, vol. 38, no. 4, 2007: 559–76.

CHALLENGE. *The Changing Landscape of European Liberty and Security* [research project and online observatory]. Available from: www.libertysecurity.org.

Chandler, David. 'The Revival of Carl Schmitt in International Relations: The Last Refuge of Critical Theorists?' *Millennium: Journal of International Studies*, vol. 37, no. 1, 2008: 27–48.

Chang, Nancy. *Silencing Political Dissent: How Post-September 11 Anti-Terrorism Measures Threaten Our Civil Liberties*. New York: Seven Stories; London: Turnaround, 2002.

'Civil Contingencies Act'. 2004. Available from: http://www.opsi.gov.uk/acts/acts2004/20040036.htm.

Closs Stephens, Angharad. 'Oppressed by Our Utopias: The Politics of Communities, Origins and Temporality'. Unpublished doctoral thesis, Keele University, 2007.

Cohen, David B. and John Wilson Wells. *American National Security and Civil Liberties in an Era of Terrorism*. 1st edn. New York: Palgrave Macmillan, 2004.

Cole, David and James X. Dempsey. *Terrorism and the Constitution: Sacrificing Civil Liberties in the Name of National Security*. 3rd edn. New York: New Press, 2006.

Connolly, William E. *The Augustinian Imperative: A Reflection on the Politics of Morality*. Newbury Park, Calif.; London; New Delhi: Sage, 1993.

Coole, Diana H. *Negativity and Politics: Dionysus and Dialectics from Kant to Post-structuralism*. London; New York: Routledge, 2000.

Council of Europe. 'Council of Europe Convention on Action against Trafficking in Human Beings (Cets No. 197)'. 2005. Available from: http://www.coe.int/t/dghl/monitoring/trafficking/default_en.asp.

——. 'Council of Europe Convention on Laundering, Search, Seizure and Confiscation of the Proceeds from Crime and on the Financing of Terrorism'. 2005. Available from: https://wcd.coe.int/ViewDoc.jsp?id = 835461&BackColorInternet = 9999CC&BackColorIntranet = FFBB55&BackColorLogged = FFAC75.

Darmer, M. Katherine B., Robert M. Baird and Stuart E. Rosenbaum. *Civil Liberties vs. National Security: In a Post-9/11 World*. Amherst, NY: Prometheus Books, 2004.

Deleuze, Gilles. *Kant's Critical Philosophy: The Doctrine of the Faculties*. London: Athlone, 1995.

——. *Foucault*. London: Continuum, 2006.

Derrida, Jacques. 'Différance'. In *Margins of Philosophy*. Chicago, Ill.: University of Chicago Press, 1982: 3–27.

——. 'Nietzsche and the Machine (in Conversation with Richard Beardsworth)'. *Journal of Nietzsche Studies*, no. 7, 1994: 7–65.

——. *Politics of Friendship*. Translated by George Collins, *Phronesis*. London: Verso, 1997.

Diken, Bülent and Carsten B. Laustsen. *The Culture of Exception: Sociology Facing the Camp*, International Library of Sociology. London; New York: Routledge, 2005.

Dillon, Michael. *Biopolitics of Security in the 21st Century: The Political Economy of Security after Foucault*. London: Routledge, 2010.

Dillon, Michael and Luis Lobo-Guerrero. 'The Biopolitical Imaginary of Species-Being'. *Theory, Culture & Society*, vol. 26, no. 1, 2009: 1–23.

Dillon, Michael and Julian Reid. *The Liberal Way of War: The Martial Face of Global Biopolitics*. London: Routledge, 2007.

Donohue, Laura K. *The Cost of Counterterrorism: Power, Politics, and Liberty*. Cambridge; New York: Cambridge University Press, 2008.

Doty, Roxanne Lynn. 'States of Exception on the Mexico–U.S. Border: Security, "Decisions," and Civilian Border Patrols'. *International Political Sociology*, vol. 1, no. 2, 2007: 113–37.

Dreyfus, Hubert L. and Paul Rabinow. *Michel Foucault: Beyond Structuralism and Hermeneutics*. Brighton: Harvester, 1982.

Durkheim, Emile. *The Elementary Forms of the Religious Life. A Study in Religious Sociology*. Translated by Joseph Ward Swain. London: George Allen & Unwin, 1915.

Ebeling, Richard M. and Jacob G. Hornberger, eds *Liberty, Security, and the War on Terrorism*. Fairfax, Virg.: Future of Freedom Foundation, 2002.

Edkins, Jenny and Véronique Pin-Fat. 'Through the Wire: Relations of Power and Relations of Violence'. *Millennium: Journal of International Studies*, vol. 34, no. 1, 2005: 1–24.

E.U. Network of Independent Experts in Fundamental Rights (cfr-cdf). 'The Balance between Freedom and Security in the Response by the European Union and Its Member States to the Terrorist Threats'. European Commission, Unit A5, 'Citizenship, Charter of fundamental rights, Racism, Xenophobia, Daphne program', of DG Justice and Home Affairs., 2003. Available from: http://ec.europa.eu/justice_home/cfr_cdf/doc/obs_thematique_en.pdf.

Falk, Richard A. *The Costs of War: International Law, the UN, and World Order after Iraq*. New York; London: Routledge, 2008.

Falkoff, Marc. *Poems from Guantánamo: The Detainees Speak*. Iowa City, Iowa: University of Iowa Press, 2007.

Foreign Affairs Committee, House of Commons. *Visit to Guantanamo Bay: Hc 44, Second Report of Session 2006–07-Report, Together with Formal Minutes and Written Evidence*. London: The Stationery Office, 2007.

Foucault, Michel. *The History of Sexuality, the Will to Knowledge*. Translated by Robert Hurley. Vol. 1. New York: Random House, 1978.

——. 'Truth and Power'. In *Power/Knowledge: Selected Interviews and Other Writings 1972–1977*, edited by Colin Gordon. New York: Harvester Wheatsheaf, 1980: 109–33.

——. *The History of Sexuality, Vol. 1*. Translated by Robert Hurley. London: Penguin, 1990.

——. 'Nietzsche, Genealogy, History'. In *The Foucault Reader*, edited by Paul Rabinow. London: Penguin, 1991: 76–100.

——. *Discipline and Punish: The Birth of the Prison*. Translated by Alan Sheridan. London: Penguin, 1999.

——. *Madness and Civilization: A History of Insanity in the Age of Reason*. Translated by Richard Howard, *Routledge Classics*. London: Routledge, 2001.

——. *The Order of Things: An Archaeology of the Human Sciences*. London: Routledge, 2001.

——. *The Archaeology of Knowledge*. Translated by A. M. Sheridan Smith. London: Routledge, 2002.

——. *'Society Must Be Defended': Lectures at the Collège de France, 1975–76*. Translated by David Macey. New York: Picador, 2002.

——. 'The Subject and Power'. In *Power: Essential Works of Foucault, 1954–1984, Vol. 3*, edited by James D. Faubion. London: Penguin, 2002: 326–48.

——. *The Birth of Biopolitics: Lectures at the Collège de France, 1978–1979*. Translated by Graham Burchell. Edited by Arnold Davidson. Basingstoke: Palgrave Macmillan, 2008.

Foucault, Michel, Donald Fernand Bouchard and Sherry Simon. *Language, Counter-Memory, Practice: Selected Essays and Interviews*. Oxford: Blackwell, 1977.

Freud, Sigmund. *Totem and Taboo: Resemblances between the Psychic Lives of Savages and Neurotics.*Translated by Abraham Arden Brill. London: George Routledge & Sons, 1919.

Friedrich, Carl J. *Constitutional Government and Democracy*. 2nd edn. Boston: Ginn, 1950.

Goldberg, Danny, Victor Goldberg and Robert Greenwald. *It's a Free Country: Personal Freedom in America after September 11*. New York: RDV Books, 2002.

Gottfried, Ted. *Homeland Security versus Constitutional Rights*. Brookfield, Conn.: 21st Century Books, 2003.

Green Cowles, Maria, James A. Caporaso and Thomas Risse-Kappen, eds. *Transforming Europe: Europeanization and Domestic Change*, Cornell Studies in Political Economy. Ithaca, NY; London: Cornell University Press, 2001.

Grey, Stephen. *Ghost Plane: The Inside Story of the CIA's Secret Rendition Programme*. London: Hurst, 2006.

Guardian. 'A Bill with Huge Powers'. *Guardian*, 20 June 2003.

Gurr, Nadine and Benjamin Cole. *The New Face of Terrorism: Threats from Weapons of Mass Destruction*. London: I. B. Tauris, 2000.

Habermas, Jürgen. 'The Horrors of Autonomy: Carl Schmitt in English'. In *The New Conservatism: Cultural Criticism and the Historians' Debate*, edited by Shierry Weber Nicholsen. Cambridge, Mass.: MIT Press, 1989: 128–39.

'Hamdan V. Rumsfeld, 126 Supreme Court 2749'. 2006.

Han, Beatrice. *Foucault's Critical Project: Between the Transcendental and the Historical, Atopia*. Stanford, Calif.: Stanford University Press, 2002.

Hansen, Lene. 'The Little Mermaid's Silent Security Dilemma and the Absence of Gender in the Copenhagen School'. *Millennium: Journal of International Studies*, vol. 29, no. 2, 2000: 285–306.

Hanssen, Beatrice. *Critique of Violence: Between Poststructuralism and Critical Theory*, Warwick Studies in European Philosophy. London: Routledge, 2000.

Hendricks, Christina. 'Foucault's Kantian Critique: Philosophy and the Present'. *Philosophy & Social Criticism*, vol. 34, no. 4, 2008: 357–82.

Hobbes, Thomas. *Leviathan*. Edited by Richard Tuck. Cambridge: Cambridge University Press, 1996.

Hobson, John M. *The State and International Relations*. Cambridge: Cambridge University Press, 2000.

Holmes, Stephen. 'Schmitt: The Debility of Liberalism'. In *The Anatomy of Antiliberalism*. Cambridge, Mass.; London: Harvard University Press, 1993: 37–60.

Hutchings, Kimberly. *Kant, Critique, and Politics*. London; New York: Routledge, 1995.

Huysmans, Jef. 'Minding Exceptions. Politics of Insecurity and Liberal Democracy'. *Contemporary Political Theory*, vol. 3, no. 3, 2004: 321–41.

——. *The Politics of Insecurity: Fear, Migration and Asylum in the EU*. London: Routledge, 2006.

International Committee of the Red Cross. 'Report of the International Committee of the Red Cross (ICRC) on the Treatment by the Coalition Forces of Prisoners of War and Other Protected Persons by the Geneva Conventions in Iraq During Arrest, Internment and Interrogation'. 2004. Available from: http://www.globalsecurity.org/military/library/report/2004/icrc_report_iraq_feb2004.htm.

Johns, Fleur. 'Guantanamo Bay and the Annihilation of the Exception'. *The European Journal of International Law*, vol. 16, no. 4, 2005: 613–35.

Johnson, Nevil. *Reshaping the British Constitution: Essays in Political Interpretation*. Basingstoke: Palgrave, 2004.

Joint Committee on the Draft Civil Contingencies Bill. 'Draft Civil Contingencies Bill, Report and Evidence'. London: The Stationery Office, 2003. Available from: http://www.publications.parliament.uk/pa/jt200203/jtselect/jtdcc/184/184.pdf.

Kant, Immanuel. 'An Answer to the Question: "What Is Enlightenment?"' In *Kant: Political Writings*, edited by Hans Reiss. Cambridge: Cambridge University Press, 1990: 54–60.

——. 'The Metaphysics of Morals'. In *Kant: Political Writings*, edited by Hans Reiss. Cambridge: Cambridge University Press, 1990: 131–75.

——. 'On the Common Saying: "This May Be True in Theory, but It Does Not Apply in Practice"'. In *Kant: Political Writings*, edited by Hans Reiss. Cambridge: Cambridge University Press, 1990: 61–92.

——. 'Perpetual Peace: A Philosophical Sketch'. In *Kant: Political Writings*, edited by Hans Reiss. Cambridge: Cambridge University Press, 1990: 93–115.

——. *The Metaphysics of Morals*. Translated by Mary J. Gregor. Edited by Mary J. Gregor. Cambridge: Cambridge University Press, 1996.

——. *Groundwork for the Metaphysics of Morals*. Edited by Allen W. Wood. New Haven, Conn.; London: Yale University Press, 2003.

Kantorowicz, Ernst Hartwig. *The King's Two Bodies: A Study in Mediaeval Political Theology*. Princeton; Chichester: Princeton University Press, 1997.

Kegley, Charles W. *The New Global Terrorism: Characteristics, Causes, Controls*. Upper Saddle River, N.J.: Prentice Hall; London: Pearson Education, 2003.

Keohane, Robert. O. and Joseph. S. Nye. *Power and Interdependence: World Politics in Transition*. New York: Little Brown, 1977.

Kersting, Wolfgang. 'Politics, Freedom, and Order: Kant's Political Philosophy'. In *The Cambridge Companion to Kant*, edited by Paul Guyer. Cambridge: Cambridge University Press, 1992: 342–66.

King, Anthony Stephen. *The British Constitution*. Oxford: Oxford University Press, 2007.

Kirkland, Andrew. 'The Weight of a Nation'. In *It's a Free Country: Personal Freedom in America after September 11*, edited by Danny Goldberg, Victor Goldberg and Robert Greenwald. New York: RDV Books, 2002: 307–10.

Laqueur, Walter. *The New Terrorism: Fanaticism and the Arms of Mass Destruction*. London: Phoenix, 1999.

Leone, Richard C. and Greg Anrig. *The War on Our Freedoms: Civil Liberties in an Age of Terrorism*. 1st edn. New York: BBS Public Affairs, 2003.

Levi, Primo. *If This Is a Man; The Truce*. Translated by Stuart Woolf. London: Vintage, 1996.

Liberty. 'Liberty Response to the Draft Civil Contingency Bill'. 2003. Available from: http://www.liberty-human-rights.org.uk/resources/policy-papers/policy-papers-2003/pdf-documents/sept-2003-draft-civil-contigency-bill.pdf.

Lukács, György. *History and Class Consciousness: Studies in Marxist Dialectics*. Translated by Rodney Livingstone. 2nd edn. London: Merlin Press, 1971.

McCormick, John. *Carl Schmitt's Critique of Liberalism: Against Politics as Technology*. Cambridge: Cambridge University Press, 1997.

Machiavelli, Niccolo. *The Prince*. Translated by Peter E. Bondanella. Oxford; New York: Oxford University Press, 2005.

MacIntyre, Alasdair C. *A Short History of Ethics: A History of Moral Philosophy from the Homeric Age to the Twentieth Century*. 2nd edn. London: Routledge, 2002.

Meisels, Tamar. *The Trouble with Terror: Liberty, Security, and the Response to Terrorism*. Cambridge: Cambridge University Press, 2008.

Mintz, Samuel Isaiah. *The Hunting of Leviathan: Seventeenth-Century Reactions to the Materialism and Moral Philosophy of Thomas Hobbes*. Bristol: Thoemmes Press, 1997.

Morris, Christopher. *Western Political Thought, Volume One: Plato to Augustine*. London: Longmans, 1967.

Morrison, Blake. 'Femme Fatale'. *Guardian*, 4 October 2003.

Mouffe, Chantal. *The Challenge of Carl Schmitt*. London: Verso, 1999.

——. *The Democratic Paradox*. London: Verso, 2000.

——. 'Carl Schmitt's Warning on the Dangers of a Unipolar World'. In *The International Political Thought of Carl Schmitt: Terror, Liberal War and the Crisis of Global Order*, edited by Louiza Odysseos and Fabio Petito. London; New York: Routledge, 2007: 147–53.

Neal, Andrew W. 'Cutting Off the King's Head: Foucault's *"Society Must Be Defended"* and the Problem of Sovereignty'. *Alternatives: Global, Local, Political*, no. 29, 2004: 373–98.

——. 'Goodbye War on Terror? Foucault and Butler on Law, War and Exceptionalism'. In *Foucault on Politics, Security and War*, edited by Michael Dillon and Andrew W. Neal. Basingstoke: Palgrave Macmillan, 2008: 43–64.

Negri, Antonio. *Time for Revolution*. Translated by Matteo Mandarini. New York; London: Continuum, 2003.

Neocleous, Mark. 'Security, Liberty and the Myth of Balance: Towards a Critique of Security Politics'. *Contemporary Political Theory*, vol. 6, no. 2, 2007: 131–49.

Nietzsche, Friedrich. 'The Wanderer and His Shadow (1880)'. In *Complete Works*. New York: Gordon Press, 1974.

O'Halpin, Eunan. 'British Intelligence and the Case for Confronting Iraq: Evidence from the Butler and Hutton Reports'. *Irish Studies in International Affairs*, vol. 16, 2005: 89–102.

Odysseos, Louize and Fabio Petito, eds. *The International Political Thought of Carl Schmitt: Terror, Liberal War and the Crisis of Global Order*. London; New York: Routledge, 2007.

——. 'Vagaries of Interpretation: A Rejoinder to David Chandler's Reductionist Reading of Carl Schmitt'. *Millennium: Journal of International Studies*, vol. 37, no. 2, 2008: 463–75.

Paglen, Trevor and A. C. Thompson. *Torture Taxi: On the Trail of the CIA's Rendition Flights*. Hoboken, N.J.: Melville House, 2006.

Paulin, Tom. 'Whose Side Are You On?' *Independent on Sunday*, 28 September 2003.

Pin-Fat, Véronique. 'The Metaphysics of the "Mysticism" National Interest and the of the Nation-State: Reading Hans J. Morgenthau'. *Millennium: Journal of International Studies*, vol. 31, no. 2, 2005: 217–36.

Posner, Eric A. and Adrian Vermeule. *Terror in the Balance: Security, Liberty, and the Courts*. New York: Oxford University Press, 2007.

Prozorov, Sergei. 'X/Xs: Toward a General Theory of the Exception'. *Alternatives: Global, Local, Political*, no. 30, 2005: 81–112.

——. 'The Ethos of Insecure Life. Reading Carl Schmitt's Existential Decisionism as a Foucauldian Ethics'. In *The International Political Thought of Carl Schmitt: Terror, Liberal War and the Crisis of Global Order*, edited by Louize Odysseos and Fabio Petito. London; New York: Routledge, 2007: 222–41.

——. 'The World Community and the Closure of the Political: How to Overcome Carl Schmitt'. Paper presented at Making Sense of a Pluralist World: Sixth Pan-European Conference on International Relations, Turin, 2007. Available from: http://archive.sgir.eu/uploads/Prozorov-prozorov_world_community_2007.pdf.

Rasch, William. 'Conflict as a Vocation: Carl Schmitt and the Possibility of Politics'. *Theory, Culture & Society*, vol. 17, no. 6, 2000: 1–32.

——. 'Introduction: Carl Schmitt and the New World Order'. *South Atlantic Quarterly*, vol. 104, no. 2, 2005: 177–83.

Rasul, Shafiq, Asif Iqbal and Rhuhel Ahmed. 'Report of Former Guantanamo Detainees. Composite Statement: Detention in Afghanistan and Guantanamo Bay'. New York: Centre for Constitutional Rights, 2004. Available from: http://www.ccr-ny.org/v2/reports/docs/Gitmo-compositestatementFINAL23july04.pdf.

Reid, Julian. *The Biopolitics of the War on Terror: Life Struggles, Liberal Modernity and the Defence of Logistical Societies, Reappraising the Political*. Manchester: Manchester University Press, 2007.

Riles, Annelise. *Rethinking the Masters of Comparative Law*. Oxford: Hart, 2001.

Robinson, K. 'An Immanent Transcendental – Foucault, Kant and Critical Philosophy'. *Radical Philosophy*, no. 141, 2007: 12–22.

Rosenau, James N. *The Study of Global Interdependence: Essays on the Transnationalization of World Affairs, Essays on the Analysis of World Politics*. London: Pinter, 1980.

Rousseau, Jean-Jacques. *On the Social Contract*. Translated by Judith R. Masters. Edited by Roger D. Masters. New York: St Martin's Press, 1978.

Sands, Philippe. *Lawless World: Making and Breaking Global Rules*. London: Penguin, 2006.

——. *Torture Team: Deception, Cruelty and the Compromise of Law*. London: Allen Lane, 2008.

Schmitt, Carl. *Political Theology: Four Chapters on the Concept of Sovereignty*. Translated by George Schwab. Cambridge, Mass.; London: MIT Press, 1985.

——. 'The Age of Neutralizations and Depoliticizations'. *Telos*, no. 96, 1993.

——. *Legalität und Legitimität*. Berlin: Duncker & Humblot, 1993.

——. *Die Diktator*. Berlin: Dunker & Humblot, 1994.

——. *The Concept of the Political*. Translated by George Schwab. Chicago, Ill.: University of Chicago Press, 1996.

——. *Roman Catholicism and Political Form*. Translated by G. L. Ulmer. Westport, Conn.: Greenwood, 1996.

——. *The Nomos of the Earth in the International Law of the Jus Publicum Europaeum*. Translated by G. L. Ulmen. New York: Telos Press, 2003.

Schneewind, J. B. 'Autonomy, Obligation, and Virtue: An Overview of Kant's Moral Philosophy'. In *The Cambridge Companion to Kant*, edited by Paul Guyer. Cambridge: Cambridge University Press, 1992: 309–41.

Schulhofer, Stephen J. *The Enemy Within: Intelligence Gathering, Law Enforcement, and Civil Liberties in the Wake of September 11*. New York: Century Foundation Press, 2002.

Serres, Michel. *The Birth of Physics*. Manchester: Clinamen, 2000.

Shapiro, Michael J. *Reading the Postmodern Polity: Political Theory as Textual Practice*. Minneapolis: University of Minnesota Press, 1992.

Shiner, Phil and Andrew Williams. *The Iraq War and International Law*. Oxford: Hart Publishing, 2008.

Simons, Jon. *Foucault and the Political*. London; New York: Routledge, 1994.

Sophocles. 'Antigone'. In *The Three Theban Plays*. Harmondsworth: Penguin, 1984: 55–128.

Sorel, Georges. *Reflections on Violence*. Translated by T. E. Hulme. London: G. Allen & Unwin, 1916.

Steyn, Johan. 'Guantanamo Bay: The Legal Black Hole'. *International and Comparative Law Quarterly*, vol. 53, 2004: 1–15.

Strauss, Leo. *The Political Philosophy of Hobbes, Its Basis and Its Genesis*. Chicago, Ill.: University of Chicago Press, 1963.

——. 'Notes on Carl Schmitt, the Concept of the Political'. In *Carl Schmitt: The Concept of the Political*. Chicago, Ill.: University of Chicago Press, 1996: 81–107.

Sylvester, Christine. *Feminist Theory and International Relations in a Postmodern Era*. Cambridge: Cambridge University Press, 1994.

Timmons, Mark. *Kant's Metaphysics of Morals: Interpretative Essays*. Oxford: Oxford University Press, 2002.

UK Government. 'The Government's Response to the Report of the Joint Committee on the Draft Civil Contingencies Bill'. London: The Stationery Office, 2004. Available from: http://www.ukresilience.info/ccbill/govtresp.pdf.

United Nations Department of Public Information. *Basic Facts about the United Nations*. New York: UN, 2000.

Vaughan-Williams, Nick. *Border Politics: The Limits of Sovereign Power*. Edinburgh: Edinburgh University Press, 2009.

Veyne, Paul. 'Foucault Revolutionizes History'. In *Foucault and His Interlocutors*, edited by Arnold I. Davidson. Chicago, Ill.; London: University of Chicago Press, 1997: 146–82.

Wæver, Ole. 'Securitization and Desecuritization'. In *On Security*, edited by Ronnie D. Lipschutz. New York; Chichester: Columbia University Press, 1995: 46–86.

——. 'The EU as a Security Actor: Reflections from a Pessimistic Constructivist on Post-Sovereign Security Orders'. In *International Relations Theory and the Politics of European Integration: Power, Security, and Community*, edited by Michael C. Williams and Morten Kelstrup. London: Routledge, 2000: 250–94.

Waldron, Jeremy. 'Security and Liberty: The Image of Balance'. *Journal of Political Philosophy*, vol. 11, no. 2, 2003: 191–210.

Walker, R. B. J. *Inside/Outside: International Relations as Political Theory.* Cambridge: Cambridge University Press, 1993.

——. 'Europe Is Not Where It Is Supposed to Be'. In *International Relations Theory and the Politics of European Integration: Power, Security, and Community*, edited by Michael C. Williams and Morten Kelstrup. London: Routledge, 2000: 14–32.

——. 'After the Future: Enclosures, Connections, Politics'. In *Re-Framing the International: Law, Culture, Politics*, edited by Richard A. Falk, Lester Edwin J. Ruiz and R. B. J. Walker. New York; London: Routledge, 2002: 3–25.

——. 'Sovereignties, Exceptions, Worlds'. In *Sovereign Lives: Power in Global Politics*, edited by Jenny Edkins, Véronique Pin-Fat and Michael J. Shapiro. New York; London: Routledge, 2004: 239–49.

——. 'Lines of Insecurity: International, Imperial, Exceptional'. *Security Dialogue*, vol. 37, no. 1, 2006: 65–82.

——. *After the Globe, before the World.* London and New York: Routledge, 2009.

Weber, Cynthia. *International Relations Theory: A Critical Introduction.* 2nd edn. London; New York: Routledge, 2005.

Weber, Max. 'Science as a Vocation'. In *From Max Weber: Essays in Sociology*, edited by H. H. Gerth and C. Wright Mills. New York: Oxford University Press, 1946: 129–57.

——. 'The Profession and Vocation of Politics'. In *Weber: Political Writings*, edited by Peter Lassman and Ronald Speirs. Cambridge: Cambridge University Press, 1994: 309–69.

Williams, Michael C. 'Words, Images, Enemies: Securitization and International Politics'. *International Studies Quarterly*, vol. 47, 2003: 511–31.

Wolin, Richard. 'Carl Schmitt: The Conservative Revolutionary Habitus and the Aesthetics of Horror'. *Political Theory*, vol. 20, no. 3, 1992: 424–47.

Wong, Kam C. 'The Making of the USA Patriot Act I: The Legislative Process and Dynamics'. *International Journal of the Sociology of Law*, vol. 34, no. 3, 2006: 179–219.

——. 'The USA Patriot Act: Some Unanswered Questions'. *International Journal of the Sociology of Law*, vol. 34, no. 1, 2006: 1–41.

Wright, George and agencies. 'Guantánamo Briton "Tortured in US Custody"'. *Guardian*, 1 October 2004.

Zehfuss, Maja. 'Forget September 11'. *Third World Quarterly: Journal of Emerging Areas*, vol. 24, no. 3, 2003: 513–28.

Žižek, Slavoj, Rex Butler and Scott Stephens. *Interrogating the Real: Selected Writings.* New York; London: Continuum, 2005.

Index

9/11 7, 11, 117, 133; and anti-terrorism policy 23; and the liberty/security discourse 8–11; policy developments since 12–13

Afghanistan 23
Agamben, Giorgio 3, 102–3, 120; on Benjamin 87–89; the exception as timeless problem 144; on happy life 142; *Home Sacer: Sovereign Power and Bare Life* 77, 78, 96; on the liberal subject 4; on pure violence 87–88; on Schmitt 86–87, 88–89, 139; on sovereign exceptionalism 79, 80, 117; on sovereignty 92, 93–94; *State of Exception* 77, 86, 96–97; on state of exception 16, 95–96; *see also* bare life; *homo sacer*
Allison, Henry 46
Althusser, Louis 137
American Civil Liberties Union (ACLU) 13
America's disappeared 11–12
Amoore, Louise 147, 148, 149
Anglo-American liberalism 63, 65, 66, 140
anomie 88, 89–92, 93–94
anti-terrorism policy 12–13; European Union 15; legal approaches 14–16; post 9/11 23; as threat to liberty 8–9
archaeological method 112–16, 118; Foucault on 4, 5; and genealogy 120–23
archaic sovereign: and right of life and death 125–26
archaic sovereign power: and disciplinary power 132–34
archive, the 118–20
Arendt, Hannah 82
Aristotle 78

artificial man: sovereign as 41
Ashcroft, John 13
Augustine 38, 39
Austin, John L. 110
authority: unlimited 72
authorization of authority 93
autonomy: freedom as 44–45, 47, 56

Bachelard, Gaston 25–26, 137
Badiou, Alain 137, 142
Balakrishnan, Gopal 62, 108, 135
bare life 78–80, 81–83, 89–92, 96, 121, 131–32
Begg, Moazzam 81
Behnke, Andreas: on Schmitt 140–41
Benjamin, Walter 22, 57, 86; Agamben on 87–89; 'Critique of Violence' 87–88; *The Origin of German Tragic Drama* 88
Bigo, Didier 143, 145
biopolitical space: concentration camps as 80–81
biopolitics 78, 82–83, 90
biopower 125–26
bios 78, 96
Blair, Tony 25
body, the 129, 130–31
Bonditti, Philippe 24
Butler, Judith 13, 147–48, 149
Buzan, Barry 100, 106, 107

Calvinism 38
Catholic Church 135
causality, laws of 39
Chandler, David: on Schmitt 137–38
Chang, Nancy: *Silencing Political Dissent: How Post-September 11 Anti-Terrorism Measures Threaten Our Civil Liberties* 11–12

Civil Contingencies Act/ Bill (2004) 18–20
Civil Defence Act (1948) 17
civil liberties 8, 9–10, 23; Hobbes on 41–44; and natural freedom 54–55; and the state 22; United States 11–14; and violence 28
civilizing mission 50
clinamen 137
cohesion: and sovereign will 49–50
commissarial dictatorship 86, 87
commonwealth: and state of nature 41
concentration camps 90–92; biopolitical space 80–81
constitutional dictatorship 92
contemporary exceptionalism 81, 116, 123–24, 126–30, 133
contract-oppression 53
covenant 40–41

death: fear of 40
democracy: and sovereign exceptionalism 14
democratic will: and sovereign will 52
Democritus 137
Derrida, Jacques: on difference 137; on practice 147; on Schmitt 68–70, 72, 74, 75
desecuritization 104–5, 106, 115
determinism: and freedom 37–38
difference 137
disciplinary power 125, 130–31; and archaic sovereign power 132–34; as productive 131
discourse 30–31, 113–14, 115–16, 119–20, 122–23
discursive formations 115, 118–20, 123–24; and modalities of power 124–25
distribution, rules of 130
domestic unity: and international pluralism 66–70
Doty, Roxanne Lynn 148–49
Dreyfus, Hubert L. 120
Durkheim, Émile 80

economics 63–64, 159 n27
emergency: definition of 17–18
emergency powers: and the Human Rights Act 19–20
Emergency Powers Act (1920) 17
emergency regulations 19–20, 30
empirical, the 142
enemy: friend/enemy distinction 58, 60, 61, 63, 66, 68, 99, 140

enlightenment 49, 50
Epicurus 137
epistemological break 137
escape: impossibility of 86–89, 93–94
ethics: communicative, and securitization theory 106–7, 108–9; depoliticizations of 63
European state system 65, 66, 136
European Union: 14–16
European Union Network of Independent Experts on Fundamental Rights 14–16, 24
event, the 137
exception, the: concept of 26; definition of, as extra-legal 30; global archipelago of 7, 123; as a metaphysical problem 58, 59, 69–70, 72, 74–75; as a philosophical problem 57, 63, 71–72, 74
use of term 22
exceptional event: historical conditions for 118–20; and nation-statist politics 103; Schmitt on 72, 74, 99, 101, 112, 138, 141
exceptional response 72, 74
exceptional sovereign 141; power 4, 102
exceptionalism: limit of liberty 54; use of term 22
executive rule 97
executive word: and the law 19

fascism 54
fictitious lacuna of the legal exception 85, 92, 102, 139
force-of-law 87
Foucault, Michel 27, 106, 112, 146, 150; archaeological method 112–16, 118; archaeology and genealogy 120–23; *The Archaeology of Knowledge* 4, 112–16, 117–20; the archive 118–20; bare life 78–80; biopolitics 78; biopower 125–26; *The Birth of Biopolitics* 143; contract-oppression 53; and crisis of rights 82; disciplinary power 125, 130–31; *Discipline and Punish* 124–25, 126, 129; discourse 113–14, 115–16, 119–20, 122–23; discursive formations 115, 118–20, 123–24; discursive formations and modalities of power 124–25; the empirical 142; genealogy of punishment 126–30; *The History of Sexuality, Volume 1: The Will to Knowledge* 125–26; medieval criminal

process 128; method of archaeology 4, 5; 'Nietzsche, Genealogy, History' 121–22; notion of tradition 114–15; *The Order of Things* 110; on practice 143–46; rules of distribution 130; '*Society Must Be Defended*' 94–95, 122, 124–25, 132, 143; the sovereign subject 83; sovereignty 4, 83–84; 'The Spectacle of the Scaffold 126; the state 140; on subjectivity 29; totalitarian theory 33; totalizing schemas of knowledge 71; truth 34; truth and power 31; war model 121–22

freedom: and civil laws 39; and determinism 37–38; Kant on 35, 44–45, 46, 47, 56, 60; and moral law 46; as necessity 48; and reason 45; and state as universal law of 56; universal 47–48, 53; *see also* natural freedom

French Revolution 29, 83

Freud, Sigmund 80

Friedrich, Carl J. 92–93

friend/enemy distinction 58, 60, 61, 63, 66, 68, 99, 140

Galtung, Johan 101

genealogical approach 125; and archaeological method 120–23, punishment 126–30

Germany: state sovereignty in 1933 32

global archipelago of exception 7, 123

God 38–39

Grossraum 136

Guantanamo Bay 7, 9, 81, 91, 123–24; and contemporary exceptionalism 126–30; creates resistance 131–32; disciplinary power 130–31; paroxysm of normality 132–33; and practice 146–47

Guardian 17

habeas corpus 83

Habermas, Jürgen 107

Hanssen, Beatrice 28

happy life 142

Hayek, Frederick von 159 n27

historical transformations 125–26, 133

Hobbes, Thomas 39, 40, 41–44, 46–47, 56; Common Power 40–41; contract-oppression 53; covenant 40–41; discourse 30; freedom 35, 48, 60; on God 38–39; *Leviathan* 38, 41, 44, 53, 55, 75; liberty and security 9, 12; liberty/security discourse 22, 42–43;

natural freedom 39–41; sovereign exceptionalism 94–95; sovereign political authority 85–86; sovereignty and security 37, 38, 42, 43; and spatio-temporal ontology 48, 50

homo sacer 79–81, 96; and sovereign 80–81

human rights 23, 82; and biopolitics 82–83; and the Civil Contingencies Act/Bill 2004 19; conventions 29

Human Rights Act: and the emergency powers 19–20

immanence 36

immaturity 49–50

inclusive exclusion 78–80, 85

individual, the 21, 28–29, 86; and the state 21; *see also* liberal subject

International Committee of the Red Cross 127

international pluralism: and domestic unity 66–70

international relations 136

Iraq 15, 23

It's a Free Country: Personal Freedom in America after September 11 (Goldberg, Goldberg and Greenwald) 13

iustitium 89

Jews, the 90

Johns, Fleur 91, 148, 149; 'Guantanamo Bay and the Annihilation of the Exception' 146–47

Joint Committee of the Draft Civil Contingencies Bill 17–18, 19

Justice and Home Affairs (JHA) 16

Kant, Immanuel 121; 'An Answer to the Question: "What is Enlightenment?"' 49; categorical imperative 45–46, 47; fact of reason 47; freedom 35, 60; freedom and moral law 46; freedom as autonomy 44–45, 47, 56; instrumental maxims 45–46; liberal society 53–54; liberal subject 4–5; liberty 55; modernity 56; noumenon 137; *Recht* 47; *Rechtsstaat* 47–48; setting up a state 51; sovereign political authority 85–86; sovereign will 51–52; sovereignty and individuality 37, 38, 52, 55; and spatio-temporal ontology 49

Kersting, Wolfgang 47
Kirkland, Andrew 13–14

Lacan, Jacques 137
law 89–90, 94; and anti-terrorism policy
    14–16; civil, and freedom 39; and the
    executive word 19; internalization of
    51–52, 53; limit of 62–63; limits of,
    and threat 58, 59; state as
    embodiment of 55
law-preserving violence 87
lawmaking violence 87
legal exception, fictitious lacuna of 85,
    92, 102, 139
Levi, Primo: *If This Is a Man* 91
liberal imperialism 64–66
liberal/legal discourse 15
liberal subject 2, 4–5
liberalism 52–56, 61–63, 72
Liberty 17, 18, 19
liberty: anti-terrorism policy a threat to
    8–9; defence of 25; immanent logic of
    36; Kant on 55; meaning of 25–26;
    political theory of 10; 'properly so-
    called' 54–55; under security 3, 9–11;
    and security 1–2, 9, 12, 52, 98, 122
liberty/security discourse 21, 92, 121;
    and 9/11 8–11; boundaries 23; and
    contract 53; Hobbes on 22, 42–43;
    problematic dualism 22; theoretical
    implications of 24–26
Lucretius 137

Machiavelli, Niccolò: *The Prince* 73,
    139–40
Marxism 108, 140
medieval criminal process 128
MI5 127
Mintz, Samuel I. 38
Minutemen 148–49
modalities of power: and discursive
    formations 124–25
modernity 52, 56, 60–61, 62, 140–41
Moore, Michael 13
moral law: and freedom 46
moral responsibility 46–47, 49
Mouffe, Chantal 14, 142
multi-culturalism 23

nation 83, 94–95
nation-state 68–70, 76, 94, 104–5, 108,
    117, 141; and the exceptional event 103
nationalism 23
natural freedom 39–41, 54–55

natural law 86, 93
nature: state of, and commonwealth 41
Nazism 125–26; juridical theory 19, 155
    n52
necessity 36, 85; freedom as 48; a space
    without law 89–90; *see also* objective
    necessity
negative freedom 22
Negri, Antonio 137
Nietzsche, Friedrich 31, 121
nomos *see* natural law
Nomos 136
normative lacuna of the legal exception
    84–86
noumenon 137

Øberg, Jan 101
objective necessity 84–85, 99, 100, 144;
    see also necessity
Odysseos, Louize and Petito, Fabio: *The
    International Political Thought of Carl
    Schmitt* 136
Oppenheimer, Franz 63

Parliament 155 n46; as sovereign 18–19
past legislation: United Kingdom Civil
    Contingencies Act (2004) 19–20
petty sovereigns 145, 147, 148
'the political' 56, 59–60, 68, 85; and
    economics 63–64; and the exception
    138
political judgement: and spatio-temporal
    ontology 50
political modernity: and sovereignty 52, 56
politics 41, 62, 66, 81–82; Schmitt on 58;
    Western tradition 45
positive freedom 22
positive law 62–63
power: exceptional sovereign 4, 102;
    political, and truth 18; Germany 1933
    32; use of by states 16
practice: Foucault's alternative 143–46;
    and Guantanamo Bay 146–47
Prozorov, Sergei 138, 139–40, 141; 'The
    World Community and the Closure of
    the Political: How to overcome Carl
    Schmitt' 142; 'X/Xs: Toward a
    General Theory of the Exception'
    141–42
punishment, genealogy of 126–30
pure violence 87–88

Rabinow, Paul 120
Rasch, William 59, 60, 62–63

'real referent' of security 102, 103, 109, 110
Real, the 137
reason: fact of 47; and freedom 45
Recht 47
Rechtsstaat 47–48, 49
relation of abandonment 78–81, 85–86, 90, 96–97
Rousseau, Jean-Jacques 44, 45
Rumsfeld memo 146

Sands, Philippe 146
Schmitt, Carl 2–3, 22, 27, 79, 86, 107, 120, 145, 150; Agamben on 86–87, 88–89, 139; 'The Age of Depoliticizations and Neutralizations' 93, 108; Behnke on 140–41; Chandler on 137–38; *The Concept of the Political* 58, 59, 61, 63, 65, 66, 68, 69–70, 72, 73–74, 92, 107–8, 136, 137, 140, 159 n4; *Crisis of Democracy* 136; depoliticization of economics 63–64; depoliticizations of ethics 63; Derrida on 68–70, 72, 74, 75; *Die Diktator* 86–87; discourse 30, 115; exception as a metaphysical problem 58, 59, 69–70, 72, 74–75; exception as a philosophical problem 57, 63, 71–72, 74; exceptional event 72, 74, 99, 101, 103, 112, 138; exceptional sovereign power 4, 102; fall of 135–37; fascism 54; friend/enemy distinction 58, 60, 61, 63, 66, 68, 99, 140; international relations 136; liberalism 61–63; modernity 56, 140–41; the nation-state 68–70, 76, 94, 104–5, 108, 117, 141; natural law 86, 93; necessity 85; *Nomos of the Earth* 136; objective necessity 144; *Political Theology* 58, 61, 67, 70, 72, 73–74, 135–36, 137, 140; politico-philosophical conditions 36–37; on politics 58; and the politics of securitization theory 102–5; positive law 62–63; problematization of the exception 136–37; prohibition on war 67; Prozorov on 138, 139–40, 141; *Roman Catholicism and Political Form* 135; on security 148; the sovereign 25, 67, 73–76, 83, 90, 99–100, 106–8, 139; sovereign decision 88; sovereign exceptionalism 66, 84, 121; sovereign nominalism 84; sovereignty 58–59, 71, 149; state exceptionalism 66; state sovereignty

32; subjectivity 29; universal problem of the exception 144; unlimited authority 72; *see also* 'The political'
Schneewind, J. B. 44, 46
Schulhofer, Stephen J.: *The Enemy Within: Intelligence Gathering, Law Enforcement, and Civil Liberties in the Wake of September 11* 12–13
Searle, John R. 102
securitization theory 3–4, 100–102, 113, 120; communicative ethics 106–7, 108–9; and discourse 114; limits of 109–12; methodological objectivism 105–6, 109; notion of tradition 114–15; Schmitt on 102–5; as selectively constructivist 109, 111; and sovereign nominalism 109
security: language and reality of 109–11; and liberty 1–2, 9, 12, 52, 98, 122; liberty under 3, 9–11; 'real referent' of 102, 103, 109, 110; Schmitt on 148; as a speech act 102
security field 111
security threats: definition of 18
Serres, Michel 137
The Situation of Fundamental Rights in the European Union and its Member States in 2002 14–15
Sophocles: *Antigone* 90
sovereign coercion 54, 55, 56
sovereign decision 88, 99, 138–39
sovereign dictatorship 86–87
sovereign exceptionalism 16, 17, 25–26, 74–75, 88, 92–93; Agamben on 79, 80, 117; and democracy 14; historical conditions for 94–95; Hobbes on 94–95; and immanence 36; Schmitt on 66, 84, 121; United Kingdom Civil Contingencies Act/Bill (2004) 20
sovereign individual 22
sovereign nominalism 75, 83–86, 103, 109
sovereign political authority 22, 29, 85–86, 94
sovereign power 128–30
sovereign response 138–39
sovereign state 65, 72, 74
sovereign subject, the 83
sovereign, the 139–40; Agamben on 92; as artificial man 41; authorization of truth 31; and bare life 96; and biopolitics 83; constitution of 92; exceptional 4; and *homo sacer* 80–81; monarchical 95; Parliament as 18–19;

petty sovereigns 145, 147, 148; and political modernity 56; right to make war 133; Schmitt on 25, 67, 73–76, 83, 90, 99–100, 106–8, 139; and subject 29
sovereign will: and cohesion 49–50; 51–52
sovereignty 31–34, 59, 63, 118; Agamben on 92, 93–94; and the Civil Contingencies Act/Bill (2004) 19–20; dispersal of 148–49; Foucault on 4, 83–84; Hobbes on 37, 38, 42, 43; Kant on 37, 38, 52, 55; limits of 44; and political modernity 52; Schmitt on 59–60, 71, 149; *see also* archaic sovereign power; executive rule
spatial exception 58
spatial/temporal ontology 23–24, 41, 48, 49, 50, 55, 68
speech acts 102, 103, 105, 106–7, 108–9, 110, 114
state exceptionalism 59, 66–70
state of exception 16, 95–96; permanent 96–98
state of nature 42
state sovereignty 32, 59, 66
state, the: and civil liberties 22; coercive 55; embodiment of liberty 55; Foucault on 140; and the individual 21, 28–29; setting up 51; as universal law of freedom 56
Strauss, Leo 41, 55; commentary on *The Concept of the Political* 61, 140
subject, the *see* individual, the
subjectivity 28–30, 120; limits of 44; modern 92
surveillance 23

'Tampere scoreboard' 16
temporal exception 58, 70–76
temporal/spatial ontology 23–24, 41, 48, 49, 50, 55, 68

terrorism: definition of 24, 30
threat: and limits of law and order 58, 59
Tipton Three 81, 91, 127–31
torture 123–24, 126–30
totalitarian theory 33
totalizing schemas of knowledge 71
tradition, notion of 114–15
Treaty of Versailles 63
truth 18, 31, 32, 34

United Kingdom Civil Contingencies Act (2004) 17–21
United States: America's disappeared 11–12; civil liberties 11–14; re-territorializing threat 24; use of torture 123–24, 126–30
United States Constitution 12, 23, 29
USA PATRIOT 11

Veyne, Paul 144, 145–46, 147, 148; 'Foucault Revolutionizes History' 1–2, 143
violence 27–28; against the subject 29

Wæver, Ole 103; desecuritization 104–5, 106, 115; and the politics of securitization theory 104; 'Securitization and Desecuritization' 100–102; security field 111; sovereign nominalism 103–5, 109; *see also* securitization theory
Walker, Rob 23, 32, 93
war 64–66, 67, 121–22, 133
war on terror 24, 135, 142, 147–48, 149
Weber, Max 59–60, 63; *Politics as a Vocation* 93
Williams, Michael C. 100, 105–9
Wolin, Richard 60

Žižek, Slavoj 137, 142
zoē 78, 80, 96

21765788R00109

Printed in Great Britain
by Amazon